Diversity, Ethnicity and Identity in South Asia

Diversity, Ethnicity and Identity in South Asia

Edited by

A.R. Momin

RAWAT PUBLICATIONS

Jaipur • New Delhi • Bangalore • Mumbai • Hyderabad • Guwahati

ISBN 81-316-0260-5

Published by
Prem Rawat for **Rawat Publications**
Satyam Apts, Sector 3, Jawahar Nagar, Jaipur 302 004 (India)
Phone: 0141 265 1748 / 7006 Fax: 0141 265 1748
E-mail: info@rawatbooks.com
Website: www.rawatbooks.com

New Delhi Office
4858/24, Ansari Road, Daryaganj, New Delhi 110 002
Phone: 011 2326 3290

Also at Bangalore, Mumbai, Hyderabad and Guwahati

Typeset by Rawat Computers, Jaipur
Printed at Chaman Enterprises, New Delhi

To

Professor J.V. Ferreira

teacher, mentor, friend

Contents

Preface

South Asia, home to nearly one-sixth of the world's population, is currently in the focus of considerable academic attention. The emergence of India as one of the fastest-growing economies in the world has sharpened the international focus on the region. South Asia is one of the most culturally diverse regions in the world and, at the same time, the site of a long-standing process of cultural hybridization and symbiosis. The region has witnessed, over the past several centuries as well as in recent years, highly significant and complex processes of ethnicization, identity construction and ethnic conflict. The present volume makes a modest contribution to the study of South Asia in the context of its pervasive diversity and complexity and the interface between change and continuity.

Four of the essays in this volume (by Parekh, Oommen, Singh, Schlesinger) were presented at an international seminar on "Cultural Pluralism, Ethnicity and Nation-Building in South Asia", organized by the Department of Sociology, University of Mumbai, as part of its platinum jubilee celebrations on December 29-31, 1995. The publication of this volume has been inordinately delayed due to unavoidable reasons. I am grateful to the contributors for their kind permission to include their papers in the volume. Three papers (by Rao, Caplan, Kloos) have been specially written for this volume. Peter Kloos, alas, is no more with us. I am grateful to his wife, Dr. Joke Schrijvers, for sending me a revised version of his paper. Dr. K. S Singh, former Director-General, Anthropological Survey of India and a dear friend of mine, passed away after a protracted illness in 2006.

Yunas Samad's paper was originally published in the *International Journal of Punjab Studies* (Vol. 2, No. 1, 1995). Grateful acknowledgement is made to Professor Samad and to the editor and publishers of the journal for permission to reprint the paper.

I am thankful to Rawat Publications for their keen interest in the publication of this volume.

A.R. Momin

Introduction

A.R. MOMIN

The prominent features of the contemporary global scenario include the intensification of the process of globalization, the salience and universal recognition of cultural diversity, the worldwide democratic upsurge, the resurgence of ethnic consciousness and identity, and the escalation of racial, ethnic, religious and cultural conflicts in large parts of the world. Most, if not all, contemporary societies can be characterized as heterogeneous and multiethnic. It is significant to note that of 185 sovereign states, which are members of the United Nations, 160 are multiethnic in composition. Robert Young has rightly remarked that "heterogeneity, cultural interchange and diversity have become the self-conscious identity of modern society" (Young, 1996: 4).

The academic engagement with heterogeneous, multiethnic societies has been informed by certain theoretical perspectives, such as pluralism and multiculturalism, and has thrown up significant issues relating to the composition, dynamics and limitations of multiethnic societies.

Pluralism and Plural Societies

The term 'plural society' has been used in the social sciences to characterize societies that are marked by the coexistence of distinct ethnic, religious and cultural groups and communities within the boundaries of a country or nation-state. Pierre Van den Berghe defines plural societies as those in which "several distinct social and/or cultural groups coexist within the boundaries of a single polity and share a common economic system that makes them interdependent, yet they maintain, to a greater or lesser degree, autonomy and discrete institutional structures in other spheres of social life" (Van den Berghe, 1973: 96). Van den Berghe maintains that pluralism exists to a greater or lesser degree in all societies.

The term 'pluralism' has been used in two distinct senses. In one sense, associated with scholars such as W. Kornhauser, S.M. Lipset and Edward Shils, pluralism has an essentially political connotation. According to this view, a pluralistic democracy is characterized by the existence of a wide variety of autonomous interest groups, which are in competition with each other in the political arena and which have a share and stake in the decision-making process. These writers consider the United States as the epitome of plural society. Shils regards pluralism as the essence of liberal democracy. He in fact equates liberalism with pluralism. Kornhauser and Lipset did not attach much importance to ethnic identifications or cleavages.

In the second sense, represented by J.S. Furnivall, a plural society is seen as characterized by the coexistence of several distinct social or cultural groups within the boundaries of an overarching political and economic system. These groups or communities, though economically or politically interdependent, enjoy a substantial measure of autonomy, especially in the spheres of family and religion. In his study of colonial Indonesia's plural society, Furnivall found that the different ethnic groups were living side by side, but their interaction was restricted to the market place. "It is a medley of people", wrote Furnivall, "for they mix but do not combine. Each group holds by its own religion, its own culture and language, its own ideas and ways. As individuals, they meet, but only in the market place, in buying and selling" (Furnivall, 1948: 307–308). Furnivall argued that Indonesian society was plural in two senses. In the first place, each of the ethnic communities comprising Indonesian society existed separately and was governed by its own religious and moral values, family and kinship system, language and culture. Secondly, the market place, which was the site of interaction and exchange among the diverse ethnic groups, was not bound by any moral or communal control. Indonesian society, like other Dutch and British colonies of South-East Asia, did not possess any shared values or ethos, which could provide a sense of unity or cohesiveness. These societies were held together by the coercive role of the state under colonial dispensation. Furnivall's study focused on societal fragmentation under the impact of colonial expansion (Furnivall, 1939; 1948).

The term 'plural society' has also been used by a group of social scientists who have studied some of the highly fragmented societies of Africa, Asia, Latin America and the Caribbean. Many of these societies are bedevilled by heightened ethnic cleavages and endemic ethnic conflicts which are rooted in specific historical and social factors such as conquest, colonialism, slavery and the oppressive role of the state.

M.G. Smith, in one of his major works *The Plural Society of the British West Indies* (1965), dealt with the highly fragmented society of the West Indies before and immediately after independence. He observed that a key feature of plural societies is the political domination of one group over the others. He pointed out that fragility and instability are generally the bane of plural societies because they lack a common social will which could be a source of unity and cohesion. Generally, pervasive social and cultural fragmentation, deep ethnic cleavages and the fragility of social bonds seem to be the characteristic features of plural societies. This is reflected in the characterization of Guatemala and Mexico by Manning Nash as 'multiple society', Van Lier's portrayal of the West Indies as 'segmental society', J.H. Boeke's representation of Indonesia as a 'dual society' and Martin Bulmer's description of Israel as a 'fractured society'.

The classical model of pluralism, as formulated by Furnivall, has stimulated a good deal of discussion and debate among anthropologists, political scientists and historians. While some scholars have taken issue with it, others have asserted its utility in different societal contexts. Many writers have emphasized the substantial extent and role of cultural hybridization in plural societies. Some scholars stress that pluralism is not just a defining feature of most societies but also a value orientation, which is reflected in the open acknowledgement and acceptance of cultural diversity, peaceful coexistence and tolerance, cosmopolitanism and respect for human rights.

Ethnicity

The term 'ethnicity' was first used in its modern sense by W. Lloyd Warner during the 1940s. By the 1980s, the term had gained wide currency in the social sciences. Ethnicity is generally defined in terms of shared past, cultural traditions, religion, languages and identity. Put simply, ethnicity connotes the positive feelings of identification with a cultural group or community. The term is derived from the Greek noun *ethnos*, which means people. One of the earliest and well-known definitions of ethnicity was given by Max Weber. He defined ethnic groups as "those human groups that entertain subjective belief in their common descent because of similarities of physical type or of customs or of both, or because of memories of colonization or migration" (Weber, 1968: 389). In the *Communist Manifesto*, Marx and Engels viewed ethnicity as a form of false consciousness and asserted that it would disappear with the emergence of the proletariat united by a common condition and shared material interests.

An early concern with ethnicity and ethnic groups was reflected in the work of sociologists of the Chicago School in the 1920s. These sociologists, notably W.I. Thomas and Robert Ezra Park, were particularly interested in the question of the assimilation of immigrants into the White, Anglo-Saxon, Protestant (WASP) mainstream of American society. They believed that, over a period of time, the ethnic identities of immigrant groups would be dissolved with the assimilation or absorption of immigrants into the American melting pot.

One of the most influential writers on ethnicity and ethnic groups has been Frederik Barth. In his widely read book, *Ethnic Groups and Boundaries*, Barth argued, from a structural-functional perspective, that ethnic groups are socially constructed and therefore attention should be focused on the boundaries that distinguish ethnic groups from one other. He suggested that the boundaries of an ethnic group are constituted through "self-ascription whereby people choose to utilize a few cultural attributes such as language, dress or style of life as the overt symbol of their distinctiveness" (Barth, 1969: 14). Barth argued that the discussion on the content and structure of ethnicity should be replaced by a consideration of the boundaries that set limits to ethnic identity. Barth's ideas have been criticized on three counts. First, his view of ethnic groups as fixed, bounded and unchanging is inadequate. Second, Barth ignores the role of cultural interpenetration, hybridization and creolization in the dynamics of ethnogenesis and in shifting the boundaries of ethnic groups. Thirdly, he fails to provide an adequate explanation for the resurgence of ethnic conflicts in the modern world.

The discussion on ethnicity has been dominated by two distinct approaches, which may be broadly characterized as primordialist on the one hand and instrumentalist or situational, on the other. According to the primordialist view, ethnic bonds and affiliations are natural, given and universal in all human societies. Furthermore, they have an overpowering, emotional and non-rational quality. The instrumentalist or situational theory of ethnicity, on the other hand, argues that ethnicity is socially constructed, a resource to be mobilized, and an instrument to be employed by particular groups in pursuit of certain goals, usually of a political or ideological nature (Geertz, 1967; Glazer and Moynihan, 1975; Rex and Mason, 1986).

Sociobiologists have attempted to explain ethnicity in terms of genetic imperatives which are assumed to operate through the mechanism of kin selection. This view is inadequate on two counts. For one thing, it fails to take cognizance of variations in manifestation of ethnicity in different historical, social and political contexts. Secondly, by ignoring the bearing of social, political and cultural factors on the process of ethnogenesis and by seeking to explain the dynamics of the construction of ethnic identity exclusively in terms of genetic imperatives, sociobiology falls a prey to biological determinism.

The project of modernity confidently asserted that ethnic affiliations and identities would gradually weaken and eventually disappear with the onward march of industrialization, urbanization, secularization and the spread of modern education. This assumption was belied by the accentuation and revival of ethnic consciousness that began to surface across large parts of the world from the late 1960s. Ethnic resurgence in the contemporary world can be seen as a response to a variety of factors, including the end of the colonial era and the emergence of new nation-states in Asia and Africa, a growing sense of marginalization and exclusion on the part of subordinated groups and ethnic minorities, accompanied by a heightened consciousness of their legitimate political and cultural rights, large-scale international migrations and the emergence of transnational diasporas, the homogenizing pressures of late modernity and globalization, and the increasing fragmentation and atomization of the modern world (Momin, 2004). The revival and reawakening of ethnic identities across the world has been greatly strengthened by the rapid, unprecedented advances in transportation and communication technologies.

A striking manifestation of the worldwide ethnic resurgence is the revival of indigenous cultural traditions in many parts of Europe and North America. In France, for example, the revival of indigenous culture is marked by the proliferation of Breton-language schools, the rising popularity of Celtic music and local cuisine, and the spread of local festivals. International tourism has also contributed to the revival and celebration of indigenous cultural traditions and local identities. More than 10 million tourists now visit Brittanny, a province of France, every year. In August 2001, Breizh Television began broadcasting in the Breton language as the country's first regional channel. The ethnic and political assertiveness on the part of Spain's Basque minority has become increasingly strident and violent in recent years.

In many parts of the world, ethnic resurgence has been accompanied by ethnic and social conflicts. Walter Connor estimates that nearly half of the world's independent countries have experienced some degree of ethnically-related dissonance (Connor, 1994; Geertz, 1967: 108–110; Epstein, 1978). The disintegration of the Soviet Union was closely associated with the suppression of religious and ethnic minorities and their forced assimilation into mainstream Russian society. Yugoslavia broke up along ethnic lines. Deep ethnic cleavages and conflicts have been conspicuous in Chechnya, Northern Ireland, Sri Lanka, India, and in several African countries (Guibernau and Rex, 1997; Denitch, 1994).

In many parts of Africa, including Sudan, Nigeria, Rwanda, Burundi, Liberia, Angola, Somalia, Congo, Sierra Leone and South Africa, ethnically-related civil wars and inter-tribal violence have taken a toll of tens of millions of lives and led to the displacement of hundreds of thousands of people. There has been a long-standing conflict between the Hutus and Tutsis in Rwanda. Following Rwanda's independence in 1962 and the assumption of power by the Hutus, the simmering conflict between the two communities intensified. On April 6, 1994, a surface-to-air missile brought down an executive jet killing the Rwandan president, Juvenal Habyarimana. Within hours of the incident Hutu militiamen and soldiers began attacking and killing Tutsis, plunging the country in an orgy of carnage and massacre. Some 8,00,000 people, mostly Tutsis and a few moderate Hutus (including, 3,00,000 children), were massacred in a space of 100 days. More than two million refugees fled to neighbouring Congo. The conflict spread into the sprawling rain forests of Congo, culminating in a deadly war that took a toll of nearly 3 million lives.

In recent years, the focus of research on ethnicity has shifted from studies of discrete ethnic groups and the delineation of ethnic boundaries to the broad process and dynamics of ethnogenesis, which involves the social construction and invention or reinvention of ethnic identity in different political, economic, social and cultural contexts, inter-ethnic hybridization and creolization, and the meaning and changing contexts of ethnic identities and their role in social and political mobilization. The idea of ethnicity, as exclusively or predominantly primordial or just a matter of subjective identification, has been largely abandoned. The earlier theoretical perspective which looked upon cultures and ethnic groups as bounded and insular with closed ethnic boundaries, is no longer considered adequate. Now cultures and ethnic groups are seen as characterized by a good deal of heterogeneity, dynamism and hybridity (Bhabha, 1994; Anthias, 2001).

Ethnicity and Nationalism

A nation is generally defined as a group of people who share common cultural traditions, language and religion, live in a clearly demarcated territory and enjoy political sovereignty (Kedourie, 1994: 1). The nation-state is a modern phenomenon which emerged in the wake of the decline of the feudal era in the 18th century. It has been inseparably bound up with the project of modernity. Anthony Smith has offered a succinct typology of conceptualizations about the origins of nationalism. The theorists of the origin of nationalism, according to him, can be grouped under four heads including the primordialists, perennialists, modernists and historical ethno-symbolists. The primordialists (such as Clifford Geertz) hold that the nation is rooted in kinship ties, language, religion and cultural traditions. The perennialists argue that nations have existed since ancient times. The modernists (such as Ernest Gellner and Eric Hobsbawm) consider the nation as an inseparable part of the project of modernity. They attach particular importance to the role of the Industrial Revolution and the emergence of capitalism in the rise of nationalism in modern times. The ethno-symbolists (such as Anthony Smith) argue that although nationalism is a product of the modern era, it derives its strength and sustenance from the myths and collective memories of ethnic communities (Smith, A., 1999: 1–19).

Historically, nationalism and ethnicity have been closely intertwined. Max Weber observed that "a nation is the political extension of the ethnic community as its members and leadership search for a unique political structure by establishing an independent state" (Weber, 1968). Ernest Gellner points out that the key factors in the formation of nations are power, education and culture. Nations, according to him, entail a culturally homogeneous population (Gellner, 1983: 95). Anthony Smith has sought to demonstrate that nationalism has had strong roots in premodern ethnicity. Nations, according to him, cannot be seen as primordial or natural but are nevertheless rooted in relatively ancient histories and in deep-seated ethnic consciousness (Smith, A., 1963; 1986; 1991). Smith argues that the ethnic community is the forerunner of the modern nation-state and views nationalism as transformed ethnicity (Smith, A., 1986: 43).

Nationalism has been one of the most potent and highly influential political and cultural ideologies of the 20th century. It has been responsible for the downfall of mighty empires and the overthrow of dictatorial regimes. Nationalism has been a source of unity, cohesion and solidarity and has provided a sense of purpose and identity to millions of people across the globe. However, as Ernest Gellner has pointed out, it has not been so sweetly reasonable nor so rationally symmetrical (Gellner, 1983: 5). Strangely, nationalism has been appropriated by diverse and even mutually antagonistic ideologies, including fascism, Nazism, socialism, liberalism and conservatism. It has been a source of societal integration as well as the suppression and alienation of ethnic and religious minorities.

Some scholars draw a distinction between political or civic nationalism, identified with common citizenship, equality, fundamental rights and democratic participation, and ethnic nationalism, based on shared descent, history, language and culture (Greenfeld, 1992: 11–13). Nationalist discourses are often embedded in ethnic narratives and myths and collective memories. Ethnic nationalism draws on the symbols and cultural traditions of the dominant national population and considers them as the mainspring of national unity and integration. On the other hand, those who do not belong to the majority population, such as ethnic and religious minorities, are excluded, suppressed and pushed to the margins of society. In some cases, they are forcibly assimilated, enslaved and even exterminated.

In the 19th century, a distinction was often drawn between the great nations, such as France, Italy, Germany, Poland, Hungary, Spain, England and Russia and smaller nationalities such as the Czechs, Slovaks, Croats, Basques, Scots, Serbians, Bulgarians and Slovenes. The great nations were seen as civilized while the smaller nationalities were viewed as primitive and barbaric, incapable of cultural or artistic development. Subsequently, many of these smaller nationalities were forcibly assimilated or incorporated into larger states as a result of colonization or conquest (Glazer, 1983; Hobsbawm, 1990). Many Western countries contain sizeable ethnic minorities and indigenous communities, such as the Bretons and the Corscians in France, the Catalans and the Basques in Spain, the Flemish and the Walloons in Belgium, the Innuits and the Lapps in Canada, the Irish and the Welsh in Britain and the Sami in the Scandinavian countries. In most cases, they were ruthlessly suppressed and forcibly assimilated into the culture of the dominant majority. In the 18th and 19th centuries, France banned the use of the Basque and Breton languages in schools. Britain pursued a similar policy towards Welsh. Canada systematically denied the cultural, linguistic and political rights of the Quebecois and the indigenous people. Such policies were aimed at depriving the ethnic minorities of their distinctive cultural identities (Kymlicka, 1998; Oommen, 1997: 135–59).

The sway of ethnic nationalism, which was often accompanied by coercive assimilation, suppression, enslavement and even genocide, is reflected in European colonization and in the processes of Hispanization, Russification and Sinification in Latin America, the erstwhile Soviet Union and China. The most horrifying consequences of ethnic nationalism were witnessed in Nazi Germany. Jews, Gypsies and Slavs were stigmatized as outsiders and excluded from public life, armed forces and state-run educational institutions. Ultimately, 6 million Jews were ruthlessly massacred. Ethnic nationalism and chauvinism were largely responsible for the violent civil war and the ethnic cleansing in the former Yugoslavia (Denitch, 1994).

The experience of most countries in the West, as elsewhere, shows that the policy of coercive assimilation has proved to be a failure in the long run. The Jews, for example, have assiduously maintained their religious and ethnic identity despite intense pressures of assimilation and homogenization as well as social exclusion and stigmatization. In Central Asia, even during the heyday of communism, most of the ethnic and religious communities, such as the Azeris, Tajiks, Kazakhs, Turkomans, Uzbeks and Kirghiz, preserved and maintained their cultural traditions and distinctive identities. The Caucasians—Chechens, Inguish, Tatars, Daghestanis—despite their racial affinity with the Russians, have always defined their separate identities on the basis of religion, culture and language.

After World War I, Italy annexed the German-speaking region of South Tyrol. Mussolini tried to forcibly assimilate the people of the region into mainstream Italian society, which was resented and resisted by the local population. Many of them chose to migrate to Austria and other countries in the face of assimilationist pressures.

Many of the national minorities in Europe have jealously guarded their distinctive identities and traditions and have launched social movements and political parties to defend their traditions and cultural rights. National minorities in Spain, such as those in the Basque Country, Catalonia and Galicia, want to be recognized as nations within Spain. Some national minorities, such as the Irish in Northern Ireland, the Corsicans in France and the Basque, have espoused violent methods to project their cultural autonomy and political aspirations.

As a nation of immigrants, the United States has long insisted on the 'swift assimilation of aliens' and has emphasized the romantic ideal of the melting pot. However, the assertion of ethnic identity on the part of the African-Americans, Hispanics and the indigenous people in the late 1960s put a question mark on the goal of assimilation. Nathan Glazer and Daniel P. Moynihan have characteristically remarked that "the point about the melting pot is that it did not happen" (Glazer and Moynihan, 1963: 289). The failure of the assimilationist model in the United

States has led to the replacement of the metaphor of the melting pot with that of the 'salad bowl' and the 'glorious mosaic', in which each racial and ethnic element in the national population maintains its distinctiveness (Glazer, 1997: 100).

Since the French Revolution, the immigrants in France were expected to forsake their culture, language and identity in favour of a homogeneous French culture and way of life. This model of assimilation worked fairly well in absorbing Spanish, Italian, Portuguese and Polish immigrants earlier in the century. But it has failed in the case of Arab, African and Asian immigrants who began entering France in substantial numbers in the post-War period. "Today integration is a total failure", says an exasperated Jean-Francois Cope, mayor of Meaux, 54 km south-east of Paris, which counts 29 different ethnic groups among its 50,000 residents.

Realizing the failure of the short-sighted policy of assimilation and homogenization, many Western countries have sought to accommodate the political and cultural aspirations of ethnic minorities. Canada, for example, has officially declared itself a multicultural state and has adopted a federal system that gives the Quebecois as well as the country's indigenous people significant, cultural, linguistic and political autonomy. Britain, Belgium, Spain and the Scandinavian countries have recognized the legitimate aspirations and cultural and political rights of their national minorities and have conceded a substantial measure of autonomy. This has led some scholars to argue that an increasing number of Western democracies are multi-nation states, rather than nation-states (Kymlicka, 1998: 76).

It is now widely recognized that Europe is a culturally diverse region. There are nearly 80 indigenous languages in the continent and 20 of them are officially recognized. Multilingualism is officially recognized by the European Union. The European Union (EU) is an extraordinary construction which has no parallel in recent history. Over 500 million people from 27 different countries have come together to create the world's first transnational political and economic space. The EU's Berlin Declaration, approved on March 25, 2007, stated: "We, the citizens of Europe, have united for the better. The unnatural division of Europe is consigned to the past. We preserve in the European Union the identities and diverse traditions of its member-states" (Momin, 2008*b*).

Identity

There has come about an unprecedented revival and reawakening of ethnic identities in many parts of the world in recent years. This revival has been strengthened by the process of globalization, the worldwide salience of cultural diversity, the accelerated pace of technological, social and cultural change, extensive international migrations and increasing contacts between different ethnic groups and cultural communities, and the growing visibility of transnational diasporas (Giddens, 1991).

One of the early formulations of identity was offered by Erik Erikson from a psychoanalytic perspective. He saw identity as an internal process by which one defines and integrates various aspects of the self. Erikson argued that it is difficult to define identity in a precise manner because it concerns a process located "in the core of the individual and yet also in the core of his communal culture, a process which establishes, in fact, the identity of these two identities" (Erikson, 1959: 22). What Erikson says, in other words, is that identity is necessarily processual and that it entails a close interaction between individual personality and participation in society. Gordon W. Allport, in his influential *The Nature of Prejudice* (1954), used the term 'identification' and suggested that it conveyed "the sense of emotional merging of oneself with others" (Allport, 1954: 293–94). A quite different kind of conceptualization of identity was developed in the sociological and anthropological tradition. Reference group theory, role theory and symbolic interactionism viewed identity as embedded in the groups to which an individual belongs and in the different roles he plays in different situations. Ralph Linton, in his *The Study of Man* (1936), introduced role theory and suggested that the concept of social role was intimately linked with that of social status. In the course of time, role theory emerged as a major theoretical perspective in sociology. The symbolic interactionist perspective emphasizes that identity is mediated and negotiated in the context of social processes and encounters. Symbolic interactionism evinces a keen interest in the way social interaction shapes the self-perception and self-consciousness of the individual. Erving Goffman's *Stigma* (1963) focuses on the centrality of identity in the consciousness of the individual. Goffman and Peter Berger played a highly important role, through their influential writings, in popularizing the sociological significance of identity. Berger emphasized that identities are not only "socially bestowed but must also be socially sustained and fairly steadily so". The multiplicity of roles, according to the sociological perspective, entails multiple identities. A major limitation of this view is that it overemphasizes social ascription as a source and determinant of identity.

The social, political and psychological turmoil resulting from World War II and the intellectual climate prevailing in the United States in the 1950s focused on the question of the survival of the person in mass society and thereby reinforced the salience of identity. The Frankfurt School, which sought to synthesize the Marxian and Freudian perspectives, launched a massive critique of mass society and highlighted personal isolation, alienation and uprootedness in the context of the gigantic structures of modern society.

The question of identity has acquired an extraordinary salience in the contemporary social science literature. Recent researches have not only taken cognizance of the universal valorization of identity but have also focused on the dynamics of identity formation and on the role and functions of identity in different social, political and cultural contexts. There is general agreement that identity is a complex, multilayered and multidimensional construct, which involves self-identification as well as ascription by others. The process of identity formation has important cognitive, affective and volitional dimensions and is significantly influenced by changing situational contexts. Generally, identities are not given once and for all, but are actively constituted and negotiated, and tend to evolve and shift. This suggests that identities are often multiple (defined by gender, race, ethnicity, class), overlapping, hybridic and contested. Lola Romanucci-Ross, George DeVos and E. Roosens have provided interesting case studies and analyses of the ways in which the identities of a wide range of ethnic groups throughout the world have evolved and changed in response to social, political and economic opportunities and constraints afforded by particular contexts (Phinny, 2000).

Identities may not always be clearly defined or perceived, but may also become blurred or confused, especially in contexts marked by hybridization or biculturation. This, for example, is the case with many young second-generation Asian and African immigrants in Europe and North America, who are situated in a kind of a cultural no man's land between the host society which does not accept them and the culture of their parents which severely restricts their freedom and with which they cannot fully identify.

As suggested in the foregoing, the process of identity formation is influenced by self-definition and self-identification as well as the perception, judgement and ascription of other people. Social recognition has a highly significant bearing on the individual's identity and self-esteem and its absence or negation is likely to have negative, adverse consequences (Taylor, 1994). This is as true of ethnic groups and cultural communities as of individuals. The integration of racially distinct immigrants, including the descendants of immigrants born and brought up in Western countries, in the larger society has become more problematic because they carry, in addition to their own self-defined identity, an ascribed identity or ethnic label, which is often negative, demeaning and stigmatizing. The African-Americans (including the children of mixed white-black parentage) are perceived and defined by the white majority not only in terms of their ethnic identity but also an ascribed identity, which stereotypes and stigmatizes them and marginalizes them from the American mainstream. It is extremely difficult, if not impossible, for most African-Americans to escape this ascribed identity (Kymlicka, 1998). Some researches in social psychology indicate that ethnic consciousness and affirmation is likely to be more pronounced among groups which experience exclusion and discrimination.

A significant theme in discussions of identity relates to national identity. According to the classical theory of the state, which was based on the assumption of a culturally homogeneous population, national identity was defined in terms of the ethos, cultural traditions and ethnic identity of the dominant national group. This view of national identity has become problematic in the context of contemporary multiethnic societies. If national identity is defined in ethnocentric, homogenizing and exclusionary terms, which has been the case until recently in most countries of Asia, Africa and Europe, it can become a source of divisiveness, conflict and discord. It is likely to engender alienation and disaffection among ethnic and religious minorities (Parekh, 2000: 237). Thankfully, an increasing number of countries now seem to be inclined to abandon the monolithic, ethnocentric and exclusionary model of national identity in favour of an inclusionary and accommodative model (Momin, 2006).

Multiculturalism

The term 'multiculturalism' as a perspective on the management of cultural diversity in multiethnic societies came into vogue in the early 1970s. Canada was the first country to adopt multiculturalism as an official policy in 1971. In Europe, multiculturalism was first adopted as an official policy by Sweden to deal with the issue of integration of immigrants. Subsequently, Britain, the Netherlands and the Scandinavian countries also adopted multicultural policies. Britain has followed a community-based model of multiculturalism, which provides for the recognition and accommodation of the rights of minority groups. The growing worldwide salience of ethnic consciousness, the great migrations of the post-World War II period (which led to significant alterations in the demographic and social composition of many Western countries), and the increasing visibility of transnational diasporas provided the social and cultural context of multiculturalism. The revival and reawakening of ethnic consciousness and identities among immigrants has been strengthened by the rapid, unprecedented advances in transportation and communication technologies.

It is useful to draw a distinction between multiculturality and multiculturalism. Multiculturality refers to the heterogeneity and diversity in the demographic composition and the ethnic and cultural profile of a country. Multiculturalism, on the other hand, is a normative political and social philosophy based on a public recognition and acceptance of ethnic and cultural diversity and a positive response to cultural difference. A heterogeneous, multiethnic society may respond to the fact of cultural diversity in two distinct ways. It may perceive cultural diversity as an impediment to national unity, integrity and cohesiveness and may thus choose to downplay it and adopt a policy of cultural homogenization. This, for example, is the case with China. Or, alternatively, it may view cultural diversity as a national asset, as a valuable source of its creative strength and dynamism, and may thus endeavour to safeguard and cherish it (Parekh, 2000: 3–5).

Multiculturalism emphasizes that cultural differences must be publicly acknowledged and accommodated in a framework of tolerance and peaceful coexistence (Taylor, 1992; Goldberg, 1994; Giddens, 1998: 136). It rejects inequality based on birth, class or caste, discrimination and social exclusion. Will Kymlicka has sought to reconcile the equal rights of citizenship with cultural diversities and the recognition of difference within the framework of what he describes as multicultural citizenship. He argues that a liberal state should respect and protect the ethnic identities of citizens. Citizenship, according to him, should be accommodative of cultural diversity (Kymlicka, 1995). Anthony Giddens maintains that a cosmopolitan outlook is the necessary condition of a multicultural society. He speaks of 'cosmopolitan pluralism' and includes it among the characteristic features of what he describes as the 'third way', which eschews the extremes of both communism or radical socialism and unrestrained free market capitalism (Giddens, 1998: 136).

The contexts of multiculturalism in Western countries on the one hand and in Asia and Africa on the other are quite different. In Europe and North America, the focus is on the integration or assimilation of immigrants into the mainstream society and the accommodation of the political and cultural rights and aspirations of indigenous national minorities. The multiethnic societies of Asia and Africa, on the other hand, are mainly concerned with striking a balance between the conflicting pressures of ethnic diversity and political unity within the overarching framework of nationalism, the mitigation of ethnic conflicts, and fostering a sense of cohesiveness in a culturally heterogeneous population.

In most European countries, immigration, cultural diversity and the integration of immigrants into the mainstream society have become sites of contestation. In many Western societies, the majority population regards the growing ethnic and cultural diversity as a threat to the cohesiveness of their societies and to their distinctive cultural traditions. By and large, immigrants in Western countries are faced with discrimination, lack of legal security, unclear citizenship status and institutionalized racism. Since the 1970s, racist sentiments and violence against immigrants and foreigners have been steadily on the increase in many European countries. The growing popularity of far-right political parties in Europe (such as the National Front in France, the British National Party, the Northern League in Italy, Vlaas Belang in Belgium and the Swiss People's Party), the recent outbreaks of anti-foreigner violence spearheaded by the neo-Nazis and other extremist groups in Germany and the emergence of racist groups in southern Europe indicate that racist sentiments and ideologies are getting strengthened (Castles, 1993; Bjorgo and Witte, 1993). In the US and in many parts of Europe, organizations that openly propagate hatred against foreigners and immigrants, such as the Ku Klux Klan and neo-Nazi groups, regularly carry out campaigns of vilification, intimidation and violence against immigrants. A central question faced by contemporary multicultural societies is: Can groups and communities maintain their cultural distinctiveness without experiencing economic, social, political and cultural marginalization (Cornwell and Stoddard, 2001: 22)?

The study of contemporary multiethnic societies has thrown up a number of contentious but highly important issues, including the relations between the dominant national population and minority groups, institutionalized racism, pressures of assimilation and homogenization, social and cultural fragmentation, the marginalization and ghettoization of ethnic minorities, the growing concern with the maintenance of cultural distinctiveness and ethnic identities on the part of ethnic and religious minorities, hybridization and creolization, political integration and representation, citizenship, human rights, national identity and transnational diasporas.

One of the significant issues in the study of multiethnic societies is the increasing salience of transnationalism. Broadly, transnationalism refers to multiple ties, interactions and networks that link large numbers of people across the borders of nation-states. Such networks are greatly strengthened by the incredible advances in transportation and communication technologies. Intensity and simultaneity are the most striking features of transnationalism. Transnational diasporas represent the most important aspect of transnationalism. The diaspora is characterized by a triadic relationship between a globally dispersed yet identity-conscious ethnic group, the countries where such groups are located, and the original homeland (Safran, 1991). Transnational diasporas represent important modes of social organization, communication and political and cultural mobilization. They play an important role in reinforcing and transmitting shared ethnic identities (Castles, 1993; Hannerz, 1996; Vertovec, 1999). Paul Gilroy has used the term 'Black Atlantic' to describe an extensive cultural network spanning Africa, the Americas, the Caribbean and Britain, which has been a source of identity, continuity and strength for millions of people of African descent (Gilroy, 1993). Transnational diasporas also serve as sites of cultural interpenetration, hybridization and creolization.

David Hollinger, in his book *Postethnic America: Beyond Multiculturalism* (1995), distinguishes two kinds of multiculturalism: a 'pluralist' model, which considers ethnic groups as permanent and enduring a 'cosmopolitan' model, which focuses on the shifting boundaries of ethnic groups and on multiple identities. As he puts it, "pluralism respects inherited boundaries and locates individuals within one or another of a series of ethno-racial groups to be protected or preserved. Cosmopolitanism is more wary of traditional enclosures and favours voluntary affiliations. Cosmopolitanism promotes multiple identities, emphasizes the dynamic and changing character of many groups, and is responsive to the potential for creating new cultural combinations" (Hollinger, 1995: 65).

The Crisis of Multiculturalism

During the past three decades, multiculturalism has enjoyed great popularity in many European countries and has enthusiastically been supported by immigrants and minority groups. However, multiculturalism has been subject to a great deal of criticism and controversy in recent years. The critics of multiculturalism point out that it presupposes a view of cultures and ethnic groups as fixed, bounded and absolute and thereby solidifies cultural difference. It ignores the role of cultural interpenetration, hybridization and creolization (Anthias, 2001). Therefore, it encourages social and cultural fragmentation and strengthens ethnic cleavages and ghettoization. Some critics accuse multiculturalism of legitimizing separatism and atomization. Civitas, a right-wing think-tank in Britain, pointed out in a report in 2005 that the concept of multiculturalism was divisive and encouraged racial hatred. Certain events at the turn of the century, including the attack on the United States on September 11, 2001, the Madrid train bombing in March 2004, the murder of the Dutch film maker Theo van Gogh in November 2004 and the terrorist attack on London's public transport system in July 2005 (carried out by home-grown, educated terrorists), have prompted an increasing number of politicians and public figures to rethink the viability of multiculturalism as a model of societal integration. Britain, the Netherlands and Denmark seem to be moving away from multiculturalism.

Trevor Philips, former head of Britain's Commission for Racial Equality, has recently suggested that multiculturalism may be outdated. He said Britain could be sleep-walking into ethnic segregation because of a failure to create common values, with some districts in the country on their way to becoming fully-fledged ghettos—black holes into which no one goes without fear and trepidation and from which no one ever escapes undamaged. A couple of years ago, the former British prime minister Tony Blair had said: "Multiculturalism is not what we thought it was. Tolerance is a must. Conform to it or don't come here. The right to be different; the duty to integrate. That's what being British means".

In 2007 Britain launched a new Commission for Integration and Cohesion, headed by an Indian-born British politician. While launching the Commission, Ruth Kelly, one of former Prime Minister Tony Blair's cabinet members, announced that the UK had moved away from a "near-uniform consensus" on the value of multiculturalism. She added that it was legitimate for Britain to support a debate whether multiculturalism has encouraged separateness. The new Commission is mandated to discuss the drawing up of "community charters", signed by community leaders, endorsing respect for democracy and the rejection of racism and violence.

The strongest criticism of multiculturalism has been launched by Europe's far-right political parties and organizations. Italy's far-right, rabidly anti-immigrant Lega Nord (Northern League) argues that to "transform Italy into a multi-racial, multi-ethnic and multi-religious country modelled after the US means to keep Italy divided".

For more than two decades, the Netherlands has espoused "tolerance of diversity" as the cornerstone of its integration policy. In the aftermath of 9/11, Dutch politicians and public figures have increasingly emphasized that immigrants must be pressurized to assimilate into mainstream Dutch society. The discourse of multiculturalism in the Netherlands is being replaced by that of integration and assimilation. In her speech during the Christmas celebrations in 2007, the Dutch Queen Beatrix made a plea for tolerance and respect for the country's minorities. She pointed out that the right to freedom of expression did not automatically mean the right to offend the religious sensibilities of minorities or other sections of the population. Geert Wilders, leader of the

Netherlands' far-right PVV Party, condemned the Queen's speech as "multicultural rubbish" and audaciously demanded that she be stripped of her constitutional position as head of the government (Momin, 2008*a*).

Multicommunitarianism

The idea of multicommunitarianism has been conceptualized in the context of present-day multiethnic societies. It seeks to bring into focus the overriding importance of societal harmony and cohesion while making an allowance for cultural diversity. Essentially, multicommunitarianism connotes living together in a framework of equality, an open recognition of cultural diversity, respect for the sensibilities of others, sharing of social, cultural and civic spaces, and societal engagement. Four core elements define multicommunitarianism: (i) equality, (ii) public recognition of ethnic and cultural diversity (and by implication, of community-specific identities and rights), (iii) shared social, cultural and civic spaces, and (iv) societal engagement (Momin, 2004; 2006; 2009).

Multicommunitarianism is conceived as an *ideal type* in the Weberian sense, a model, a set of characteristics defining the configuration of a type of societal arrangement. The basic theoretical premise underlying the perspective of multicommunitarianism is the universal dialectic of diversity and unity, of differentiation and syncretization. This dialectic is reflected in the realm of ideas, in the historical process, and in social and cultural processes. The 18th century German philosopher Gottfried Wilhelm Leibniz dwelt on this idea in a philosophical framework while the celebrated German philosopher Hans-Georg Gadamer emphasized the salience of this idea in the context of Europe. Jawaharlal Nehru, India's first prime minister, observed that the idea of unity-in-diversity represents the essence of Indian civilization. Interestingly, the motto of the European Union is *In varietate concordia* (united in diversity).

Multicommunitarianism draws on the strengths of multiculturalism and communitarianism and, at the same time, seeks to transcend their inherent limitations. While multiculturalism focuses on the recognition and accommodation of ethnic and cultural diversity in the public domain, the central concern of multicommunitarianism is to foster and strengthen common bonds and linkages among people with diverse cultural and religious backgrounds. Communitarianism rightly criticizes the tenet of radical individualism and emphasizes that a good society rests on a balance between liberty and the social order, between individual rights and social responsibilities. However, the problem with communitarianism is that it rests on the premise of a homogeneous society, which has become problematic in the present era.

II
South Asia

South Asia, which comprises the seven states of India, Pakistan, Bangladesh, Nepal, Sri Lanka, Bhutan and Maldives, covers a large geographical area, has a hoary past and contains a huge, heterogeneous population. The population of South Asia exceeds one billion, comprising nearly one-sixth of the global population. The region is characterized by an enormous range of racial, ethnic, linguistic, religious and cultural diversity. Some of the most ancient racial groups of mankind and some of the oldest languages are to be found in South Asia. All the major world religions as well as many of the most primitive, animistic beliefs and rituals are found here. While Hinduism, Buddhism, Jainism and Sikhism originated in the Indian subcontinent, Judaism, Christianity, Islam and Zoroastrianism have had a long presence in the region. One of the oldest Jewish communities, the Bene Israel, has been living in India since the 1st century AD. Christianity reached the Indian subcontinent in the first century of the common era. Muslim traders, scholars and saints began arriving in India and Sri Lanka in the first century of the Islamic era (7th century AD). The advent of Zoroastrianism in India can be traced to the 10th century. South Asia has witnessed a great deal of interaction, hybridization and syncretism in ideas, languages and dialects, cultural patterns, arts and crafts and folklore.

South Asia has experienced a long and extensive process of colonial intrusion. Following Vasco da Gama's discovery of the sea route to the east in 1498, European colonial powers systematically weakened and finally destroyed the old trading networks. In the course of time, the English, the French and the Dutch challenged the Portuguese trade monopoly and ultimately the British East India Company ousted the rival colonial powers.

Following the failure of the Indian uprising of 1857, British colonial rule was established over large parts of the country. The Portuguese reached the island of Sri Lanka in the early decades of the 16th century. They were permitted to build a fort and were also given trade concessions. In less than a century they were in control of most parts of Sri Lanka. They were joined and ousted by the Dutch in 1658, who, in turn, were defeated and forced to leave the island by the British in 1796. Sri Lanka was liberated from colonial rule in 1948. Nepal, Sri Lanka and Bhutan experienced colonial rule and domination for varying lengths of time (Schwartz, 1978: 49–64).

The independence of the Indian subcontinent from colonial rule in 1947 was followed by one of the most horrifying massacres in human history. More than a million people—including Hindus, Muslims and Sikhs—were brutally killed on either side of the border. Nearly 12 million people were uprooted and displaced and thousands of women were kidnapped and dishonoured.

Politically, South Asia presents a fragmented scenario with shades of military dictatorships, monarchy and democratic rule. Political instability as well as extensive democratization have been the striking features of the region. Both India and Pakistan celebrated the 61st anniversary of their independence in August 2008. India has enjoyed political stability and democratic rule since independence. The Constitution of India provides for a federal polity, an independent judiciary and a multi-party system of democracy and has been a key instrument in safeguarding the country's democratic institutions and people's fundamental rights. Drawing upon India's cultural heritage as well as the constitutional and legal experiences of several Western countries, the Constitution provides the defining features of the state and society in India in terms of equality, citizenship, fundamental rights, social justice and secularism. It recognizes the rights of ethnic, religious and linguistic minorities, including their personal laws and religious and educational institutions. India has enjoyed political stability and civilian rule since its independence in 1947. An independent judiciary and autonomous public institutions, such as the Election Commission, have greatly strengthened the country's democratic fabric. Judicial activism has played a highly important role in securing people's fundamental rights, in checking the violation of constitutional norms by corrupt, partisan and insensitive governments, and in preventing environmental degradation.

It took nine years for Pakistan's constitution to be agreed upon and drafted. Shortly after the promulgation of the constitution in 1956, Pakistan came under military rule. Frequent, long and agonizing spells of authoritarian military rule have invariably been accompanied by political instability and the suppression of human rights and civil liberties. In fact, political instability and the fragility of democratic institutions have been the hallmark of Pakistan since its creation. In October 1999 General Parvez Musharraf seized power by ousting a civilian government. Following the terrorist attack on the United States on September 11, 2001, Pakistan became a close ally of the US-led war against global terrorism, which caused widespread resentment in the country, resulted in the escalation of violence and deepened political polarization. In November 2007, General Musharraf sacked the Chief Justice of the Supreme Court and clamped emergency in the country. Benazir Bhutto, a former Prime Minister, was assassinated in a bomb attack in December 2007, plunging the country in turmoil and instability. In parliamentary elections held in February 2008, General Musharraf's supporters were defeated by the opposition Pakistan People's Party and the former Prime Minister Nawaz Sharif's Muslim League. The two parties formed a coalition government, with Pakistan People's Party's Yusuf Raza Gilani as Prime Minister and Asif Ali Zardari, Benazir Bhutto's husband, as President. General Musharraf resigned under the threat of impeachment.

Bangladesh is the youngest state in South Asia. Its secession from Pakistan in 1971 was accompanied by violent upheaval and turbulence which shook the Indian subcontinent to its foundations. The creation of Bangladesh was inspired by linguistic and cultural nationalism. The Constitution of Bangladesh, promulgated by its first Prime Minister Sheikh Mujeebur Rahman in 1972, rests on the principles of democracy, nationalism, socialism and secularism. Bangladesh fell under military rule a few years after its creation. In 1979, the country experienced a brief spell of civilian rule under President Zia, which was cut short by his assassination in 1981. General Hossain Mohammad Ershad ruled the country for nine years, which undermined the country's nascent democratic institutions. The military regime of General Ershad was overthrown in consequence of a massive popular uprising in

1990. Since its creation, Bangladesh has been plagued by political uncertainty, fragility of democratic institutions and widespread corruption.

The political scenario in Bangladesh during the past three decades has been marked by a long-standing rivalry and feud between the Awami League, led by Sheikh Hasina Wajid (daughter of Sheikh Mujibur Rahman), and the Bangladesh Nationalist Party, led by Begum Khaleda Zia (General Ziaur Rahman's daughter). Sheikh Hasina Wajid was Prime Minister from 1996 to 2001 while Begum Khaleda Zia was Prime Minister between 1991 and 1996 and again from 2001 to 2006. The acrimony between the two parties, which is often attributed to an ego clash between the two "Begums", has often erupted into violence. Violent clashes between the supporters of the two parties led to the cancellation of elections in January 2007 and the imposition of a state of emergency. Dr Fakhruddin Ahmed, a former head of the Central Bank, took over as head of the interim government, with the backing of the military, in June 2007. The caretaker government launched a massive drive against graft and corruption. In the recent elections held on December 29, 2008 Sheikh Hasina Wajid's Awami League secured an overwhelming majority and came into power again.

Nepal has been under the sway of a hereditary monarch for more than two centuries. A multi-party democracy under a constitutional monarchy was established in 1951. Since the late 1990s a civil war, spearheaded by Maoist insurgents who were bitterly opposed to the monarchy, has devastated the country. More than 12,000 people have been killed in clashes between government forces and Maoist guerrillas and nearly 1,00,000 people have been displaced. In April 2006, Nepal's major political parties joined hands with the Maoists in organizing countrywide mass demonstrations for the restoration of democracy. This compelled King Gyanendra to relinquish power and reinstate parliament. In early 2007 the Maoists joined an interim government.

In the April 2008 elections, the Maoists emerged as the largest group in parliament and a new Marxist-dominated government took office in August 2008. The Constituent Assembly took a historic decision to abolish the 239-year-old monarchy. Nepal was declared a republic in May 2008, with Ram Baran Yadav, a doctor by profession, as the first president and Pushpa

Kamal Dahal, popularly known as Prachanda, as the new prime minister.

The Himalayan kingdom of Bhutan has been almost cut off from the rest of the world for centuries. Sir Ugyen Wangchuk, a powerful provincial governor, assumed the reign of government in 1907 and was designated the first hereditary king of the country. In 1949 India and Bhutan signed the Treaty of Peace and Friendship, which provided that India would not interfere in Bhutan's internal affairs. Bhutan became a member of the United Nations in 1971. Jigme Singye Wanchuck, who ascended the throne in 1972, was a great votary of education, democratization and modernization. He voluntarily stepped down in December 2006, appointed his son, Khesar Namgyel Wangchuck, as his successor, and decreed that the country should follow the path of democracy. The first general elections were held in March 2008, in which the royalist Bhutan Peace and Prosperity Party secured 44 of the 47 seats in the new parliament. Bhutan thus emerged as the world's youngest democracy with a constitutional monarchy. Jigme Thinley became the country's first elected prime minister. The new king—the last monarch in South Asia—has pledged to follow in the footsteps of his father who had made democratization and development his foremost priorities.

In Sri Lanka, a democratic government was established in the wake of the end of colonial rule in 1948. The first government espoused socialist policies but worked to safeguard and strengthen the dominance and interests of the majority Sinhala population. Sinhalese was declared the official language of the country. Tension between the majority Sinhala population and the long-established Tamil minority has been simmering for decades, which erupted in a civil war in the 1980s. Tamil Tiger militants carried out deadly suicide bombings in Colombo in the 1990s. The violent clashes between government forces and the LTTE have left more than 60,000 people dead and more than 200,000 displaced.

A ceasefire was agreed in 2002, but regular attacks and counter-attacks and suicide bombings continued unabated. The expiry of the ceasefire in January 2008 saw a renewed upsurge in clashes between government forces and Tamil separatists, leaving scores of people dead on both sides. The latest development is that the government forces have almost wiped out the LTTE and have taken possession of the areas controlled by LTTE.

Around the 5th century BC, Maldives came to be inhabited by settlers from Sri Lanka and southern India. Islam reached the archipelago, through Arab traders, in 1153. For nearly eight centuries Maldives was an independent Muslim sultanate. In the 16th and 17th centuries the islands came under the control of the Portuguese and the Dutch. Subsequently, it became a British protectorate from 1887 to 1965. Following a referendum, the sultanate was abolished in 1968 and the islands became a republic. Ibrahim Nasir became the first President of the country and held office from 1968 to 1978. He was succeeded by Maumoon Abdul Ghayoom, who held the reigns of power for nearly three decades, winning six consecutive elections. Maumoon's reign was marked by political repression. Following the November 2008 elections, Mohammad Nasheed, a former political prisoner, was sworn in as the country's new President on November 11, 2008.

Economic Growth

In the medieval period, India was famous as the world's richest region, the land of gold and precious jewels. In 1600, when the East India Company was founded, India accounted for 22.5 per cent of the global GDP while Britain's share was only 1.8 per cent. Colonial rule led to the decline and impoverishment of the Indian economy and undermined the cultural traditions and self-confidence of the people.

India, Bangladesh and Pakistan, which are among the top ten most populous nations in the world, have come a long way since independence. In the whole of South Asia, India has experienced the most dramatic economic growth. During the past five years, India's economic and financial integration with the global market has accelerated at an unprecedented pace. The country's foreign reserves have risen to an enviable $250 billion and raised annual economic growth from around 4 per cent in the four decades before the early 1990s—when the process of wide-ranging economic reforms and liberalization started—to more than 9 per cent in 2007. The country's real GDP growth has experienced an annual average of nearly 9 per cent in the past five years. Even, in the recent recession, the growth rate has not been affected much as in the developed economies of the world. It is poised to maintain an annual growth rate of around 7.5 per cent in the coming years. Similarly, foreign direct investment has grown from about $100 million in the early 1990s to about $16 billion today. As a result of extensive economic reforms, the balance of payments has turned into a surplus of almost $50 billion. Perhaps, the most striking development has taken place in telecommunications. Today, there are more mobile phones in the country than landline phones, with 200 million subscribers and 6 million more being added each month. India is today one of the world's fastest growing economies. On a purchasing power parity (PPP) basis, India is today the fourth largest economy in the world after the US, China and Japan. It is on the verge of overtaking Japan to become the third largest economy in the world. It is estimated that India will overtake the US in about 2050, as measured in dollar terms. India is poised to become the fastest-growing economy in the world by 2008–30, averaging an annual expansion of 6.3 per cent. Per capita income in the country, which was Rs 255 in 1947, has risen to Rs 33,283 in 2007–08. It is estimated that India's per capita income will increase to 35 times the present level by 2050. According to Goldman Sach's BRIC Report—which provides comparative economic projections in respect of Brazil, Russia, India and China—India is the only BRIC economy which will sustain an average of above 5 per cent growth rate through the next 45 years. The country is thus speedily moving in the direction of sustainable growth.

Despite being a poor and economically backward country in 1947, Pakistan's economic growth was better than the global average from the 1950s to 1980s. However, the 1990s witnessed a slowdown in the economy due to political turmoil and instability. Pakistan registered a growth rate of 7 per cent during the past four years. In its June 2006 Economic Survey, Stanley Morgan, the world's leading finance consultant, included Pakistan in its list of major markets in the world economy. Pakistan's gross domestic product (GDP), in terms of PPP, is estimated to be $439.7 billion, while its per capita income stands at $2,803. Though Pakistan's GDP growth rates have been steadily on the increase over the past five years, experts are of the opinion that it will be extremely difficult, if not impossible, for the country to sustain a high growth rate. High economic growth has not led to any substantial reduction in poverty. According to the reports of the World Bank, the United Nations Development Programme and the Asian

Development Bank, the poverty rate in Pakistan is between 23–28 per cent.

In the past few years, Bangladesh has made substantial progress in the alleviation of poverty, in reducing population growth and in economic development. The poverty rate fell from an estimated 74 per cent in 1973–74 to 40 per cent in 2005. The country is expected to achieve the United Nations' Millennium Development Goal (MDG) of reducing poverty by half by 2015. The economy of Bangladesh—the third largest in South Asia—has grown on an average of 5.5 per cent since 2000 and reached 6.7 per cent in 2006, while per capita growth has increased from 1 per cent in the 1980s to the current 3.5 per cent (Yunus, 2007: 105–6).

Since its creation in 1971, Bangladesh continues to be under the shadow of poverty and economic backwardness. The country's economy is largely based on agriculture and it is the third largest rice-producing country in the world. The country's foreign exchange earnings are largely derived from the garment and jute industries. Bangladesh's per capita GDP stands at $2,300. Nearly half of the country's 158.6 million people live below the poverty line. The current unemployment rate is nearly 35 per cent.

Nepal's economy is largely based on agriculture, which accounts for about 40 per cent of the GDP, and livestock farming. Approximately, three quarters of the population are engaged in agriculture. The country's economic development is hampered by a multiplicity of factors, including its landlocked and hilly terrain, lack of resource endowment, and absence of comprehensive development policies and programmes. With per capita GDP of $1,500—the lowest in South Asia—Nepal is one of the poorest countries in the world. About 82.5 per cent of Nepal's population of 28.2 million is living below the international poverty line of $ 2 per day. According to World Bank estimates, the poverty rate in Nepal has become worse in the past two decades. Nepal's absolute monarchy ended in 2006 but the path to democracy is fraught with formidable obstacles and challenges.

Sri Lanka has been famous for the production and export of tea, coffee, rubber and coconuts. Its per capita GDP is $4,700—the highest in South Asia. It has an annual growth rate of 7.4 per cent. In the mid-1970s Sri Lanka began to shift away from socialist policies and the economy was gradually opened to global competition. However, two decades of civil war have greatly undermined the economy as well as the country's democratic institutions.

Bhutan is one of the world's smallest and least developed economies. Nearly 90 per cent of its people depend on agriculture and forestry for their livelihood. The country's per capita GDP is $1,969. The economy is closely tied up with India through trade and monetary exchange.

The economy of Maldives, which is largely dependent on tourism and fishing, has registered a growth rate of over 7.5 per cent for more than a decade. Tourism is Maldives' largest industry, which accounts for 28 per cent of the GDP. The country's per capita GDP is $3,900—the second highest in South Asia, the highest being that of Sri Lanka at $ 4,700. The tsunami disaster in December 2004 had a catastrophic impact on the economy, as a consequence of which the GDP came down to 3.6 per cent. However, it quickly recovered and now enjoys a robust growth rate.

Climate Change and Development

Economic growth, human development and environment are closely intertwined. The Nobel Laureate Amartya Sen has rightly observed: "Development cannot be divorced from ecological and environmental concerns. Indeed, important components of human freedoms—and crucial ingredients of our quality of life—are thoroughly dependent on the integrity of the environment." The UNDP's *Human Development Report 2007/2008* focuses on the challenges of climate change and on worldwide responses and strategies to cope with them.

The 2007 report of the United Nations' Intergovernmental Panel on Climate Change (IPCC) presents a grim scenario of the looming environmental crisis and its alarming consequences for human settlements, agricultural productivity, water resources and health. The detrimental consequences of climate change are largely an outcome of short-sighted policies and reckless lifestyles, to which the industrialized countries are the major contributors. High-income OECD countries, with just 15 per cent of the world's population, account for almost half of the emissions that are a major cause of climate change. The per capita emissions of India, for example, are a mere 1/30th or 1/40th of the emissions in the US or Europe.

The IPCC report further points out that sea levels are likely to rise by at least 40 cm by 2100, inundating vast areas on the coastline, including some of the most densely populated cities, and forcing millions of people to migrate to safer areas. Glacier and snow melting in the Himalayas will lead to flooding, with devastating consequences for human settlements and agricultural productivity. Temperatures in South Asia are expected to rise by as much as 1.2 degrees Celsius, resulting in a fall in agricultural activity and increasing the prospects of drought in many areas. Crop yield in South Asia could decrease by up to 30 per cent by the middle of the present century. An estimated 60 million people living in the low-lying coastal areas of the region could be displaced as a result of consequences flowing from global warming by the end of the 21st century. Coastal cities like Mumbai and Kolkata are especially vulnerable to the prospects of flooding.

India is likely to be seriously affected by decreasing rainfall, caused by global warming and glacier melt in the Himalayas, which will adversely impact the country's river systems. With the drying up of rivers, water tables will fall and the gross per capita water availability in the country may decline by one-third by 2050.

Bangladesh is vulnerable to frequent flooding and cyclones. Nearly 40 per cent of the country's land surface is flooded during the monsoon season, causing large-scale devastation and leaving hundreds of thousands of people homeless. Global warming is likely to result in higher temperatures, enhanced monsoon precipitation and increase in cyclone intensity. Sea levels in the Bay of Bengal are rising, posing a serious danger to about 20 per cent of the country's land surface which lies about three feet or less above sea level. Kofi Annan, former UN Secretary-General, has warned that a significant portion of Bangladesh is likely to disappear completely by the end of the 21st century (Yunus, 2007: 204). The IPCC report projects that Bangladesh may lose approximately 1,000 sq km of cultivated land due to rising sea levels.

Nepal's high dependence on natural resources and its lack of resources to deal with the consequences of climate change make it quite vulnerable to the environmental catastrophe. The Himalayas, which overshadow the central and northern parts of the country, constitute a threatened ecosystem. Weather-related extreme events, such as excessive rainfall, longer drought periods, landslides and floods, are increasing in frequency and magnitude, posing a serious threat to irrigation, water supply systems, infrastructure and health.

In Sri Lanka, the sea level is expected to rise by half a metre over the next two decades, leading to flooding in some areas and droughts in others. A major part of Jaffna, which lies on the northern tip of the island, may be submerged when the sea level rises. Climate change will have dire consequences for agriculture, water resources and health.

The IPCC report projects that, with the erosion of ice sheets and the expansion of warming seawater, sea levels are likely to rise worldwide by up to two feet by 2100. Maldives is the lowest high point on earth: the natural ground level anywhere in the islands does not exceed 2.3 metres. Sea levels around the Maldives have risen by about 20 cm in the past century, and the UN estimates that they will rise by a further 58 cm by 2100. The islands were inundated by unusually high tides in 1987 that caused extensive damage. The Asian tsunami of December 2004 left a trail of devastation in the islands. Any sea level rise could have a devastating effect on the people of Maldives and may in fact endanger the very survival of the country.

Mohammad Nasheed, the new president, recently told the BBC that he planned to establish an investment fund with some of the earnings from tourism, which could be used to purchase land—either in Sri Lanka or India—to relocate the entire population of Maldives in the event of a dangerous rise in sea levels. This seems to be an extremely complex and problematic proposition, which involves issues of sovereignty, national borders and international law. The government is also mulling over another, comparative more feasible, alternative. It plans to construct a new island, Hulu Male, where the population of some of its lowest-lying atolls, as well as the capital Male, could be relocated.

Human Development

Mahbub ul Haq's authoritative and illuminating study *Human Development in South Asia* (1997) reveals that South Asia is the poorest, the most illiterate, the most malnourished and the least gender-sensitive region in the world. The region has the lowest adult literacy rate (49%) in the world—lower than that of Sub-Saharan Africa (57%). Over 400 million illiterate adults, who comprise nearly half of the world's illiterate people, are found in South Asia. Nearly two-thirds of the region's adult female population is illiterate. More than 50 million children in South Asia, who comprise nearly two-fifths of world's children, do not attend school. South Asia has the dubious distinction of having the largest number of people in the world who are living in absolute poverty. South Asia and Sub-Saharan Africa have the lowest levels of per capita income in the world. In 1991, there were 52 countries where the expectation of life at birth was below 60 years—46 of these countries (88% of the total) were in South Asia and Sub-Saharan Africa (Haq and Haq, 1997).

South Asia has the highest incidence of annual maternal deaths in the world. Every year, around 1,88,000 women die from complications in pregnancy and child birth. The majority of births in the region occur at home in rural areas without qualified medical help or adequate health care facilities. The region's high maternal mortality rates account for almost half of all maternal deaths worldwide. In South Asia, India has the largest number of annual maternal deaths (1,17,000 or 540 per 1,00,000 live births), followed by Afghanistan (26,000), Bangladesh (21,000) and Pakistan (15,000). Some studies suggest that children who are left motherless are 10 times more likely than their peers to die within two years of their mother's death.

A UNESCO report points out that throughout South Asia there is a huge disparity between impressive economic growth and dismal performance in respect of human development indices. A recently released report by the UN and Asian Development Bank points out that India is lagging behind in eradicating extreme poverty and hunger, in achieving universal primary education, in promoting gender equality, in reducing maternal and infant mortality and in combating malaria and other diseases.

Despite formidable impediments and challenges, South Asian countries have made considerable progress in human development. India's high and sustainable economic growth has significantly impacted the human development index. According to World Bank data, India's poverty rate (the proportion of population living below $1 a day in PPP terms) dropped from 45 per cent (413 million) in 1994 to 34.3 per cent (371 million) in 2004. The spectre of famine, which used to frequently haunt the country in the early years of independence, has been banished. Epidemics like plague, smallpox, measles, whooping cough and cholera, which used to take a heavy toll of human life in the early decades of independence, have been brought under control.

Bangladesh has done rather well in human development, especially in health care. Infant mortality rates in the country fell by more than half (from 100 to 41 per 1,000 children) between 1990 and 2006. The mortality rate for children under five has been brought down to 52 per 1,000, compared with 87 in India and 98 in Pakistan. More girls than boys now attend secondary schools in the country.

Bhutan's former king, Jigme Singye Wanchuck, became internationally known for enunciating the concept of "Gross National Happiness", which emphasizes that it is people's well-being and happiness, and not Gross National Product (GNP), which provides an index of real development. The concept of Gross National Happiness is premised on four principles: sustainable development, environmentalism, good governance and the preservation of Bhutan's cultural values.

The UNDP ranks Bhutan 133rd out of 177 countries on the Human Development Index, but the Happy Planet Index of the New Economics Foundation, a London-based think-tank, ranks the country 13th. A pilot survey conducted in 2008 by Bhutan's GNH Commission (formerly the Planning Commission) suggested that more than two-thirds of people in Bhutan could be classified as being happy.

Ethnic Diversity

India is the seventh largest nation in the world in terms of area, comprising 2.2 per cent of the earth's surface, and also the second most populous country where 15.7 per cent of the global population resides. In Asia, India occupies 7.5 per cent of the territory and contains over a quarter (over 26%) of the continent's population. Indian society is characterized by an extensive and wide range of diversity. This diversity is reflected in the ethnic and social composition of the country's population, its multiplicity of languages, religious beliefs and practices, and customs and traditions. In terms of religious composition, 80.46 per cent of India's population is Hindu, 13.46 per cent Muslim, 2.34 per cent Christian, 1.87 per cent Sikh, 0.41 per cent Jain and 0.65 per cent of other faiths. According to the People of India (PoI) project, there are 325 community-specific languages and dialects in India, which belong to five language families. These languages are written in 25 different scripts. There are as many as 2,795 communities and about 80,000 segments with their respective titles and surnames (Singh, 1992).

Though an overwhelming majority of Pakistan's population (95%) follows the Islamic faith, significant ethnic, linguistic, cultural and sectarian diversities exist in the country. Pakistan's population consists of four major ethnic groups: Punjabis (60%), Sindhis (12%), Pukhtuns (14%) and Baluch (4%). The distribution of these four groups roughly corresponds to the country's provincial boundaries. Refugees (*Mohajirs*), who migrated from India in 1947 or shortly thereafter, comprise about 8 per cent of the population (Ahmed, 1983, 1997). Christians and Hindus comprise, respectively, 2 per cent and 1.8 per cent of the population.

The population of Bangladesh comprises Muslims (86%), Hindus (13%) and tribals (1%). There are significant religious, linguistic and cultural variations in the country's tribal population. The population of Sri Lanka is composed of the Sinhalese (82.7%), who are mostly followers of Buddhism, Tamil-speaking Hindus (8.9%) and Muslims (7.7%). The population of Nepal is composed of Nepali Hindus (86.5%), Buddhists (7.8%) and Muslims (3.5%). Christians and Jains constitute less than one per cent of the country's population. The Task Force on the Nepal Foundation for the Upliftment of the Nationalities (1991) has identified 61 ethnic groups in Nepal. The Commission for the National Language Policy Reform (1994) identified more than 70 languages and dialects in the country. Bhutan's population is composed of three major ethnic groups, namely, the Bhutia, who constitute about 50 per cent of the population, the Nepalese (Gurung), who constitute about 35 per cent of the population, and the Sharchops, who are about 15 per cent of the country's population. In Maldives, though the entire population follows Islam, significant racial, ethnic, linguistic and cultural diversities exist. The population of Maldives is of mixed Sinhalese, Indian and Arab descent. The majority of people speak Divehi (Maldivian), which has a close structural affinity with the Sinhalese language of Sri Lanka.

The fact that religion plays a highly significant role in South Asia is reflected not only in the religious beliefs and rituals, cultural traditions and behaviour patterns of the people but also in its association with the state. Thus, while Islam is the official religion in Pakistan and Maldives, Hinduism is the official religion in Nepal and Mahayana Buddhism is the official religion in Bhutan. In Bangladesh, during the regime of General Ziaur Rahman, more emphasis came to be placed on the country's Islamic identity. India and Sri Lanka have no official religion and have adopted secularism as a matter of state policy.

South Asia has witnessed extensive migrations and intermingling of people and cultures since ancient times. The processes of migration, adaptation and indigenization gave rise to a great deal of cultural exchange, hybridization and syncretism. This is reflected in large-scale miscegenation, languages and dialects, customs and traditions, beliefs and rituals, arts and crafts, and folklore. Historically, the Indian subcontinent has occupied a pre-eminent position in South Asia. A distinct and richly textured composite civilization emerged in the Indian subcontinent as a result of prolonged interaction and exchange between Hindu, Buddhist, Islamic and Western traditions. Indian history, civilization and cultural traditions have left a deep and enduring impress on the region. Nepal has developed a composite, syncretistic Hindu-Buddhist culture.

Ethnicity and Identity

Though ethnic identities in South Asia appear to be conspicuously salient, they cannot be considered as fixed, bounded and static. Centuries of cultural interaction and exchange among different ethnic groups and religious communities have resulted in the overlapping, blurring and hybridization of identities. Ethnic affiliations and identities in South Asia often cut across regional, religious and even national boundaries. The Kashmiri identity, for example, is shared in common by the people of Kashmiri descent on both sides of the Indo-Pakistan border as well as by the Kashmiri diaspora in Europe and North America. Similarly, the Sindhi identity is shared not only by the Sindhi Muslims and Hindus in Pakistan but also by the Sindhi migrants and their descendants in India and the transnational Sindhi diaspora.

Ethnicity and inter-ethnic relations in South Asia have been greatly influenced by social, political and economic processes and are often characterized by contestation and conflict. The factors that led to the secession of Bangladesh from Pakistan—economic disparity between the two wings of the country, the dominance of the Punjabi oligarchy in politics, military and the civil services, and the grossly disproportionate representation of the Bengali-speaking Muslims in all sectors of national life—were articulated in ethnic terms. Sheikh Mujeebur Rahman espoused Bengali nationalism based on Bengali language and culture. Thus, ethnicity played a crucial role in articulating the sense of alienation and discrimination felt by the people of East Pakistan and in political mobilization (Jalal, 1995, 1997). Subsequently, ethnic resentment and alienation among the Sindhis, Pukhtuns and Baluch in Pakistan was manifested in demands for independent Pukhtunistan, Sindhistan and Azad Baluchistan. In October 1998, at a conference of Sindhis, Baluch and Seraikis, it was decided to launch Pakistan Oppressed Nations Movement (PONM). The conference issued a joint statement in which Pakistan was declared a multinational country.

The Indian subcontinent suffered the horrifying consequences of partition in 1947 in which ethnicity and religion played an important role (Pandey, 2003). In Sri Lanka, the ethnic conflict between the majority Sinhalese and the Tamil separatists has been violent for many years (Kaferer, 1998). Bhutan witnessed ethnic tensions in the 1990s following the enforcement of an earlier citizenship act, which rendered many members of the minority Nepali community, who are concentrated in the southern part of the country, stateless. Following the eruption of violence, tens of thousands of ethnic Nepalis fled to Nepal between 1988 and 1993. Some 1,00,000 refugees from Bhutan live in the UN-supervised camps in Nepal. In contrast with other countries in South Asia, Maldives has been a haven of peace and tranquillity. A shared religion (Islam) and a common language (Divehi) have played an important role in the integration and cohesiveness of the country.

By and large, nationalist discourses in South Asia have been embedded in ethnic narratives and myths. The majoritarian view of nationalism has often surfaced on the political scene in most parts of South Asia and has encountered resistance from ethnic and religious minorities. Since the 19th century, one can discern two distinctive and contrasting strands in the nationalist discourse in India. One of them may be characterized as ethnonationalism or Hindu nationalism, which is premised on a conflation of nationalism and the ethos and religious and cultural traditions of the majority Hindu population. The other strand is based on a set of political principles, including equality, citizenship, fundamental rights and secularism. Bankim Chandra Chatterjee (1838–1894) was one of the early exponents of Hindu nationalism. He argued that the national character must be built only on the edifice of the national religion which, in the case of India, is Hinduism. Aurobindo Ghosh, Dayanand Saraswati, Bipin Chandra Pal, Lala Lajpat Rai and Lokmanya Tilak argued in favour of combining nationalism with Hindu revivalism. Tilak extolled the assumed superiority of the Aryan race and justified the Aryan conquest of non-Aryan races with whom they came in contact in the wake of their migration. He argued that "the common factor in Indian society is the feeling of *Hindutva*" (Heimsath, 1964: 141). V.D. Savarkar, the founder of Hindu Mahasabha, was a protégé of Tilak. He believed that Hindus and Muslims were two nations. He greatly admired the Italian fascist leader Giuseppe Mazzini (1805–1872) and translated his autobiography into Marathi. One can scarcely fail to notice in Savarkar's writings the calculated construction of a virile, aggressively communal Hindu self which is intolerant of other religious traditions (Basu et al., 1993). Savarkar's ideas greatly influenced K.B. Hedgewar, who founded the Rashtriya Swayamsewak Sangh (RSS) in 1925. M.S. Golwalkar, one of the prominent leaders of the RSS, distinguished five criteria which, in his view, define a nation: land, race, religion, culture and language (Jaffrelot, 1997, 1996; Anderson and Damle, 1987; Chatterjee, 1994). The RSS has always identified Indian culture and Indian nationalism with the ethos and cultural traditions of Brahmanical Hinduism and has excluded non-Hindus from its ambit. Mahatma Gandhi described the RSS as "a communal body with a totalitarian outlook" (Pyarelal, 1956: 440).

Since its inception, Pakistan has been trying, without much success, to reconcile its avowed Islamic identity with Western notions of the nation-state and democratic governance and the ethnic aspirations and identities of its major constituents. The consequence is that it has a confused, unclear sense of national identity (Jalal, 1997: 123; Mallick, 1998: 152–55; Jahan, 1973: 121–38). In Bangladesh, Islamic and Bengali identities have been closely intertwined in the articulation of national identity (Phadnis, 1989: 108). The Constitution of Nepal recognizes the country as a multiethnic and multilingual country but declares

Nepali as the only official language, which is resented by the country's linguistic and religious minorities.

III
The Volume

Bhikhu Parekh examines the complex interface between cultural diversity and political unity in the context of contemporary multi-ethnic societies. Tracing the trajectory of the modern state, Parekh points out that the emergence of the state in Europe in the 16th century was accompanied by a culturally homogeneous society. In the course of time, the European states were constituted in accordance with this assumption and when the state was exported or appropriated in non-Western contexts the dominant theory of the state followed in its wake. According to this theory, the state should have a clearly defined territorial boundary, a unitary and homogeneous source of sovereignty, a single system of rights and obligations, a culturally homogeneous national population, a unitary conception of citizenship, a single, homogeneous identity, uniform legal space, and a uniform mode of relating the citizen to the state. The dominant theory of the state presupposes a culturally homogeneous society, political uniformity and a culture of individualism.

Launching a cogent critique of the dominant theory of the state, Parekh points out that it tends to be insensitive to cultural diversity and to the perceptions, identities and aspirations of ethnic and cultural minorities. He argues that by abstracting away cultural, religious and other differences the dominant theory of the state impoverishes the state and deprives it of a creative and mutually enriching dialogue with its constituent communities. He points out that this model of the state has lost its value and relevance in the context of multiethnic societies, which is what most societies are today.

T.K. Oommen's paper deals with a critique of the concepts of pluralism and plural society in the context of South Asia. He criticizes some of the major theorists of pluralism, such as J.S. Furnivall, Anthony Smith and Van den Berghe, for their inconsistencies and contradictions, for their tendency to confuse the polity with society, and for their typology of plural societies. Oommen argues that the existing conceptualizations of multiethnic societies are inadequate in many empirical contexts. He suggests that we need to clearly distinguish between four types of societies on the basis of their constituent elements: homogeneous, heterogeneous, hierarchical and plural. He also argues that a distinction should be drawn between plural society and pluralism. Pluralism, according to him, is not just a social reality but also a value orientation. He is critical of the doctrine of homogenization because it is antithetical to the spirit of democracy and pluralism. He maintains that "the option before democratic societies is not the escape route of homogenization but the reconciliation of the competing demands of equality and identity".

Against this theoretical backdrop, Oommen turns to an analysis of the contemporary social and political scenario in India. He argues that state intervention in India is selective and partisan in regard to the question of conversion, which erodes the meaning of secularism. He also argues that, notwithstanding the constitutional guarantee, the state sometimes discriminates between citizens on the basis of religion, as in the case of protective discrimination. Similarly, the state unfairly differentiates between religions of Indian origin and religions of alien origin, which denies the identity of the latter. This discrimination, Oommen argues, has created a wedge between the majority Hindu population, who are considered insiders, and the minorities who are regarded as outsiders. He suggests that the state should accept the legitimacy and equal importance of all its constituent components and ensure their dignified coexistence.

Aparna Rao's paper is concerned with an explication and analysis of the changing contours of ethnicity and identity and the dynamics of the relationship between individual and group identities in the context of a pastoral nomadic community, the Bakkarwal and Gujar, in the state of Jammu and Kashmir. Rao maintains that in all societies identities, which are often multiple and fluid, are chosen by or imposed upon individual along their gender-specific life-spans. She points out that identity formation is a processual phenomenon. Similarly, she argues that ethnicity is not an inert 'thing' but a cognitive system of relations and representations. Collective identities, according to her, are a result of both primordial ties and specific historical and cultural processes.

Rao seeks to reconstruct the process of ethnogenesis in the case of the Bakkarwals by showing how the group evolved into a community over a period of time and how their ethnic identity underwent significant changes after 1947. Highlighting the linkage between the multiplicity of identities and the changing situational contexts, she demonstrates that religion, language and cultural traditions, in the changed context of competition for resources and the compulsions of electoral politics, played a highly important role in identity formation in the case of the Bakkarwals in the post-partition scenario. Rao provides a nuanced account of the conflict experienced by the Bakkarwals and Gujars both within—the conflict between their ethnic identity and religious identity—and outside—the conflict between the Bakkarwals and the dominant Kashmiri Muslim population. She shows how a new, overarching Gujar identity, encompassing Muslim, Hindu and Sikh segments of the community, emerged in the 1980s. She also highlights the role of politics in heightening ethnic cleavages and in the manipulation of ethnic identities for electoral gains.

Yunas Samad's paper focuses on the linkage between ethnicity and national identity in the context of Pakistan. He views the process of identity formation or identification as fluid, contested and dynamic. He argues that though official nationalism in Pakistan was premised on an essentialized idea of Islam, the relationship between religion, ethnicity and nationalism was never clearly worked out and that this ambiguity and confusion lies at the root of the crisis in Pakistan's national identity. He argues that Pakistani nationalism and ethnicity were closely intertwined in a dynamic relationship, and that Pakistani nationalism did not displace old regional, tribal and ethnic loyalties but subsumed them. However, according to Samad, Pakistani nationalism failed to accommodate ethnic identifications in the long run. Furthermore, he points out, Muslim nationalism in Pakistan was not a homogeneous phenomenon; three stands—separatist, federal and confederal—ran through the nationalist discourse.

Samad argues that he domination of the state and society in Pakistan by the Punjabis—nearly 80 per cent of the personnel in the army and 55 per cent in the federal bureaucracy were from the Punjab—led to fundamental distortions in Pakistani society and fuelled ethnic resentment and conflict and separatism. He points out that the Punjabi domination of Pakistan did not benefit all Punjabis. The benefits accrued largely to bureaucrats, army personnel, landlords, and some sections of the peasantry. Samad points out that groups that were excluded from the power structure, such as the people of East Bengal, Sindh and Baluchistan, used ethnicity as an instrument for the legitimation of their resistance and separatism. He thus highlights the political role and use of ethnicity. Samad also throws light on the process of Islamization set into motion under General Zia-ul Haq's regime and its repercussions on Pakistani society, particularly on women and on religious and sectarian conflicts.

Peter Kloos attempts to show how the process of nation-building may be thwarted by ethnic strife. He argues that ethnic violence poses a serious threat to the unity and integrity of the nation-state. Kloos focuses on this issue in the context of the steady growth in violence in the post-independence history of Sri Lanka and the role of violent youth movements in the escalation of violence. He examines the origins and dynamics of two youth movements, one belonging to the Sinhala majority and the other to the Tamil minority, and points out that both the movements were a manifestation of disaffection, discontent and resentment on the part of unemployed youth. After independence in 1948, the ethnic cleavages in Sri Lanka were accentuated, largely as a result of the partisan policies of the Sinhala-dominated political elite. The growing tension and conflict between the Sinhala and the Tamils resulted in recurrent violent confrontations and ultimately culminated in a bloody civil war in 1983.

Kloos points out that the Sinhala youth movement—JVP—was inspired by revolutionary Marxist ideas, while the Tamil movement, LTTE, aimed at secession from Sri Lanka and the establishment of an independent Tamil state. He examines the commonalities as well as differences between the two movements, noting that though both indulged in reckless violence, which was mainly directed against the government, their goals and social organization were quite different. While the revolutionary JVP espoused Sinhala chauvinism, the separatist LTTE's overriding objective was to resist Sinhala dominance and to establish an independent Tamil state.

Lionel Caplan's paper focuses on the processes of identity formation and creolization in the context of the Anglo-Indian community located in the city of Chennai. Caplan points out that though the Anglo-Indians imagine themselves, and are perceived by others, as a distinctive community, they in fact may be viewed as a socially and culturally differentiated group. Their heterogeneity is reflected in language, class distinctions, food habits and dress and behaviour patterns. Caplan also notes that there are significant continuities between the cultural practices of the

Anglo-Indians and those of other ethnic groups and communities in the city. He points out that the boundaries separating the Anglo-Indians from the British on the one hand and from Indians on the other were and continue to be extremely porous and are easily traversed.

Caplan describes the phases through which a sense of community and identity evolved and underwent changes, especially after the independence of the country. During the colonial period, the Anglo-Indians identified themselves with the British in respect of descent, denial of maternal ancestry and culture. The British attitude towards the Anglo-Indians was a mixture of patronizing, condescension, exclusion and even hostility, depending on political exigencies. In the course of time, the Anglo-Indians began to realize that they were a distinct social group, separate from the British as well as from the local population. The identification with the British gradually weakened with the passage of time. In the post-independence period, cultural influences from the wider Indian society, including intermarriages between the Anglo-Indians and other groups, have grown even more evident. All these influences have brought about a creolized, hybrid culture.

Caplan questions the assumption of closed, homogeneous and chaste cultures existing within clear ethnic boundaries and emphasizes that we need to pay more attention to cultural diversity both within and across the lines dividing ethnic groups. He argues that in India's urban centres the processes of ethnic integration and closure seem to occur simultaneously.

K.S. Singh's paper discusses the relationship between India's characteristic and pervasive diversity, the growing ethnic consciousness and articulation and movements for autonomy in the context of tribal society. Focusing on the Jharkhand movement in the Chotanagpur and Santal Pargana regions in the state of Bihar (now Jharkhand), Singh points out that in the 1980s there emerged a growing consciousness of a common regional heritage on the part of tribal as well as non-tribal communities in the region. This consciousness was strengthened by the marginalization and alienation of all communities in the region. Gradually, the ethnic dimension was replaced by the regional perspective, which was dominated by concerns for development, empowerment and autonomy. In the course of time, these concerns paved the way for political mobilization which in turn led to the movement for a separate state of Jharkhand. He thus draws attention to the transition from a relatively homogeneous ethnic (tribal) identity to regional, composite identity in the context of Jharkhand.

Singh also examines the issues of ethnic resurgence, shifting identities, political mobilization and the growing clamour for autonomy among the tribal communities in North-Eastern India. He points out that myth-making plays an important role in the formation of ethnic movements. He highlights the instrumental dimensions of ethnicity, especially in the case of the Bodos of Assam, as well as the linkage between ethnic identity and autonomy. He discusses the various models which seek to accommodate ethnic and regional aspirations in the country within the framework of India's federal polity. He argues that one cannot be indifferent or oblivious to the widespread and growing desire on the part of different groups and communities in the country for a share in the power structure. He then examines the viability of three distinct approaches or models, namely, development authorities (which failed to have any impact), autonomous councils, and the creation of smaller, separate states. He favours a combination of autonomy and protectionism to accommodate the ethnic and regional aspirations of the people, especially in the context of tribal society.

Lee Schlesinger's paper covers a wide spectrum ranging from the interface between religion and identity to tolerance and secularism in the context of village life in India. He explores these issues, highly important as they are, through an intersection between biography and the changing dynamics of a village in Maharashtra which he has studied. Schlesinger is critical of the notions of cultural pluralism and ethnicity which, he believes, have been derived from the Western context, and points out that these terms are generally used as homogenizing notions and that they do not really convey or capture the reality of South Asian villages. Furthermore, he says, they are not in consonance with the history, values and traditions of South Asia. He considers secularism, cultural pluralism and ethnicity as bourgeois concerns.

Schlesinger points out that the village is far from a closed or isolated place. Rather, it is exposed to ideas and forces from the larger society. He argues that in order to understand the dynamics of village life in South Asia, we need to focus on community identity and values which deeply affect, sustain and organize people's day-to-day lives. The focus, in other words, should be on unravelling the complexity of localized living in the context of religion, community and identity, particularly in the village setting. Schlesinger chides Indian social scientists for not paying sufficient attention to the integrative role of popular religions, such as the cult of Sai Baba in Maharashtra.

The essays in this volume cover a fairly wide range of interrelated themes, including the theory of the state, nationalism (including the two main variants of ethnic nationalism and political or civic nationalism), ethnicity, identity, multiethnic societies, pluralism and multiculturalism, and national identity. It is worthwhile to identify and highlight certain points or themes which run through most if not all of the essays.

First, there is a universal and growing recognition of the ubiquity and salience of cultural diversity across the world, within nation-states, and within ethnic groups and cultural communities. Parekh and Oommen call for a reconceptualization of the state and of multiethnic societies in the light of the pervasiveness and salience of cultural diversity. A corollary of the above is that forced homogenization and uniformity are to be eschewed because there is no necessary correlation between cultural uniformity and political unity and because it is self-defeating in the long run. As Bhikhu Parekh points out, "political unity does not require cultural homogeneity and is best preserved in a climate of flourishing and self-confident cultural diversities" (Parekh, 1997).

Second, identities, both personal and collective, are often multiple, fluid, processual, overlapping, shifting and hybrid, rather than given once and for all, fixed, bounded, homogeneous or insular. Identities are defined, mediated and constructed in social and cultural contexts which are often changing. Often, ethnicity is employed by individuals and groups as a means or instrument for the furtherance of economic, political or cultural goals and for social and political mobilization. Most of the essays in this volume are based on a critique—explicit or implicit—of static, essentialized, monolithic notions of culture and ethnicity, and of ethnic absolutism.

Third, ethnicity appears to be a Janus-faced phenomenon in that is has positive as well as negative and socially disruptive consequences. This is particularly evidenced in the career of ethnic or majoritarian nationalism. National identity in many countries of South Asia, as elsewhere, has been defined in ethnocentric, exclusionary and even xenophobic terms. The conflation of ethnicity and nationalism has often brought about social disharmony, ethnic strife, and disaffection and alienation in most parts of the world, including South Asia. Many scholars therefore argue that the national identity of multiethnic societies should be defined in political rather than ethnic or cultural terms, that it should be inclusionary rather than exclusionary, flexible and accommodative rather than closed and solipsistic, cosmopolitan rather than ethnocentric (Momin, 2006).

References

Ahmed, Akbar S. (1983), *Religion and Politics in Muslim Society: Order and Conflict in Pakistan*. Cambridge: Cambridge University Press.

—— (1997), "Tribes, Regional Pressures and Nationhood" in Victoria Schofield (ed.), *Old Roads, New Highways: Fifty Years of Pakistan*, pp. 139–155.

Allport, Gordon (1954), *The Nature of Prejudice*. Reading, Mass.

Anderson, W. and S. Damle (1987), *The Brotherhood in Saffron: The RSS and Hindu Revivalism*. New Delhi.

Anthias, Floya (2001), "New Hybridities, Old Concepts: The Limits of 'Culture'", *Ethnic and Racial Studies*, 24 (4), pp. 619–41.

Barth, Frederik (1969), *Ethnic Groups and Boundaries*. Boston, MA: Little Brown.

Basu, Tapan et al. (1993), *Khaki Shorts, Saffron Flags: A Critique of the Hindu Right*. Delhi: Orient Longman.

Berghe, Pierre van den (1973), "Pluralism" in J.J. Honigmann (ed.), *Handbook of Social and Cultural Anthropology*. Chicago: Rand McNally, pp. 959–77.

Bhabha, Homi (1994), *The Location of Culture*. London: Routledge.

Bjorgo, T. and R. Witte (eds.) (1993), *Racist Violence in Europe*. London: Macmillan.

Castles, S. (1993), *Racism: A Global Analysis*. Wollongong: University of Wollongong.

Chatterjee, Partha (1994), *The Nation and Its Fragments*. Delhi: Oxford University Press.

Connor, Walter (1994), *Ethnonationalism: The Quest for Understanding*. Princeton: Oxford University Press.

Cornwell, Grant H. and E.W. Stoddard (eds.) (2001), *Global Multiculturalism: Perspectives on Ethnicity, Race and Nation*. London: Rowman and Littlefield Publishers.

Denitch, Bogdan (1994), *Ethnonationalism: The Tragic Death of Yugoslavia*. Minneapolis: University of Minnesota Press.

Epstein, A.L. (1978), *Ethos and Identity: Three Studies in Ethnicity*. London: Tavistock.

Erikson, Erik (1959), *Identity and the Life Cycle: Selected Papers*. New York.

Furnival, J.S. (1939), *Netherlands India: A Study in Plural Economy*. Cambridge: Cambridge University Press.

—— (1948), *Colonial Policy and Practice: A Comparative Study of Burma and Netherlands India*. London: Cambridge University Press.

Geertz, C. (1967), *Old Societies and New States: The Quest for Modernity in Asia and Africa*. New York: Free Press.

Gellner, Ernest (1983), *Nations and Nationalism*. Oxford: Basil and Blackwell.

Giddens, Anthony (1991), *Modernity and Self-Identity*. Stanford: Stanford University Press.

—— (1998), *The Third Way*. Cambridge: Polity Press.

Gilroy, Paul (1993), *The Black Atlantic*. London: Verso.

Glazer, Nathan (1983), *Ethnic Dilemmas:1964–1982*. Cambridge, Mass: Harvard University Press.

—— (1997), *We Are All Multiculturalists Now*. Cambridge, Mass: Harvard University Press.

Glazer, Nathan and Daniel P. Moynihan (1963), *Beyond the Melting Pot*. Cambridge, Mass: Harvard University Press.

—— (eds.) (1975), *Ethnicity: Theory and Experience*. Cambridge, Mass: Harvard University Press.

Goffman, Erving (1963), *Stigma: Notes on the Management of Spoiled Identity*. New Jersey: Prentice Hall.

Goldberg, D.T. (ed.) (1994), *Multiculturalism: A Critical Reader*. Oxford: Blackwell.

Greenfeld, L. (1992), *Nationalism: Five Roads to Modernity*. Cambridge, MaGDP ss: Harvard University Press.

Guibernau, Montserrat and Rex John, (eds.) (1997), *The Ethnicity Reader: Nationalism, Multiculturalism and Migration*. Cambridge: Polity Press.

Hannerz, U. (1996), *Transnational Connections: Culture, People, Places*. London and New York: Routledge.

Haq, Mahbub ul and Khadija Haq (1997), *Human Development in South Asia*. Karachi: Oxford University Press.

Heimasath, Charles H. (1964), *Indian Nationalism and Hindu Social Reform*. Princeton, New Jersey: Princeton University Press.

Hobsbawm, Eric (1990), *Nations and Nationalism since 1780: Programme, Myths and Reality*. Berkeley: University of California Press.

Hollinger, David (1995), *Postethnic America: Beyond Multiculturalism*. New York: Basic Books.

Jaffrelot, Christophe (1997), "The Idea of the Hindu Race in the Writings of Hindu Nationalist Ideologues in the 1920s and 1930s: A Concept between Two Cultures" in Peter Robb (ed.), *The Concept of Race in South Asia*. New Delhi: Oxford University Press.

Jahan, Raunaq (1973), *Pakistan: Failure in National Integration*. Dacca: Oxford University Press.

Jalal, Ayesha (1997), "Ideology and the Struggle for Democratic Institutions" in Victoria Schofield (ed.), *Old Roads, New Highways: Fifty Years of Pakistan*. Karachi: Oxford University Press.

—— (cd.) (1995), *Democracy and Authoritarianism in South Asia*. Cambridge: Cambridge University Press.

Kaferer, Bruce (1998), *Legends of People, Myths of State: Violence, Intolerance and Political Culture in Sri Lanka and Australia*. Washington D.C.: Smithsonian Institution.

Kedourie, Elie (1994), *Nationalism*. 4th Edition. Oxford: Basil Blackwell.

Kymlicka, Will (1995), *Multicultural Citizenship*. Oxford: Oxford University Press.

—— (1998), "American Multiculturalism in the International Arena" *Dissent* (Fall), pp. 73–79.

Linton, Ralph (1936), *The Study of Man: An Introduction*. New York.

Mallick, Ross (1998), *Development, Ethnicity and Human Rights in South Asia*. New Delhi: Sage.

Momin, A.R. (2004), "Multicommunitarianism in a Fragmented World" *Asia-Europe Journal*, Vol. 3, pp. 445–459.

—— (2006), "India as a Model for Multiethnic Europe", *Asia-Europe Journal*, Vol. Vol. 4, pp. 523–537.

—— (2008a), "The Crisis of Multiculturalism in Europe" (Lecture delivered at the Institute of Sociology, Graz University, Austria on 17 April, 2008).

—— (2008b), "Towards a Multicommunitarian Europe" (Lecture delivered at the Department of Sociology, Bonn University, Germany on 27 April, 2008).

—— (2009), "Multicommunitarianism: A Perspective on Living Together in a Multiethnic Society" (*forthcoming*).

Oommen, T.K. (1997), *Citizenship, Nationality and Ethnicity*. Cambridge: Polity Press.

Pandey, Gyanendra (2001), *Remembering Partition*. Cambridge: Cambridge University Press.

Parekh, Bhikhu (1997), "Managing Multicultural Societies", Convocation Address, University of Delhi.

—— (2000), *Rethinking Multiculturalism: Cultural Diversity and Political Theory*. London: Macmillan.

Phadnis, Urmila (1989), *Ethnicity and Nation-Building in South Asia*. New Delhi: Sage.

Phinney, Jean S. (2000), "Ethnic Identity" in Alan E. Kazdin (ed.), *Encyclopaedia of Psychology*. New York: Oxford University Press, Vol. 3, pp. 254–59.

Pyarelal (1956), *Mahatma Gandhi: The Last Phase*. Ahmedabad.

Rex, J. and D. Mason (eds.) (1986), *Theories of Race and Ethnic Relations*. Cambridge: Cambridge University Press.

Safran, William (1991), "Diasporas in Modern Societies: Myths of Homeland and Return", *Diaspora*, Vol. 1, pp. 83–99.

Schwartz, Joseph E. (1978), *A Historical Atlas of South Asia*. Chicago: The University of Chicago Press.

Singh, K.S. (1992), *People of India: An Introduction*. Calcutta: Anthropological Survey of India.

Smith, Anthony (1963), *Theories of Nationalism*. London: Duckworth.

—— (1986), *Ethnic Origins of Nations*. Oxford: Blackwell.

—— (1999), *Myths and Memories of the Nation*. Oxford: Oxford University Press.

Smith, M.G. (1965), *The Plural Society of the British West Indies*. London: Sangsters.

Taylor, Charles (1992), *Multiculturalism and the Politics of Recognition*. Princeton, New Jersey: Princeton University Press.

—— (1994), "The Politics of Recognition" in A. Gutmann (ed.), *Multiculturalism*. Princeton, New Jersey: Princeton University Press.

Vertovec, Steven (1999), "Conceiving and Researching Transnationalism", *Ethnic and Racial Studies,* 22 (2), pp. 447–62.

Weber, Max (1968), *Economy and Society*. Los Angeles: University of California Press.

Young, Robert (1996), *Colonial Desire: Hybridity in Theory, Culture and Race*. London: Routledge.

Yunus, Muhammad (2007), *Creating a World without Poverty: Social Business and the Future of Capitalism.* New York: Public Affairs.

1

The Dialectic of Unity and Diversity in a Multicultural State

BHIKHU PAREKH

In this paper I intend to maintain the following thesis. For the past three centuries a specific theory of the state has gained political and philosophical ascendancy and provided the model of a properly constituted state. The theory is based on the assumption of a culturally homogeneous society, and becomes a source of disorder, injustice and violence when applied to culturally heterogeneous societies. If we are to cope with the problems thrown up by these societies, we need to replace it with one far more sensitive to cultural diversity.[1]

Every territorially organized human society has several basic features.[2] *First,* its members are born, live, work, raise their families and die in a more or less clearly demarcated territorial area. Since their personal and collective life-histories are tied up with it, they build up a moral and emotional relationship with it. The territory is not an external or passive background to their collective existence but an integral part of their way of life. And, although its borders are historically contingent, they are not merely lines on the map or on the ground but bound up with its self-definition, and hence morally not arbitrary. *Second,* its members have some shared sense of collective identity, including who they are, how they are related to each other, who does or does not belong to their society, and how to behave towards both. *Third*, every organized society has a reasonably well-defined structure of authority specifying who is entitled to speak and act on its behalf, to make collectively binding rules, and to settle inevitable conflicts and disagreements. *Fourth*, it has some machinery for enforcing its decisions and a system of sanctions—be they a religious curse, social ostracism, physical punishment, temporary or permanent suspension, expulsion, or physical elimination. *Finally*, every society is necessarily multidimensional in the sense that its members engage in a wide variety of such vital activities as material production, defending their lives and property against invaders, and initiating the young into their way of life. No society ever is or can be concerned merely with the maintenance of order, for order is a condition and context of substantive human activities and has only a derivative significance.

For convenience I shall use the term 'polity' to refer to such a territorially organized society united in terms of common subscription to a shared system of authority. The polity represents the way a society constitutes itself in order to achieve internal order, external security and such other collective objectives as it considers important, and refers to its political form. The structure of a polity is shaped by the wider society's views on how it wishes to live, what collective goals it wishes to pursue, what activities may or may not be coerced, and so on. And, these in turn are shaped by such interrelated factors as its history, level of technological development, economic and social structure and culture. Since different sections of society generally have different interests and entertain different conceptions of how it should be organized, the kind of polity a society throws up reflects either the views and interests of the dominant group or, more often, an inherently tentative compromise between those of the contending groups. Not surprisingly, different societies in history have thrown up different kinds of polity which, while sharing the five features sketched above and other related to these, define and combine them differently. Europe alone has given rise to such different kinds of polity as the Greek polis, the Roman civitas and empire, and the medieval kingdom. The rest of the world has given rise to many more.

The modern state, as we know it today, began to emerge in the late 15th and early 16th centuries in response to important economic, social, cultural and other changes. Different social groups with different interests and expectations sought to shape it in specific ways, giving rise to much political struggle and philosophical discussion concerning its structure, functions, and place in social life. Over time, one particular model or theory of the state gained political and philosophical ascendancy. Although other views were never completely silenced and sometimes found eloquent spokesmen, they remained marginal. The dominant theory of the state drew upon several pre-existing intellectual traditions and represented a broad compromise between conflicting views about its nature, constitution, functions and role in social life. Although it had a strong liberal orientation, it was also shaped by other bodies of ideas. And, although the rising bourgeoisie and the professional classes were its greatest champions, the dominant view of the state also included the self-understanding and claims of other social classes. For convenience, and in order not to identify it with a specific political or philosophical doctrine, I shall simply call it the dominant theory or model of the state.

As the dominant theory shaped the structure, design, procedures, institutions and objectives of states, it no longer remained just a way of understanding them but became inscribed in their very structure. Since states have to survive in a real world and must make messy compromises, hardly any of them conformed to the model. However, the model remained their inspiration and standard of judgement, and they all strove in their own different ways to measure up to its requirements as much as they could. Once European states came to be constituted along the lines of the dominant model, the latter appeared to offer a true account of the real 'nature' of the modern state. Like all human institutions, the state, of course, has no nature, to which our understanding of it can be expected to conform. It is what its members make of it in the twofold sense of how they understand it and how that understanding shapes their conduct. The modern state could have taken several different forms. The fact that it generally took a particular form has to do not with its inherent 'nature' or an imaginary historical teleology but with the fact that a specific form of understanding it became politically and philosophically dominant.

Once European states came to be constituted along certain lines, it was widely argued that only such states were properly so called, and that differently constituted states were not different kinds of state but perversions of it, indeed not states at all. What was only a contingent historical form of polity came to be presented as its only possible form, and a specific theory of it came to be seen as the only true account of its 'nature'. When the state was exported outside Europe, the dominant theory followed it as its inseparable shadow. Anxious to develop into modern states, citizens of non-European societies dared not risk exploring alternative models lest they should be considered backward or pre-modern. In this respect, the United States represented a remarkable attempt to break away from the European model. It dispensed with the centralized notion of sovereignty and introduced a federal mode of structuring the polity including plural systems of law, and did not even insist on a common American citizenship until after the Civil War. However, its experiences were largely ignored by the dominant theory of the state, some of whose spokesmen thought rather poorly of it and believed that over time it was bound to evolve into a polity closely resembling the European state.

The basic outlines of the dominant model of the modern state are broadly as follows. In pre-modern Western and non-Western politics, territory played a marginal and largely instrumental role in the life of the community. A community was distinguished by its way of life, and the latter not the territory was the primary object of loyalty. African tribes moved from one place to another with their gods, and used them to ensure continuity of identity. Traditional Muslim societies defined themselves in terms of their ways of life not their territory and carried their 'personal' laws with them, these laws and practices being regarded as an integral part of their identity just as much as their bodily features. That was why, such minorities as Jews and Christians enjoyed the right to lead their traditional ways of life without interference by the ruler under the Millet system established by the Ottoman Empire. This was also broadly the case in traditional Hindu societies and, with some variations, under the Roman Empire and in medieval Europe. In most of these societies the land on which a community was settled derived its importance from the fact that it was the place where the community's gods lived, where its holy places were located, where its ancestors were buried, and so on. Although its boundaries were reasonably clear, they remained relatively porous.

In the modern state land is largely secularized and conceptualized in the culturally neutral language of territory. The secularized view of the territory paves the way for its exclusive political and moral appropriation by the state. Territory is primarily seen as the site of the formation of the state; its central buildings and places are those with political significance; and its physical space is structured in terms of historically evocative and politically important events and memories. Territory is the material basis, the body, of the state and is unambiguously marked off, so that there is little doubt in the minds of both its members and especially the outsiders where the state begins and ends.[3] Since territory represents the physical expression and extent of the state, an attack on it is perceived as an attack on the integrity of the state itself. The natural and other resources lying within the territorial bounds of the state are its property, with which it may do what it likes and to which outsiders have no moral claim. The modern conceptions of private property and the individual's relation to his body inform the state's relation to its territory, and developed in tandem with it. It is striking that, unlike many of their predecessors, almost all the theorists of the modern state start by postulating a body of men cut off from the rest of mankind, occupying a neatly bounded territorial unit, and creating a structure of civil authority by an act of collective will. The rest of mankind enters the picture only after the state is created, and that too in the form of similarly isolated political units.

The modern state is internally unified, freed of physical and legal barriers to the movement of people and goods, and forms a homogeneous and clearly bounded unit of physical and legal space. To enter its territory is to enter its jurisdiction and to be subject to its authority. Unlike in many a pre-modern polity, the individual does not carry his *professio juris* and laws with him wherever he goes. Law is *lex terrae* and binds all falling within its jurisdiction, irrespective of their consent or volition. Unlike almost all the earlier polities, the modern state offers protection to everyone who happens to be within its territorial boundaries, irrespective of whether or not they are its full members. In Athens, such protection was a political privilege available only to the citizens, and the outsider required a citizen patron to qualify for it. In the feudal polity the protection and the right to claim indemnity against attack or harm were limited to those owing fealty to the lord. The minimum and largely guaranteed physical protection to all within its territorial jurisdiction is almost unique to the modern state.

The territory defines the corporate identity of its members and gives it a distinct name. Britain is not where the British live, rather the British are those who live in Britain. It is hardly surprising that the inhabitants went with the territory and were subjected to the laws of whoever acquired it. Unlike most pre-modern societies which were socially exclusive and denied citizenship to those who did not share their ways of life, the modern state can accommodate total strangers and might even be exclusively composed of them. Territory is also the basis of political representation in it. Earlier polities were either innocent of representative institutions or defined these in non-territorial terms. Even, the feudal assembly, which comes moderately close to modern representative institution, consisted of individuals who were potentates standing at the centre of networks of linkages involving vassals of various removes. In the modern state the representative assembly consists of men and women who represent not clusters of relations or functions but territorially demarcated constituencies.

In many earlier polities individuals had multiple identities such as the ethnic, the religious, the social and the territorial, and saw themselves as belonging to several collectivities, some of them extra-territorial. These identities and the concomitant loyalties, which were not always hierarchically graded, were accepted as an inescapable feature of social life and regarded as sources of important rights and duties, limited the ruler's authority. The modern state is almost unique in privileging the territorial identity. Its members do, of course, have multiple identities, affiliations and allegiances, but the territorial identity is overarching and dominant. When a state is at war with another, all ties between their citizens are suspended. Their scientists, scholars and artists are not at liberty to claim that since they form a universal community and are not at war with their counterparts in the enemy country, they should remain free to travel there unhindered. Nor are ordinary citizens permitted to cross the border to meet their relations, visit holy places, or attend important religious and social functions in countries with which their own is at war.[4] Unlike its earlier counterparts, the state territorializes and totalizes human relations and activities, and gives them a wholly new dimension. It is a compulsory association in the three-fold sense that every individual belongs to one of the many states in which mankind is neatly parcelled out, that no one may leave or enter it without is permission, and that everyone within its boundary is subject to its jurisdiction unless granted exemption.

The modern state represents a historically unique mode of relating its members and creating a united polity. It abstracts away such socially differentiating elements as social status, ethnic, regional, religious and other identities and economic circumstances, individualizes, equalizes and defines its members in the barest possible manner as self-determining agents capable of choice and will, and unites them in terms of their subscription to a common structure of authority. Not surprisingly, the modern state feels deeply uneasy in the presence of well-organized ethnic, religious and other communities lest they should introduce differences, subvert the principle of abstract equality, and set up rival foci of loyalty. Unless it is compelled to do so, as is the case in many plural societies, it rarely invests such communities with rights, gives them a legal and political status, or allows its citizens to place their loyalties to them on a part with their allegiance to the state. And, when political necessity compels it to do so, its members feel deeply troubled as if they had committed a political sacrilege.

The authority of the modern state is not a collection of discrete rights and prerogatives; rather they are all aspects or attributes of a unitary, basic and overarching power called sovereignty. Almost all earlier polities were characterized by plural systems of authority, each with its own distinct source, character and manner of functioning. And often they all had to agree before a decision became binding. As for the specifically legal authority, it too was plural, consisting of different and mutually irreducible powers, each valid within a specific area. In the modern state the different systems of authority are all rationalized, homogenized, centralized, and hierarchically arranged. Although the idea of supreme power is to be found in all pre-statal polities, it is quite different from the modern idea of sovereignty. Unlike the earlier form of defining and constituting supreme power, sovereignty refers to a rationalized system of authority, is unitary and impersonal in nature, is the source of all legal authority exercised within the state, is not legally bound by traditions, customs and principles of morality, and is not subject to a higher internal or external authority.

As an autonomous and self-contained institution, the state has its own distinct identity and mode of operation. It is composed of institutions such as the executive, the civil service, the judiciary, the standing army and the police, which uniquely belong to it and are assiduously guarded against popular pressure. It has its distinct sources of wealth collected through taxes, and neither by contributions negotiated with its subjects (as under feudalism), nor by drawing on the ruler's own wealth, selling offices or claiming share in the proceeds of military, colonial and commercial ventures of its citizens (as under the absolute monarchy). The modern state relates and speaks to its subjects in its own distinct language, the language of law. And being self-contained, it relies on its own self-generated sanctions for the enforcement of the law. In the modern state law is abstracted from all other forms of social control, given a distinct and uniquely privileged status, and is enacted or made. As Bodin, one of the earliest theorists of the modern state, pointed out, it is the only polity in history to regard legislation and not adjudication as its primary function. Not surprisingly, it is historically unique in defining supreme power or sovereignty in legislative terms and insisting that its citizens should be subject to no other laws than those made, acquiesced in or endorsed by it. The power to make laws therefore became the subject of the most intense political battles, and its history is for all practical purposes the history of the modern state. The modern state's primary task is to establish and maintain not order *per se* but law-based order, that is, order as defined by and arising out of obedience to laws. Since it is primarily a legal and impersonal institution and articulated in terms of law, it is expected not only to require its citizens to obey its laws but also to respect and obey them itself.

As an autonomous institution the state is inspired by one central concern, namely, to hold itself together, to safeguard its legal and territorial integrity, to maintain order. It may or may not pursue other objectives although it invariably does, but it must maintain order. And even if it successfully pursues other objectives, it is largely judged by its capacity to maintain peace. It is so identified with the maintenance and creation of order that it is blamed for and feels threatened by every act of disorder. As such it enjoys the legal monopoly of the right to use force. Without such a monopoly it cannot subdue forces of disorder functioning singly or collectively. And, since it is a law-governed institution, it is expected to use force in a measured, rule-governed and institutionalized manner. Thanks to its exclusive responsibility to maintain order, it is uniquely identified with the criminal law, and is a party to all disputes involving physical harm or disorder. In many polities including classical Athens, Rome during part of its history, and early feudalism, murder, arson and so on were subject to private action brought by the victim or his family, and false testimony was treated as a tort. This is unthinkable in the modern state.

As a homogenized, rationalized, integrated and hierarchically structured set of institutions and powers, enjoying both the monopoly of the authority to use force and the capacity for indefinite elaboration and expansion, the modern state can undertake activities beyond the wildest dream of its predecessors, and naturally arouses great expectations. Not surprisingly, its emergence, consolidation and expansion entailed egregious internal and external violence, exceeding that perpetrated by almost any other institution past or present. Its rulers dismantled long-established religious, cultural and other communities in pursuit of a culturally homogeneous and easily governable community. Since they had massive force at their disposal, the latter became their first means of recourse. And since they were convinced that the state represented the only truly rational mode of constituting the polity and modernizing society, they felt morally justified in their use of force. They also fought wars of territorial expansion and reached out to distant societies in the Americas, Australia and elsewhere where their representatives thought little of murdering millions of native people in order to modernize or civilize them by establishing state-like institutions. Since the state can be 'captured' or taken over and 'used' as an instrument of large-scale social transformation, it encouraged revolution, a distinctly modern phenomenon. As different from riot, rebellion and revolt, revolution presupposes a volitionalist view of political power, independence of the state from society, the state's right to intervene in social life, readily mobilizable armed forces, the capacity to formulate and pursue large and long-term goals, etc. Although some of these pre-conditions obtained earlier, the presence of them all is unique to the modern state.

The state represents the principle of universality within society. First, all those who are within its territorial boundaries are subject to its jurisdiction and entitled to its protection. Second, everyone who satisfies its requirements of citizenship is invested with equal rights and obligations. Third, whatever their ethnic, religious and other differences, all citizens are equally subject to the law. And fourth, unlike all other institutions which are deemed to be narrowly based on sectional in their concerns, the state represents the community as a whole and speaks and acts in its name. It is concerned with what is common or universal to all its members. The latter may belong to different religious, ethnic and cultural groups, but the state transcends such differences and only concerns itself with what all its citizens qua citizens share in common. The common interests, which they are all supposed to share, irrespective of their cultural, ethnic and other affiliations, include such things as life, liberty, property, legality and civil order.

Since the state represents what is common to all its citizens, some form of public-private distinction is built into its very structure. What is common belongs to the public realm; what varies with the citizens belongs to the private realm. Since nothing relating to the citizens' lives lies outside the legal reach of the state, the private realm does not fall outside the state's jurisdiction as it did in almost all pre-modern societies. The public-private distinction is not between what lies within and what lies outside the jurisdiction of the state, for that is ruled out by the principle of state sovereignty. Rather, the private realm is one where the state generally does not, and if citizens think that it should not, intervene, whereas the public realm is one where it does and where they think that it should intervene. The distinction between the two is therefore normative and not ontological, a matter of policy and not of the 'inherent' nature or boundary of the state. In classical Greece and Rome, the family was outside the jurisdiction of the state, and its head derived his authority over its members not from the state but from customs and traditions. In the modern state the family is an integral part of the state, which confers on its head such authority as he is deemed to require to ensure order within it.

Given that the state is taken to represent the principle of universality, to be its citizen or full member is to rise up to and incarnate its universality. Citizenship is considered to be an unmediated relationship between the individual and the state in the sense that one is its member directly and not by virtue of one's membership of specific associations and communities. To be a citizen is to abstract away and transcend one's ethnic, religious and other particularities and to think and act only as a member of the state. As a citizen, one has no religion, ethnicity, caste, tribe or family. Citizenship is an autonomous and free-standing public status, and represents a realm where members of the state interact as equals in a difference—blind manner. As a public status, citizenship carries two basic obligations, to pursue shared common interests in preference to narrow personal and sectional interests, and to deliberate about them not in terms of ethnic, religious and other reasons but collectively shared and sharable public reasons. It is assumed that when citizens deliberate about common interests from a common standpoint and in terms of common reason, they would have little difficulty reaching an agreement.

Since citizenship involves abstracting away socially generated differences, all citizens are related to the state in an identical manner. Once their ethnic origins, religious affiliations, political biographies, and all such sources of difference are excluded, they are homogenized and there is nothing to distinguish them from each other. Since they are all identically related to the state, the grounds of their obligations to it—be they consent, gratitude or fair play—are the same for all. It is striking that hardly any political thinker has entertained the possibility that different groups of citizens might be obligated to the state on different grounds.

Given the unique structure of the modern state, its relation to both the wider society and the government is quite different to that in pre-modern polities. The state splits the unity of society and government characteristic of the earlier polities, inserts itself in the space so created, and reconstitutes and relates the two in a novel manner. It mediates between the two but, like all mediating entities, it first deconstitutes and then reconstitutes them on its terms. As Hobbes and, at a different level, Rousseau emphasized, the state is only possible when members of a society 'renounce' or dissolve their traditional forms of life and set up or 'generate' a new collectivity capable of conferring on them a new identity. The creation of the state involves a qualitative transformation in the relations between its members, and the concomitant supersession of one set of ties by another.

Unlike the pre-modern polities in which political authority was embedded in the collective life of the community, the modern state forms an autonomous and self-contained world and its authority is indigenous to it. It may not intervene in the substantive activities of its subjects, but none of these is immune to its regulative control. And even when it does not direct them, they all occur within the framework of rights and obligations created by it. Society requires norms and rules, and since in a modern society the state is more or less the only stable, comprehensive and authoritative source of them, the modern state is more or less the sole basis of unity in modern society. This means that the state is both co-extensive with and narrower than society: the former because every member of society and their every relationship and activity fall under the state's jurisdiction, the latter because the state does not incorporate society but retains its distance from it.

Since the modern state stands in an extremely complex and elusive relationship to society, it is hardly surprising that the relationship has resisted adequate conceptualization and is often expressed in suggestive but loose metaphors. The state is said to 'transcend', 'stand above', 'hover over', 'stand outside' and 'dominate' society.[5] Each of these metaphors makes an important point, but misinterprets it or misses out others equally important. The state stands outside society in the sense that it is self-contained and has its source of authority within it. However, it is not wholly outside society for its legitimacy and effectiveness depend on the society's beliefs and values. It is above society and transcends it in the sense that it enacts and enforces laws binding on the latter and is run by a professional body of men not continuously accountable to society. However, it is not wholly above society for it is subject to the constraints of economic and social forces wielding the power to paralyze and even destroy it. Although the state is formally outside society and transcends it, it is very much 'in' it and both shapes and is shaped by it.

Like the modern state's relation to society, its relation to government is extremely complex. Since the modern state is historically unique, so is the form of government possible within it. Indeed one might say that unlike most earlier polities in which rulers ruled but rarely governed, the institution of government, a well co-ordinated, systematic and carefully planned system of rule and administration, is unique to the modern state. The state is activated by and acts through its government, even as the activities of the latter react upon and strengthen or weaken the state, but the two are not identical. Governments come and go, but the state remains. They may collapse and there may be no government, yet the state continues if only for a short while. Forms of government may change, but the identity of the state remains unaltered. Monarchical, parliamentary and presidential governments are all forms of government, but do not represent different modes of constituting the state. Federal and unitary forms of government refer to both state and government depending on how they are defined. Democracy is an ambiguous concept. For liberals it is a form of government; for radicals it is a form of the state and some of them such as Marx and Bakunin even regard it as its antithesis. Again, a rebellion against a government is not necessarily a rebellion against the state; the head of government is not the head of the state; such things as 'national' anthem and national flag pertain to the state and not to the government; and crimes against the latter are not all crimes against the state. To occupy an office of the state is to acquire the authority inherent in it. Elections confer legitimacy but not authority on the occupants of such offices.

The modern state stands in a deeply ambiguous relationship to democracy. Historically speaking, the state emerged as a form of polity that sought to avoid the two extremes of absolute and personalized rule on the one hand and popular sovereignty on the other.[6] As against the former, theorists of the state argued that all authority was derived from the people and should be exercised in their interests. As against the latter, they argued that people permanently 'alienated', 'transferred' or 'renounced' their sovereignty to the state, and that it was to be exercised according to the law and only by the authorized representatives of the state. If the term 'democracy' is taken to mean that all authority is derived from the people and should be exercised in their interest, then, the modern state cannot only accommodate it but presupposes it as its very basis. But if 'democracy' means that the people are active and self-determining subjects who ought to conduct their collective affairs themselves, then, the state is inhospitable to it. Those in charge of the state see themselves as guardians of people's real and long-term interests and are deeply suspicious of the latter's ability either to define these interests clearly or to pursue them against the pressures of shifting opinions and organized interests; democracy is based on opposite assumptions. The conflict between the assumptions underlying the modern state and democracy has dominated European history since the 19th century, and was resolved differently in different countries.

Broadly speaking, the compromise everywhere followed a common pattern. The state was loosened up to make room for democracy after the latter was defined in narrowly legislative terms, and the institution of the popularly elected legislature was enshrined at the heart of the state. Not the people themselves but their elected representatives were accommodated within the state, and that too on condition that once elected they would not as a rule be constantly accountable to and recallable by their electors. Even this compromise has not proved wholly acceptable to the agencies of the state, which continue to feel possessive or at least protective about it and view the 'politicians' in the legislature and their political parties with deep suspicion. In France, where the suspicion is most acute, the uneasy constitutional relationship between the legislature and the rest of the state remains a subject of much recurrent public debate. In the Netherlands, both are seen as equally important 'powers' or 'pillars' of the state and have managed to establish a reasonable harmonious working relationship. In post-war Germany, the idea of the 'party state' has gained ascendancy, and political parties, seen as the agents of integrating the state and democracy, both form the political will of the state and supervise its efficient execution. In almost all Western states the constitutional compromise between the state and democracy is heavily biased towards the former.[7]

This is hardly surprising. The state has traditionally been constructed and run from top downwards rather than bottom upwards as is to be expected in an organization that began as an apparatus of ruling under absolute monarchy. Although it has opened up under popular pressure and accommodates a representative form of government, the latter remains severely circumscribed by the state's abstract and autonomous character. It transfers to the elected representatives, and not to the people, almost all the powers long enjoyed by the absolute monarchy. The representative or liberal democracy signifies the kind and degree of democracy possible within the framework of the state. Since a full-blooded democracy involves active citizen participation in the conduct of public affairs and requires a polity constituted from bottom upward, it is possible within the framework of the modern state only to a limited degree.

II

In the light of the above discussion, the following features are central to the state as defined by the dominant model of it:

First, the state is identified with and claims proprietary jurisdiction over a specific territorial area, and privileges the territorial identity and loyalty along the lines discussed earlier.

Second, the state is sovereign. Indeed, as Hobbes put it, sovereignty is the 'soul' of the state, and the latter is unimaginable without it. Basically to say that the state is sovereign is to say three things. First, no area of social life is in principle exempt from the jurisdictional reach of the state. Second, the state is the source of all legal authority within its territory. And third, it is not formally or legally subject to any internal or external power in the conduct of its affairs. Sovereignty may be located in a single institution as in the case of the British parliament, or divided among different units as in a federal state, or subjected to a complex system of checks and balances. However, none of these detracts from its three essential features mentioned above. Contrary to what some writers have maintained, federal states represent not novel ways of bypassing sovereignty, but different ways of decentring, decentralizing and distributing it.

Third, the state is an association of individuals, who constitute its ultimate ontological units and who are the sole bearers of rights and obligations. Families, tribes, religious and ethnic communities, and other such social collectives enjoy no political status and receive no official recognition from the state.

Fourth, the state is expected to have a singular and unambiguous identity. This is achieved when the constitution, which defines the structure, institutions, powers and functions of the state, rests on a coherent and homogeneous set of legal and political principals. A constitution that enunciates a mixed body of principles or allows different parts of the country to be governed by different principles gives the state a hybrid or confused identity, and creates what Pufendorf called *corpus irregulare monstro simile* (an irregular body, like that of a monster).

Fifth, citizens of the state enjoy equal rights. And since their social, cultural and other differences are abstracted away, equal rights mean identical or uniform rights. The state is a homogeneous legal space within which its members should be able to move about freely and carry exactly the same rights and obligations. There are neither 'no-go' areas within the state nor ones where its citizens enjoy different rights from their counterparts elsewhere.

Sixth, if the state is federally constituted, its component units are all expected to enjoy equal rights and powers. If their rights and powers were to differ, there would be not only inequality between them but also between their members who would now enjoy different rights in different parts of the country, thereby detracting from the principle of equal citizenship and the homogeneous legal space.

Seventh, citizenship is a unitary, unmediated and homogeneous relationship between the individual and the state. Since it involves abstracting away cultural, religious, ethnic and other identities and seeing oneself solely as a member of the state, all citizens are directly related to the state and not through their membership of intermediate communities. They are also identically related to it and not each in his or her own way. In the dominant view of the state, the latter requires homogeneous citizens as its necessary human correlates.

Eighth, members of the state constitute a single people or community. In a democratically constituted state, the majority of them speaks and acts in the name of them all.[8]

I outlined above some of the basic features of the dominant theory of the modern state. This view of the state clearly presupposes a culturally homogeneous society, as would become clear if we carefully examined each of the eight features.

The *first* feature requires that the citizens of the state are all agreed that their territorial identity should be privileged over their cultural, ethnic, religious and other identities. If some of them took a different view, the state would not be able to accommodate them.

The *second* feature presupposes that they all agree that the legal authority should be superior to all others, that the state should enjoy the monopoly of it, that every area of life should be in principle subject to the jurisdiction of the state, and that the interests of the state regulate and override the demands of other identities. It also presupposes that what the citizens share in common with each other is to them far more important than what they share with their fellow-religionists or fellow-ethnics outside their territorial boundaries, and that they are so prepared to trust their state to look after their vital interests that they would not like its internal affairs to be subject to the intervention or even the influence of external agencies.

The *third* feature, which makes the individual the basic unit of the state, presupposes a culture of individualism, and implies that citizens of the state are all agreed in defining themselves primarily as individuals rather than as members of specific ethnic, religious or cultural communities.

The *fourth* feature presupposes that they are all agreed on what principles should inform the nature, structure and functions of the state, what fundamental rights they should all have, and how their collective political identity should be defined. It also presupposes that the state does not consist of territorially concentrated minorities who might wish to conduct their affairs and design their institutions on different principles from the rest of the country.

The *fifth* feature requires that members of the state are equally willing and able to abstract away their cultural and other differences and to define their citizenship in autonomous terms. This in turn presupposes that they relate to their culture, ethnicity, religion, etc., in an identical manner and assign them a more or less equal value. Given the obvious cultural and other differences between individuals, equal rights can mean identical rights only if the differences are more or less equally inconsequential to them.

The *sixth* feature presupposes that all the constituent units of a federal state have basically the same needs, are identically circumstanced, and have broadly the same histories, traditions and characters. If they were different in these and other respects and wished to preserve them, they would obviously need and press for different powers.

The *seventh* feature implies that all citizens, and all communities to which they might belong, share identical conceptions of the state, have broadly similar histories and backgrounds, relate to the state in the same manner, and ground their obligation to it in an identical principle.

The *eight and final* feature clearly presupposes a culturally and ethnically homogeneous community. If a state consisted of several different communities and was heterogeneous in its nature and composition, then, the principle of majority would become deeply problematic. The largest community would invariably form a majority within the state, and exercise domination over others.

According to the dominant view of it, then, the state should have a single identity, a single and homogeneous source of sovereignty, a single system of basic rights and obligations, a single and homogeneous people, a unitary conception of citizenship, a uniform mode of relating the citizen to the state, and so forth. The unity of the state rests on the uniformity of views on these and related matters, and is deemed to be threatened if the uniformity is absent. This means that although the state can accommodate a wide variety of differences, they should not be such as to rule out substantive agreement on its identity, system of rights, the nature of citizenship, etc. If they are, they have to be eliminated by educational, economic, cultural and, when necessary, coercive means.

The assumption that political uniformity is the indispensable basis of political unity is to be found in all major writers from Hobbes to Rawls. They do, no doubt, disagree about the degree and extent of political uniformity. Some want unity of religion, ethnicity, language, etc., whereas others think differently. However, hardly anyone has questioned the assumption itself, not even the founding fathers of the American Constitution. The federation they created assumed that although the constituent states could have different legal systems, constitutions, etc., they all shared a basic commitment to the same body of rights defined and applied in a more or less identical manner.

Since the dominant model assumes a basic political uniformity, and since the latter constitutes a central defining feature of nationhood, the modern state has an inherent tendency to become a nation. It is often suggested, mistakenly in my view, that the nation-state is a result of the nationalists hijacking the state, for this does not explain why they were able to hijack it at all, why states after states proved willing accomplices, and why this did not happen to pre-modern polities. It is also worth nothing that hardly any state, and any theorist of it, has managed to resist nationalist aspirations. They might have been hostile to ethnic or religious nationalism, but not to its so-called civic variety. Although the latter is more open and less tribal, it too is inspired by a search for political uniformity, without which the state is supposed to lack unity and a common sense of belonging. The modern state is not as innocent an institution, and as different from nation, as is generally imagined.

Like any theory, the dominant model of the state makes sense in a society that satisfies its basic presuppositions and is culturally homogeneous in the manner it requires. In culturally heterogeneous or deeply divided societies, which is what most societies are today, the value and validity of the model are severely limited. Indeed if the state were to be constituted and to conduct its internal and external affairs along the lines laid down by the dominant theory, it would become an instrument of injustice, oppression, even disorder and defeat its basic objectives. In such societies the state clearly needs to be constituted very differently. There is nothing intrinsically valuable or sacrosanct about the modern state. It is just an institutional form developed during a specific historical period to achieve conditions considered desirable by its members. If they today desire different conditions, or believe that these are better achieved by different institutional forms, they should explore alternatives without the slightest feeling of unease.[9] The point would become clearer if we took some contemporary examples to show why such an exploration is vitally necessary, and why the failure to undertake it out of inertia, fear or misplaced nostalgia is the source of many of our problems.

III

More or less ever since their colonization, Indians of Canada were confronted with a stark choice: either to get assimilated into the mainstream liberal way of life and receive full rights of citizenship, or to stick to their way of life and forfeit the rights. Not surprisingly, hardly anyone opted for the former alternative. Rather than respect their choice, the colonial government introduced a system of compulsory residential schools in which the Indian culture was severely suppressed. Even then only a few Indians chose to trade away their way of life, as seen in the fact that between 1857 and 1920 only 250 of them sought enfranchisement.

During the 1950s and 1960s the political climate changed, and the Hawthorn-Tremblay report of 1966 proposed that Indians could have both the normal rights of Canadian citizenship and the additional ones required to retain their way of life. The fact that this was called 'citizen plus' showed the continuing hold of the dominant theory of the state. Strictly speaking, the additional rights did not privilege them for, given their circumstances and needs, they required them to enjoy equal citizenship with the rest of their fellow-Canadians. However, since all citizens were assumed to be entitled to exactly the same rights, the additional ones given to Indians were seen as a privilege, no doubt justified but nevertheless a privilege.

Not surprisingly, the liberal Prime Minister Traudeau's White Paper of 1969 argued that the proposal violated the liberal principles of equality and common citizenship, and demanded that the separate Indian status be abolished and Indians speedily absorbed into the mainstream society. While it was eventually dropped in teeth of opposition, many felt deeply uneasy and restored the basic ideas of the White Paper in the 1982 Charter of Rights and Freedoms. The Charter basically translated the dominant theory of the state in the Canadian context and had in mind not just the Indians but also, and especially, Quebec. It assumed that political unity required political uniformity, that is, unity of views on such matters as national identity, the nature of citizenship, and the content of fundamental rights. Since the Charter provided that uniformity, Charter patriotism, a precursor to Habermas's constitutional patriotism, was to be the sole basis of Canada's unity. All Canadians were citizens of Canada. Citizenship involved abstracting away their cultural, religious, ethnic and other differences, and relating to the Canadian state in a uniform and direct manner. The state took no account of cultural and other differences among its citizens, and was culturally neutral. Citizenship consisted in possessing certain basic rights and freedoms, which were uniform throughout the country and admitted of no violation or modification. Subject to their constraints, Canadians were free to organize their personal and interpersonal affairs the way they liked, all provinces were equal and enjoyed equal powers. They were political sub-units of the Canadian state, open alike to all citizens, and not ethnic homelands of specific communities however large their numbers. The Canadian state was the sole source and guarantor of the basic rights of citizenship, and hence the ultimate object of allegiance and loyalty. Since only the federal government spoke and acted in its name, it was the primary bond between all Canadian citizens. Canadians were one people and shared a common sense of belonging because they all alike share a common loyalty to the Charter.

Although Tradeau's vision as embodied in the Charter had its strengths, it was also flawed. The Charter was presented as culturally neutral, but in fact the rights and freedoms it stressed embodied a predominantly liberal individualist view of political life. Since the aboriginal peoples and Quebec did not share that view, they could legitimately complain of injustice and double standards. Furthermore, the Charter's political liberalism expressed and was continuous with the way of life as lived by the liberals. So far as others were concerned, it created a disjunction, a hiatus, between their normal way of life and their political life. Since they could not fully identify with the Charter, it could not form the basis of their patriotism and loyalty to the Canadian state. Again, given the deep historical inequalities between the Anglophones and the rest of Canadians, the formal equality asserted by the Charter was bound to have unequal consequences for the latter. The aboriginal peoples could hardly retain their way of life in competition with the vastly more powerful Anglophone culture. And, the generalized pan-Canadian bilingualism could hardly counter the pressure on the Francophones in Quebec and elsewhere to assimilate into Anglophone Canada. Both groups needed collective action to preserve their ways of life, and that was ruled out by the Charter. The gap between them and the advocates of the philosophy of the Charter would become clearer if we briefly examined the public discourse on their demands.

Although Canada has done much to accommodate the aboriginal aspirations, the path to it was uneven and bitterly contested, and the earlier unease about the integrity of the liberal values and the unity of the Canadian state still persist.

In order to preserve their way of life within the Canadian state, the aboriginal leaders made several demands of which the following are illustrative:

(i) The right to self-government, including the right to make their own laws and follow their own customs in certain areas to exercise control over their resources, especially land, to make policies relating to health, education and the promotion of their languages and cultures, to adopt a criminal justice system based on tribal courts aiming at reconciliation and rehabilitation, and so forth

(ii) Citizens of the rest of Canada should not be allowed to settle in large numbers in aboriginal territories and buy land there.
(iii) Members of aboriginal communities should not be at liberty to sell their lands to outsiders, and should lose their rights to communal lands and other facilities if they choose to marry outsiders.
(iv) The aboriginal people should be free to follow their own traditional system of election rather than adopt the conventional liberal form.
(v) The aboriginal right to self-government is not derived from the Canadian state but forms part of a treaty arrangements, and can be regulated but not abrogated by the Canadian state.

The response of much of the rest of Canada, based as it was on the dominant model of the state, was for long predictably hostile to almost all these demands.[10]

(1) was rejected on three grounds: (a) Since the kind of self-government demanded by the indigenous people involves far more powers than are enjoyed by the provinces, it privileges the aboriginal communities and violates the principle of the equality of the provinces. (b) It gives the indigenous government the authority to impose unacceptable restrictions on its members' basic rights as guaranteed by the Canadian Charter of Rights and Freedoms, and violates both the principle of the equality of citizens and the liberal character of Canada. (c) It creates a confused, three-tier and messy federation that rests on no clear principles of distribution of powers.

(2) was rejected on two grounds: (a) It violates the basic rights of Canadian citizens to move about freely within their country and to buy and sell property. (b) It establishes differential systems of rights in different parts of the country and offends against the principles of the homogeneity of the legal space and equal rights of citizens.

(3) was rejected on three grounds: (a) It denies to members of the indigenous community some of the basic liberal rights and is profoundly illiberal. (b) It gives them less rights than to other Canadian citizens and offends against the principle of the equality of citizens. (c) For obvious reasons, it violates the principle of the homogeneity of the legal space and detracts from the singularity of the Canadian state.

(4) was rejected on the ground that the indigenous community's mode of election was not sufficiently open and free, and offended against one of the basic principles of liberal democracy.

(5) went against the principle of the sovereignty of the state and simply could not be entertained.

While some of these objections reflect legitimate moral and political anxieties which should not be lightly brushed aside, they are not unanswerable. (1a) makes sense only if equality of the provinces of the territorial units is defined in formal and abstract terms. If equality is defined in terms of powers required to meet their different needs and circumstances, it is perfectly consistent with a differential system of powers. The powers might be different, but so long as they are equally adequate to their needs, the principle of the equality of the provinces is not violated.

As for (1b), is raises difficult questions. Since we cannot consider them all, a few words should suffice. The Canadian Charter of Rights and Freedoms basically lays down the familiar list of liberal rights. What if the indigenous people do not accept it, or do so subject to their right to reinterpret and vary some of its provisions? If they do not agree to it, they cannot be bound by it on liberal grounds. It might be argued that the rights are central to human dignity and well-being and ought to be respected by all. Although there is much to be said in support of this view, one needs to appreciate that human well-being and dignity can be defined in several different ways and imply different system of basic rights and freedoms. Rather than unilaterally impose liberal rights and freedoms, the Canadian state needs to enter into a dialogue with the aboriginal people with a view to arriving at a minimum body of principles that all its citizens, including the latter, can agree upon and be required to respect. If no such agreement is forthcoming, the Canadian state should wait and rely on educational and other forms of pressure to evolve a consensus. Furthermore, all rights, including the fundamental ones, can conflict and need to be prioritized and traded-off. Since this can be done differently by different communities, the latter should be free to do so in a manner that both best coheres with their ways of life and is acceptable to their members and to the country at large.

Sometimes it is argued that since the rights laid down by the Charter enjoy the endorsement of the overwhelming majority of Canadian citizens, the indigenous people should respect them. The argument makes sense only if we accept the idea of the homogeneous people lying at the basis of the dominant theory of the state, and there is no obvious reason why we should. Since society implies a shared way of life and constant interaction, Canada, which includes different ways of life and communities, is not a single society but made up of several societies. And insofar as the indigenous communities are, or at least see themselves as, distinct peoples who, although Canadians, are also Inuit, Metis, etc., Canada is not a single and homogeneous people. The indigenous peoples are part of Canada in the sense that they live within its territorial jurisdiction and largely identify with the country, but they are not a part of Canada in the sense of sharing its dominant way of life. Since the Canadians are not a single and homogeneous people, the standard liberal theory of legitimacy needs to be revised. In a culturally and ethnically heterogeneous society the concept of majority needs to be defined not in abstract and mechanical but communally mediated terms, and the decisions of the national majority, that is, of the majority of the majority community cannot be allowed automatically to override the views of the majority within the constituent communities and peoples.

As for (1c) there is no obvious reason why a federation should necessarily be two-tier or symmetrical, and not allow different forms of government to its different territorial units. Powers should be related to needs and circumstances, and vary with the latter.

As for (2a), it makes sense only if we accept that Canadians have a basic right to settle and buy property wherever they like in Canada, a view the aboriginal peoples reject. Since the rest of Canada agrees that the aboriginal people should be free to preserve their ways of life, it should accept such essential restrictions as this entails. There is no good reason either why the right to reside where one likes or to buy and sell property there should be considered a fundamental right. And if the Canadian Charter makes it a fundamental right, it should permit exemptions to the aboriginal people both because it conflicts with their equally basic right to preserve their way of life and because it does not enjoy their consent.

As for (2b), there is no reason why the state should represent a homogeneous legal space. If its constituent communities have different needs, face different problems or entertain different conceptions of the good, they need differential systems of rights. To disallow this in the name of a homogeneous legal space is to be unfair to them. And, since the homogeneous legal space is created by institutionalizing a specific conception of the good, its imposition also involves an element of cultural intolerance and worse.

As for (3a), it confronts the aboriginal people with a liberal list of inviolable rights and demands that they respect them. As we saw, the demand is unfair. As for 3(b), denying the members of the aboriginal community the right to sell land, etc., does give them less rights in the sense that they cannot do some of the things that their counterparts elsewhere can do. However, if they value these rights less highly than their right to preserve their way of life, their decision deserves respect. The level at which equality ultimately matters and should be established is not that of specific rights but the general right to lead a life of one's choice. And, if that entails variations in specific rights, as it is bound to do when ways of life differ, the principle of equality is not violated.

As for 3(c), we have already seen that the principle of homogeneous legal space cannot be elevated to the status of an inviolable moral principle. It presupposes a relatively homogeneous community whose members share a common conception of the good life and have broadly similar needs, and has not only little relevance but becomes a source of injustice when these conditions do not obtain. As to the argument that the Canadian state should rest on a single body of constitutional principles and possess a singular identity, there is, again, no obvious reason why this should be so. The identity of a state should reflect its members' self-understanding. If a state consists of different communities holding divergent conceptions of their collective life, its identity needs to be plural.

As for (4), the Canadian state is right to insist that elections among the aboriginal people should be fair and free. However, this does not mean that they should conform to the standard liberal pattern. Since the aboriginal people are unused or antipathetic to the ideological and political polarization lying at the basis of the party system and more at home with the consensual method of decision-making, they should be free to follow the latter provided that it meets the norms of freedom and fairness. The fact that decisions are made only by male tribal elders does not warrant state intervention unless there is a widespread demand for change. And, (5) assumes that sovereignty should have a single source. There is no obvious reason why this should be true of every state. In Canada, as in many other countries, the indigenous people enjoyed 'sovereignty' before they were conquered, and their relations with the colonising settlers are governed both by treaties and, since these were often contracted under duress, by the moral principles informing international law. In such countries the state has plural sources of sovereignty and needs to respect their constraints.

Like the aboriginal demand for self-government, Quebec's demand to be recognized as a distinct society enjoying the power to protect its way of life has aroused considerable controversy. In the eyes of its French-speaking majority, it is not just a province where most people happen to speak French, but a society with a distinct culture, history, legal system, mode of incorporation into the Canadian state, collective self-understanding, etc., in short, a distinct identity which it has both a right and a duty to preserve. With that objective in mind, Quebec made specific demands. It asked the rest of Canada to recognize its distinctness, to enshrine it in the Canadian Charter and Constitution and to define the Canadian national identity in bicultural terms. This would publicly affirm its status as a co-founder of the Canadian federation, recognize it as Francophone homeland, enable it to identify with the Canadian state, mark it out from other ethnic groups that have subsequently immigrated to Canada, and authorize the Canadian Supreme Court to take its distinct needs into account when interpreting and judging the constitutionality of its laws. It would also enable the Quebecois to belong both to *la nation Quebecois* and to the Canadian state and to enjoy mediated citizenship without feeling or arousing in the rest of Canada a deep sense of moral unease. Quebec has also asked for several powers such as the power to control immigration, to make laws necessary to preserve French language, and to require that unlike the Anglophones the Francophones and Allophones may not send their children to English language schools. It also asked that the Charter and all future constitutional amendments should apply to it only if its government and National Assembly consent to them, and that three seats on the Canadian Supreme Court should be reserved for Quebeckers.

After considerable resistance and protracted negotiations, some of these demands were met. In addition to Quebec's distinct legal system, which has long been constitutionally recognized, it has power over immigration, a right to take measures necessary to promote French language subject to the provisions of the Charter, three seats on the Canadian Supreme Court, its own pension plan, diplomatic representation abroad, and so forth. Some of these, however, were seen by the rest of Canada as unprincipled concessions reluctantly made by it to avoid Quebec's secession. Many of Quebec's other demands still remain unmet. Meech Lake Accord of 1987, which recognized Quebec as a 'distinct society' and the Francophone presence as a 'fundamental characteristic' of Canada, failed to be ratified by all the provincial legislatures in time and seemed to enjoy the support of barely 20 per cent of Canadians outside Quebec around the time of its ratification.

There are all kinds of reasons, some perfectly understandable, why the rest of Canada was unwilling to meet Quebec's demands, but they do not concern us. What interests us are the kinds of arguments some of its leaders advanced with considerable popular support. The argument overlap with those made against the aboriginal demands and reveal the hold of the dominant theory of the state.

(i) The national identity of the state should be singular and unambiguous for otherwise it becomes nebulous and lacks the power to unite and evoke the undivided loyalty of its citizens. To accept Quebec's French identity as part of Canada's national identity and to make its preservation one of its central national purposes is to put Canada and Quebec on an equal footing and to treat them as equally worthy objects of allegiance. This not only threatened the unity of the state but also violated its cultural neutrality.

(ii) In a federal state all its constituent provinces should be treated equally. Quebec asks for a privileged status, and that offends against the principle of the equality of the provinces.

(iii) To be a citizen of the state is to transcend ethnic, cultural, linguistic and other differences and to be directly and identically related to it. In defining Canadian citizenship in a dual and mediated manner, Quebec violates this fundamental principle. All Canadians are 'above all' Canadians, and none can be a *Quebecois* first and a Canadian secondarily or even both at once. As Trudeau often told Quebecers, they had to choose between Canada and Quebec, two alternative not complementary objects of allegiance.

(iv) Canada is a liberal state as reflected in its Charter of Rights and Freedoms. Quebec's demand to restrict individual rights in order to preserve its French identity has a collectivist thrust and detracts from Canada's liberal character. When it is pointed out that Quebec's respect for fundamental rights is just as strong as that of the rest of Canada, that it has its own *Charte des Droits* which in some respect is more liberal than its national counterpart, that it generally seeks to restrict only the relatively unimportant rights, and that it too is and wishes to remain a liberal society albeit in its own different way, it is argued that all parts of Canada should subscribe to the same basic rights, define and prioritize them in the same way, and be liberal in a more or less identical manner. The asymmetrical federation demanded by Quebec might not only lead to the dissolution of the Canadian state but already represents its partial dissolution and surrenders the very idea of a single nation.

(v) Citizens of a state should enjoy equal rights and freedoms regardless of where they live. Quebec's demands entail restrictions on individual rights that do not obtain in other parts of the country, and offend against the principle of equal citizenship. The state symbolizes a homogeneous legal space within which it citizens should be able to move with equal ease and entertain identical expectations. Quebec's demands violate this principle and virtually create a state within a state.

(vi) The state represents a single and united people, and the majority decisions are binding on all its members. Since the *Quebecois* are a minority within Canada, they are wrong to demand equality of status with the rest of Canada, let alone dictate to it the pattern of its constitutional arrangements. They should have the democratic grace to accept such systems of rights as the majority of their countrymen have agreed upon.

Each of these objections draws on the dominant theory of the state and assumes its truth. In so doing they systematically fail to appreciate both the justice of some of Quebec's demands and the need of rethink the nature of the state in a culturally diverse society.

(1) is mistaken because the identity of the state in a culturally plural society cannot be simple and homogeneous. Since only a plural identity enables its diverse communities to identify with the state and to see in its symbols and defining principles the reassuring public affirmation of their histories and culture, it alone can command their loyalty and allegiance.

(2) is mistaken because it fails to appreciate that when provinces are different in their circumstances and needs, to treat them uniformly is to treat them not equally but unequally. Indeed to call them all provinces is to impose a uniform identity on what are otherwise very different collectivizes, and to misconceive their nature. Quebec is not so much a province as a national society or a territorially concentrated national minority, and qualitatively different from the rest. Furthermore, like any federal state, the Canadian state acknowledges that since different provinces are unequally endowed in their natural and human resources, the poorer ones need to be given additional resources, as is evident in its policy of equalization payments. The Canadian Constitution Act, 1982 also rightly allows provinces with higher than average unemployment to prefer their own residents to migrants from other provinces. If the principle of equality can take account of economic differences, there is no obvious reason why it should not also take account of cultural differences. Here, as elsewhere, the dominant theory of the state is sensitive to economic but not to cultural needs, and reveals its biases.

(3) is mistaken because there is no reason why we should accept unitary and unmediated citizenship as the only valid way to define it. Although I cannot argue the point here, one might also observe that national citizenship is likely to be richer and more secure if it is grounded in and vitalized by the narrower communities that provide meaning to citizens' lives.

(4) assumed a uniform model of liberalism, and does not allow for the obvious fact that basic liberal values can be interpreted, traded off and realized differently in different communities.

(5) makes a similar mistake and confuses equality with uniformity. As for (6), we have already seen why it is flawed. The Quebecois are not a numerical minority but a people in the conventional sense of the term. To argue that the majority of Canadians speaks in the name of all Canadians and automatically overrides the majority of Quebecois is to give one people unjust moral precedence over another.

To say that Quebec has a legitimate case is not to say that all its demands are just or even reasonable, or that it has pursued them with the requisite degree of sensitivity to the deepest fears and anxieties of the rest of Canada. Some of its nationalist spokesmen have so heavily privileged their Quebecois identity over the Canadian, and taken such pleasure in reducing Canada to a weak, amorphous, unstable and largely instrumental state, that the rest of Canada has sometimes wondered why it should risk unravelling their state in order to accommodate Quebec. However, our concern here is not to arbitrate on these and other issues, but simply to highlight the kinds of conceptual obstacles the dominant theory of the state puts in the path of an open-minded dialogue.

IV

The Canadian situation is replicated in many other countries as well. And, in almost every case, the basic principles of the dominant theory of the state are asserted as sacred and inviolable, resulting in considerable injustices to minorities, political instability, and the vicious cycle of secessionist movements provoking and in turn being provoked by state repression. Take the case of India. The Indian Constitution wisely granted the Muslim-majority state of Kashmir a special status as long ago as 1950, including the right to have its own constitution, a greater autonomy than other Indian states, and symbols of quasi-independent statehood. Almost since then, and increasingly so in recent years, many have attacked this on broadly the same grounds as those advanced by the rest of Canada against Quebec.

The Indian Constitution, again, rightly gave its 60 million tribal people considerable legal, cultural and administrative autonomy of the kind demanded by the aboriginal people of Canada. It also gave the subsequently created three tribal states the kind of autonomy and preferential financial regime not available to other Indian states, recognized their customary laws, and denied other Indian citizens the right to settle and buy land there. Although these policies have not aroused the kind of opposition that Kashmir's special status has, they are constantly subverted in practice by government agencies and business corporations, often with the support or at least the connivance of the central and state governments.

At independence India faced a problem that has no analogue in Canada and elsewhere. Born in the trauma of the partition of the country and fearful of alienating its religious minorities, the Constitution of India decided to continue the colonial policy of leaving the minorities free to be governed by their own personal laws in such matters as marriage, divorce, custody and guardianship of children and inheritance. Although the state retains formal jurisdiction over these matters, it is not at liberty to alter them without the explicit consent of the communities concerned. In all other matters such as the criminal law and the laws relating to the economy, the Indian state enjoys full powers to make such laws as it deems necessary. The Constitution had hoped that all Indian citizens would one day be governed by a single personal law or civil code, but neither set the time limit nor provided the necessary mechanism. Although it laid down a largely liberal list of fundamental rights, it remained ambiguous about whether the minority personal laws were subject to their constraints. The subsequent Supreme Court judgments ruled that they were not.[11]

This system of limited legal pluralism has become a subject of considerable debate, especially in relation to Muslims. Hindu nationalists and an influential body of liberals have argued that the system violates such principles as common citizenship, equal rights and equality before the law, and militates against the unity of the Indian state. In the light of our discussion it should be obvious that it does no such thing, and that the criticisms levelled against it make sense only if we accept the dominant theory of the state upon which they are based. In a culturally plural society the basic principles of a common civil code are not easy to agree upon, especially those relating to the culturally central area of the family life; and any precipitate attempt to legislate them is likely to end up imposing majority values and practices on the rest of the population and provoking disorder. This is not say that a single civil code might not be desirable in India, but rather that the case made for it from within the dominant theory of the state is unconvincing.

V

The modern state is a remarkable and truly original historical achievement. It evolved in response to the specific historical needs, pressures and collective self-understanding of the West European people, and has proved a mixed blessing. It liberated its members from narrow group identities and loyalties, and gave them a wider object of allegiance and a larger space for collective action. It also created an unprecedented area of individual liberty and established an admirable regime of personal liberties and rights. It institutionalized equality, the rule of law, procedural and impersonal justice, and so on, and based the conduct of collective affairs on easily intelligible and publicly debatable principles of rationality.

While the emancipatory potential of the state is beyond doubt and should not be allowed to be obscured by the politically naive post-modernist debunking of it, the historical fact remains that the dominant model of it is predicated upon, and has over the centuries vigorously striven to establish, a culturally homogeneous society. Although liberal, conservative, communitarian, nationalist, Marxist and other theorists of the state have offered different substantive views concerning its nature, social basis and functions, they have all in their own different way assumed that it requires a single conception of the good life, unmediated and homogeneous citizenship, a single language of public discourse, a single source of sovereignty, a single political identity, and so forth. This was true even of Hobbes, the most minimalist political theorist in the history of Western thought, as is evident in his justification of the state, his list of natural laws, his discussion of the ends of civil and criminal legislation, and his insistence on the sovereign's right to provide an authoritative interpretation of Christian theology.

Our situation and self-understanding today are quite different. Differences concerning how we should conduct our personal and collective lives are deep and pervasive. They often have ethnic, religious or linguistic bases, and cannot be suppressed. What is no less important, we are increasingly beginning to appreciate that by abstracting away cultural, religious and other differences, the dominant model impoverishes the state and deprives it of a creative and mutually enriching dialogue with its constituent communities. For these and related reasons we need to reconceptualize the state and replace the dominant theory with what I might call a pluralist and culturally sensitive theory of the state.

Such a pluralist theory of the state would need to do three things.[12] *First*, it should sensitively redefine and, when necessary, replace such concepts as sovereignty, people, majority, citizenship, equality (both of individuals and of groups) and national identity, in term of which almost all modern theories of the state are articulated.

Second, it needs to challenge such standard assumptions as that every state must have a singular constitutional identity, a single political culture, a uniformly applied system of rights, a homogeneous legal space, a uniform system of criminal justice, and identically empowered constituent units. Every state requires a shared body of principles and values, especially a multicultural state in which they often constitute the only basis of unity. But if the principles and values are to serve their intended purpose, they should be thin enough to be acceptable to all the constituent communities, and should additionally allow adjustments to their different traditions and ways of life.

Third, while plurality and differences deserve greater recognition than they have received from the dominant theory of state, they can also become sources of division and disunity. Indeed, as the recent experiences of Eastern Europe and parts of Asia and Africa demonstrate, an indiscriminate and unprincipled indulgence of differences is the surest way to political disintegration and chaos. The pluralist theory of the state therefore needs to explore new modes of political unity that respect and cherish diversity, bring them into a creative interplay, prevent them from becoming frozen and rigid, and evolve a shared, open and collectively acceptable regime of rights and obligations. Contrary to the central assumption of the dominant model, the state alone cannot carry the burden of uniting and holding together such complex and divided societies as ours. Indeed, since it is the site of political contestation, the more it tries to unite society and the greater the powers it acquires, the more is its role contested and the greater the disunity it paradoxically creates. The pluralist theory of the state needs to find ways of both decentring and recentring the state, of both respecting the identities of its constituent communities and using their moral and emotional resources to renew its own legitimacy and authority.[13]

As I have argued at various places in this paper, all states have to come to terms with cultural diversities. Although they sometimes try to suppress them, they do not often succeed and over time work out ways of coming to terms with them. Indeed there is hardly a state that fully conforms to the dominant model as I have outlined it. However, the model continues to be thought of as a norm, and departures from it are seen as deviations regrettably made necessary by the exigencies and recalcitrance of political life. My concern has been to argue that rather than try to live up to the dominant model, we should bring it in harmony with political reality and develop a theory of the state that does greater justice to the countless ingenious ways in which human societies reconcile the equally legitimate and sometimes conflicting demands of unity and diversity.[14]

Notes

1. I am most grateful to Professors Douglas Verney and Brian Walker for their helpful comments on an earlier draft of this paper.
2. For the first section of this paper I have drawn on my *The Nature of the Modern State*, in D.L. Sheth and Ashis Nandy (eds.), *The Multiverse of Democracy*. Delhi: Sage, 1996.
3. Since I am primarily concerned with the state, my interest in these features is largely heuristic. Hence, my discussion of them is highly schematic and sketchy.
4. Although all writers on the state mention territory, hardly any of them appreciates and analyses its unique moral and ontological importance.

5. In many earlier polities, such claims were generally respected.
6. These metaphors are particularly common in the Marxist discourse on the state.
7. For further discussion, see Quentin Skinner, *Foundations of Modern Political Thought*, Cambridge: Cambridge University Press, 1979.
8. For further discussion, see Kenneth Dyson, *The State Tradition in the Western Europe*, Oxford: Martin Robertson, 1980.
9. For a discussion of some of these ideas, see James Tully, *Strange Multiplicity: Constitutionalism in An Age of Diversity*, Cambridge: Cambridge University Press, 1995.
10. Cited in J.R. Miller, *Skyscrapers Hide the Heavens: A History of Indian-White Relations in Canada*, revised edition, Toronto: University of Toronto Press, 1990, p. 207.
11. For a useful summary of liberal reactions to the indigenous demands, see Augie Fleras and Jean Leonard Elliott, *The Nations Within: Aboriginal—State Relations in Canada, the United States and the New Zealand,* Toronto: Oxford University Press, 1992, Part I, especially chapters. 5 to 8.
12. The Indian Constitution is a delicate balance of liberal and non-liberal principles and gives the Indian state a complex and multiple identity.
13. Although Charles Taylor, Joseph Carens, James Tully and Will Kymlicka have offered perceptive critiques of the dominant theories of the state and constitution, none of them has so far provided a well-considered alternative.
14. I have explored these ideas in 'A Misconceived Discourse on Political Obligation', *Political Studies*, June 1993; 'Citizenship and Political Obligation' in Preston King (ed.), *Socialism and the Common Good* (London: Frank Cass, 1996); 'Cultural Pluralism and the Limits of Diversity', *Alternatives*, December 1995 and 'Cultural Diversity and Liberal Democracy' in David Beetham (ed.), *Defining and Measuring Democracy* (London: Sage Publications, 1994).

2

Plural Society and Pluralism in South Asia

A Conceptual Refinement and an Empirical Explication

T.K. OOMMEN

In contemporary social science there are two broad conceptions of plural societies and pluralism which are anchored to research done in two different empirical situations—the 'pre-modern' colonial and post-colonial societies and the modern industrial societies. The intellectual ancestry of these conceptualizations is readily traceable to J.S. Furnivall and Alexis de Tocqueville. Those who followed Furnivall are mainly social and cultural anthropologists and they may be designated as cultural pluralists. The Tocquevillean line was pursued largely by political scientists and political sociologists who may be labelled as political pluralists. That is, the conceptualization of pluralism and plural society is tempered by several factors—the property of the empirical situations in which the researches are done and the intellectual, ideological and disciplinary orientations of the researchers. In this paper I propose to argue that we need to re-conceptualize the notions of plural society and pluralism not only because of the inherent ambiguities in the prevailing conceptualizations but also because of their inadequacy to be applied to several other empirical situations. The viability of the proposed conceptualizations is demonstrated with special reference to South Asian polities.

I

The classic description of plural society by Furnivall based on the colonial situation which he analyzed reads thus:

> Each group holds by its own religion, its own culture, its own ideas and ways. As individuals they meet but only in the market place, in buying and selling … . There is a plural society, with different sections of the community living side by side, but separately within the same political unit. Even in the economic sphere there is a division of labour on racial lines. (1948: 308)

That is, in Furnivall's plural society, the co-existence of the different segments, usually of racial collectivities, one native and the other alien, is not voluntary but brought about through the force imposed by the colonial power from the outside. Further, given this lack of 'integration' plural societies are unsuited for nationalism and hence democracy. "Nationalism within a plural society is itself a disruptive force, tending to shatter and not consolidate its social order" (Furnivall, 1939: 468). By implication, only in societies which are voluntarily constituted and are homogeneous, democracy can be institutionalized and nurtured. However, such a position is not sustainable in the light of empirical evidence. The most 'successful democracy' in the world, the United States of America, is not a voluntarily constituted polity if one takes into account the manner in which the original inhabitants of the US territory and the Blacks in the anti-bellum South were incorporated. And, the 'biggest democracy' in the world, viz., India, is utterly heterogeneous and plural.

M.G. Smith (1960: 763–77) was one of the earliest analysts who extended and reformulated the concept of plural society following Furnivall. In doing this, he distinguishes between three types of societies—homogeneous, heterogeneous and plural. Some have criticized the notion of homogeneous society on the ground that in all 'national' societies regional, rural-urban, ethnic and class differences exist and therefore a homogeneous society is an exception rather than a rule (see Braithwaite, 1960: 816–31).

However, such a view confuses between social stratification and cultural and racial heterogeneity. All societies, including homogeneous ones, are undoubtedly stratified based on a multiplicity of factors. But, the nature of elements contributing to stratification and heterogeneity are qualitatively different, although, of course, they may often operate conjointly in specific societies.

There are, however, two fundamental problems with Smith's analysis. One is that he defines society as a political unit; a territorial area with its own governmental institutions. That is, he conflates polity and society. The danger of this conflation is all too evident when one notes that the same society may be divided into the territories of two or more states (e.g., Basques, Bengalis, Koreans, Punjabis, Kurds) and several societies may belong to the territory of the same state (e.g., Soviet Union or Czechoslovakia before their break up, Indian Union, Pakistan).

The second fundamental problem in Smith's analysis is the encapsulation of institutions into culture and vice versa. In fact, he maintains that the core of a culture is its institutional system. Although he suggests that society and culture are not coterminus, Smith distinguishes the cultural plurality of different societies (that is, polities) based on a categorization of institutions which he designates as 'compulsory', 'alternative' and 'exclusive'. If the total population of a society shares the entire institutional system, it is a homogeneous society. The typical examples of these are pre-modern societies. In heterogeneous societies people share the same set of basic institutions but they also participate in different systems of alternate and exclusive institutions. Modern industrial societies are heterogeneous societies, according to Smith. In contrast, the groups in plural society practices very different systems of compulsory institutions, that is, cultural plurality and social plurality co-exists. The typical examples of this type are the 'new nations' which are invariably post-colonial societies.

Smith (1971: 415–58) later listed three basic deficiencies in the conceptualization of plural society made by Furnivall. First, its total identification and restriction to modern colonial situation and multi-racial societies. Second, its correlated confinement to tropical latitudes. Third, its restriction to the phase of individual expansion and *laissez-faire* capitalism by Europeans. Smith expands on the notion of plural society and refers to pluralism as the condition in which there is formal diversity in the basic system of institutions such as kinship, education, religion, property and economy and recreation but not government. This is so because, "Given the fundamental differences of belief, value and organization that connote pluralism, the monopoly of power by one cultural section is the essential pre-condition for the maintenance of the total society in its current form" (Smith, 1965: 86).

Although Smith wanted to extend and improve upon Furnivall's conceptualization, it seems to me that he has not achieved the goal in spite of the typology of societies he has proposed. While Smith has extended the notion of plural society to wider empirical contexts, the *differentia specifica* between plural and non-plural societies is not made clear.

Despres (1967: 20–21) advanced the following criticisms about Smith's conceptualization: (1) the 'elusive distinction' between society and culture, (2) the difficulty in differentiating the heterogeneous society from the plural society based on the criteria provided, and (3) the 'spurious' nature of the analytical distinction made between the compulsory, alternative and exclusive institutions to denote expressions of culture. However, he contends that with some modification of Smith's view it is possible to construct a systematic model of plural society. According to Despres:

> … the definition of the plural society must take into account two related sets of factors: (1) the extent to which specified groups are culturally differentiated in terms of specific institutional activities, and (2) the level at which institutional activities serve to maintain cultural differentiation as the basis for socio-cultural integration. (1967: 22)

Having rejected Smith's categorization of societies based on differential participation of the population in three types of institutions—compulsory, alternative and exclusive—Despres distinguishes between minimal or local cultural sections which serve to maintain cultural differentiation between groups at local levels and maximal or national cultural sections which integrate institutional activities of similar cultural groups and differentiate them from other cultural groups at the national level. Invoking this distinction Despres distinguishes between homogeneous societies wherein minimal cultural sections and the least amount of cultural variations exist, heterogeneous societies wherein local or minimal cultural sections exist with some variations, and plural societies in which maximal or national cultural sections exist.

The distinction that Despres makes between homogeneous and heterogeneous societies is vague and ambiguous as it does not specify the *differentia specifica* between the two. And, the confusion in distinguishing between the heterogeneous and plural societies becomes evident when he designates the United States of America as heterogeneous and Nigeria as plural. The US is a heterogeneous society because it contains many cultural groups such as the Irish, the Polish and the like, which are integrated at the local levels but are not linked through institutional structures such as religious associations, labour unions or political parties, according to Despres. In contrast, Nigeria is a plural society because the Ibo, the Yoruba and the Hausa are not only culturally differentiated and locally integrated but are linked through institutional structures such as political parties which serve to maintain their cultural differences at the national level.

There are several difficulties with the conceptualization proposed by Despres as is evident from its application to the two cases. First, the US and Nigeria are not societies but polities in which a large number of societies co-exist. Most polities in the contemporary world are multi-national, poly-ethnic, multi-religi -ous and/or multi-racial. That is, like Smith, Despres also conflates polity and society.

Second, the US consists of immigrant groups and communities, save the original inhabitants, all of whom retain part of their cultural baggage but have shed part of it. Nigeria consists of different tribes (nations) firmly anchored to their ancestral homelands and perhaps each of them could have become separate polities (that is, societies in the sense in which Despres uses the term) but for the colonial intervention. The different nations of Nigeria have become interest groups within the multi-national polity of Nigeria so as to wrest a better deal from the state. In all probability their cultural integrity cannot be kept in tact because of emigration from and immigration into the homelands of different peoples. That is, the local groups are also involved 'nationally'.

Third, the constituent units of Nigeria are homogeneous communities and the comparable groups in the US are only the Native American tribes. Finally, the examples that Despres invoke from the US are the wrong ones because the Blacks, Catholics or the Jews have all-US political, cultural and/or economic associations, institutions and movements which integrate them as collectivities. That is, both the tribes (national groups) and the religious and racial groups of the US are involved both in local and 'national' institutions. To conclude, the distinction between the heterogeneous and plural societies based on the types of institutions in which the constituting groups in a polity participate is not a viable basis of distinguishing these societies.

Another important contributor to the debate on pluralism is Van den Berghe (1971: 67) for whom plural societies are characterized by two basic features: "(1) segmentation into corporate groups that frequently, though not necessarily, have different cultures or subcultures; and (2) a social structure compartmentalized into analogous, parallel, non-complementary but distinguishable sets of institutions". Further, Van den Berghe contents that there are two types of pluralistic societies: the democratic and the despotic. The latter type is ruled by a despotic minority whose rule lacks "... consensus on both values legitimizing the existing polity and norms regulating political behaviour. Plural societies ... are primarily held together by coercion and the latter largely results from the superiority of the dominant group in the technology of violence" (1971: 73).

In contrast, democratic plural societies have a consensual value system enshrined in their constitutions and articulated through their institutions. While constitutional guarantees are important what matters are the substantive realities of life. It is the actual state of affairs which is decisive for sociological purposes. Therefore, what matters are not legal-formal guarantees, important as they are, but praxiological gaps which are bound to exist even in a democratic plural society. Hence, Van den Berghe concludes: "I believe that pluralism is intrinsically associated with conflict and relative lack of consensus and integration" (1971: 79).

If Furnivall's conceptualization of plural society was anchored to the empirical situation of the tropical, colonial, multi-racial societies, Smith, Despres and Van den Berghe refined the notion and extended it to other empirical contexts such as slave and multi-racial societies, both colonial and post-colonial. In contrast, the Tocquevillean conceptualization of pluralism is based on an entirely different type of empirical situation, that which grew out of multiplicity of collectivities competing in the political arena through the instrumentality of parties and associations, institutions and mobilizations. The typical cases which represent such situations are capitalist liberal democracies of the United Kingdom with its multi-national and migrant populations, and the United States of America which is poly-ethnic and multi-racial.

Tocqueville (1956) having observed the persisting turmoil in France, the country of his birth, and the land of the great revolution, was eager to locate the sources of stable and successful democracy which obtained in the US. He found that there existed a number of 'secondary powers', that is, voluntary associations, and these associations along with the autonomy of local authorities (e.g., municipalities) served to prevent the authoritarianism of the central state and helped to stabilize democracy. Thus, voluntary associations are recognized as countervailing powers which sustain political pluralism in democratic societies.

Political pluralists argue that voluntary associations are instruments which sustain democracy; and associations are formed based on a wide variety of factors including race, religion, caste, region and the like. The US, the most 'successful' democracy in the world, is hailed as a country of joiners and the American propensity to form voluntary associations is universally acclaimed (see, for example, Bryce, 1910; Hsu, 1963).

Students of community power, who have dealt with the relationship between the structural differentiation and dispersion of power in communities, have argued that political pluralism is conductive to democracy. For instance, Simpson and Simpson write:

> In communities with a large number of differentiated interest groups, community power is pluralistic and resembles the national power structure. In communities which are less differentiated or when potentially differentiated interest groups are poorly organized—including most small towns—power is apt to

> be monolithic, with a small business dominated elite exerting most of the effective pressure on government decisions. (1964: 380)

Sayre and Kaufman (1960) discovered that party leaders, the elected and appointed public officials, organized bureaucracies, the numerous non-governmental associations, the mass media officials and agencies of other governments—all exert influence in the governance of New York City, thereby suggesting that the heterogeneity and structural differentiation of the city had inevitably resulted in the enlargement of its power pool and dispersion of power. Rogers argues that "... the structural differentiation and increased complexity and heterogeneity that accompany industrialisation contribute to a pluralistic power structure" (1964: 402). Dahl (1961: 85) refers to the dispersion of political resources in New Haven in the wake of industrialization and the consequent dispersed inequalities and the emergence of specialized leadership resulting in a pluralistic power structure.

Some theorists (e.g., Van den Berghe, 1971: 67–81) refer to cultural pluralism as the conflict model and to political pluralism as the equilibrium model. The essential source of conflict in the first type—the culturally plural society—is located in the fact that a demographic, racial and cultural minority dominates over the majority in every aspect of life. This domination is made possible through their economic and technological superiority. This situation necessarily breeds conflict between the two parties and the resolution of conflict is possible only by doing away with the very sources of conflict, namely, the domination of the minority over the majority. But viewed historically, a large number of such societies have continued for a long time as 'stable' societies, the dominated majority rarely revolting against the dominant minority either because the value of self-governance was not internalized by it or because it does not have the requisite striking power.

On the other hand, it is not true that societies grouped under the equilibrium model—the democratic plural societies—did not have any conflict. In fact, the thesis of political pluralism, which propounded the idea of integration being achieved through multiple affiliations of individuals to a variety of institutions and associations, almost entirely ignored the racial minorities, particularly the black populations of these societies. And, consequently, conflict which is almost endemic in these societies has been ignored. In fact, conflict is more visible in the democratic plural societies as compared with the despotic plural ones. Thus, conflict and equilibrium are common to both types of plural societies. Therefore, to label these societies in terms of one of these features is inadequate, nay misleading. In the light of these considerations I suggest that we need to distinguish between the two types of societies based on the *quality* of equilibrium which obtains in them. The culturally plural societies are characterized by *coercive* equilibrium and the politically plural societies are informed by *consensual* equilibrium. Admittedly, the real challenge faced by culturally plural societies is to transform their equilibrium from a coercive to consensual one and that of the politically plural societies is to sustain the prevailing consensual equilibrium.

It is important to underline this point because Van den Berghe insists that culturally plural societies are inherently conflict-ridden as noted above. This evaluation is also endorsed by Kuper who writes: "By pluralization ... I mean an increasing accentuation of plural division based on race and ethnicity and an intensification of conflict between the plural sections, whereas de-pluralization here denotes a diminishing salience of ethnic and racial pluralism" (1971: 459).

De-pluralization is a process by which total identities dissolve into particular identities, that is, as citizens, as members of classes and as primordial collectivities individuals and groups act differently, based on contextual variations. This postulation is based on a particular conception of pluralism which needs to be questioned. Further, by implication, these theorists are suggesting that only homogeneous societies can be conflict-free—a proposition beset with dangerous implications and which erodes the very basis of genuine pluralism.

Three general conclusions emerge from the discussion so far. *First*, there is no consensus among theorists about the conceptualization of different types of societies. The heterogeneous societies of cultural pluralists are plural societies for the political pluralists. There is no consensus even among the cultural pluralists regarding the definitions of the three types of societies—

homogeneous, heterogeneous and plural. *Second,* the pronouncements regarding the relationship between pluralism and democracy are diametrically opposite. To cultural pluralists, pluralism destabilizes the social order, it is antithetical to the very ethos of democracy. By implication, they plumb for homogeneity for sustaining democracy. To political pluralists, pluralism is the very essence of democracy. Understandably, social heterogeneity is the natural soil on which authentic democracy will survive and prosper. *Third,* neither cultural nor political pluralists have addressed the all-important issue of institutionalized inter-group inequality as an inherent feature of hierarchical societies.

In the light of these points I want to make the following suggestions: *First,* we must clearly distinguish between four types of societies—homogeneous, heterogeneous, hierarchical and plural—based on the nature of the elements which constitute them—their internal social milieu. *Second,* the distinction between plural society and pluralism should be clearly maintained. In fact, the route through which plural societies can become democratic is to accept the value of pluralism. Third, the doctrine of homogeneity should be abandoned as it is antithetical to the spirit of both democracy and pluralism.

All societies are stratified based on age, gender and class. But, if a society's population is drawn from the same race, religious and/or linguistic group, it may be viewed as *homogeneous*. Conversely, the multi-racial, multi-national, multi-religious and poly-ethnic polities are *heterogeneous.* In this type of polity there is a possibility of inequality becoming a formal feature based on race (South Africa, until recently) or caste (India, before 1947), which render them also hierarchical societies. That is, heterogeneous polities with institutionalized inequality are hierarchical. But, a heterogeneous polity need not be hierarchical as racially and/or culturally diverse groups in the polity may have socio-economic equality. In the cases of homogeneous, heterogeneous and hierarchical polities, however, the internality of the constituting elements is not questioned. Thus, the American 'Negro', the Indian 'untouchable' and the Greek 'slave' were all accepted as essential and useful internal elements, although they were utterly unequal as compared to other elements. In contrast, the internality of one or another segment in a plural polity is questioned, that is, a *plural society* is polarized between insiders and outsiders. Sometimes, the insiders may be marginalized (e.g., the First Nations in the New World) and the outsiders become dominant and sometimes the outsiders may be marginalized and deprived of their rights (e.g., Indians in Fiji, or guest workers in Western Europe). It is necessary and useful to recognize the distinctions between these polities for the clarity of analysis. It is of signal importance to note that the first three types are not either or but additive types. That is, culturally diverse (heterogeneous) polities are also stratified. The hierarchical polities are stratified and heterogeneous. Finally, the plural polities are stratified and heterogeneous but may or may not be hierarchical but have a social segment whose internality to the system is questioned.

Further, I want to suggest that pluralism is not a social fact but a value-orientation, which indeed is based on the fact of diversity/heterogeneity. Viewed thus, political pluralism connotes a societal situation in which a multiplicity of interest groups with differing social backgrounds compete in the political arena for power and pelf; however, they are all insiders to the society. Whereas in homogeneous societies individuals, occupational groups, classes, gender and age-groups constitute the building blocks, in heterogeneous and hierarchical societies, racial, religious, caste, regional and linguistic collectivities will come to constitute additional building blocks, thereby rendering them more complex. In heterogeneous societies, if these building blocks enjoy socio-economic equality, the primary concern would be in sustaining identity. In hierarchical societies equality is the central concern. In a plural society in so far as identity is the source of inequality both identity and equality acquire saliency.

Finally, as I have argued elsewhere (Oommen, 1992: 154), homogenization is not admissible for three reasons. *First,* to homogenize often means to establish the hegemony of the dominant collectivity, annihilation of the weak and minority collectivities or at best their assimilation into an artificially contrived cultural mainstream, leading to the eclipse of their identity. *Second,* most polities, as they are constituted, draw their population from diverse sources. Therefore, annihilation and assimilation entail endangering the principles of maintaining diversity and developing pluralism. *Third*, contemporary societies are constantly exposed to alien influences and hence characterized by frayed edges and loose textures. If anything, the ongoing process of globalization would intensify this trend. In such a situation, the only viable option is to accommodate diversity, foster pluralism and nurture inter-group equality.

The point I am making is that the option before democratic societies is not the escape route of homogenization but the reconciliation of the competing demands of equality and identity.

II

Broadly speaking, South Asia may be identified as the region of Indian civilization presently divided into eight states. While they differ as post-colonial polities in terms of the history and degree of institutionalization of democracy, they share several common features. *First*, political pluralism, that is, the articulation of interests by a multiplicity of groups exists in all of them. *Second*, they are all stratified and seven of them (except the atoll state of Maldives) are heterogeneous. *Third*, some of them have hierarchical societies in that the caste system with its most abominable practice of untouchability still persists. However, even the most orthodox Hindu elements grudgingly acknowledge the need to consolidate the Hindu society, eradication of untouchability being a pre-requisite for this. Finally, South Asian polities are plural in the sense in which I have conceptualized 'plural society', that is, the distinction between 'insiders' and 'outsiders' is widely prevalent and practised. If hierarchy institutionalizes inequality, plurality problematizes identity—that is, internality of some of the elements to the polity. Of these two, I suggest, identity is the more formidable problem to 'build' South Asian polities because the moment the internality of a section of the population is questioned the polity tends to crack.

The insider-outsider polarization in South Asian polities is primarily discerned in terms of religion and language. Of the two, the religious identity is more unsettling and hence I shall focus on it in this paper. The linguistic identity will be referred to only when it exists in conjunction with religious identity. The populations of South Asian states are drawn from different religions although all of them have one dominant religion as is evident from Table 1.

Table 1

Population (in percentage) of South Asia by Religion (mid-1980)*

Name of the Country	*Hindu*	*Muslim*	*Buddhist*	*Christian***	*Others*
India (N=694,309,000)	78.8	11.6	0.8	3.9	4.9***
Bangladesh (N=84,803,000)	12.7	85.9	0.6	0.5	0.3
Pakistan (N=82,952,000)	1.3	96.8	0.0	1.8	0.1
Burma (N=35,195,000)	0.9	3.6	87.2	5.6	2.7
Sri Lanka (N=15,465,000)	16.0	7.2	66.9	8.3	1.6
Nepal (N=14,232,000)	89.6	3.0	6.1	0.0	1.3
Bhutan (N=1,327,000)	24.6	5.0	69.6	0.1	0.7

* Compiled from the data provided by Barrett, David, B. (ed.) *World Christian Encyclopedia*, Nairobi: OUP, 1982, pp. 165, 179, 202, 370, 507, 542, 635.

** The percentage of Christians is inflated as it includes 'Crypto-Christians' (Crypto-Christians are affiliated to Church but unknown as such publicly to the state or society). For example, in India, Crypto-Christians are estimated to be 1.1 per cent of the total population, leaving the percentage of professing Christians at 2.8 per cent which approximates the official count. Crypto-Christians and animists are usually counted as Hindus in India.

*** Out of this, nearly 2 per cent are Sikhs.

The South Asian countries may be divided into three categories based on their dominant religious collectivities: Hindu (India and Nepal), Muslim (Pakistan and Bangladesh) and Buddhist (Bhutan, Burma and Sri Lanka). The state divide based on Hinduism and Islam came into being after the colonial exit. British India was divided into the states of India and Pakistan in 1947 after prolonged and bloody inter-religious conflicts between Hindus and Muslims. While Pakistan gave formal legitimacy to Islam as the state religion, the Indian state opted for secularism, which meant according equal respect to all religions. But religion as the sole determinant of state formation could not be sustained for long in the case of Pakistan also (see Varma and Narain, eds.,

1972). Thus, in 1972, after 25 years of its emergence, Pakistan was split into two nations, this time based on geography and language, although both the new states—Pakistan and Bangladesh—are populated predominantly by Muslims.

As the basis of state formation changed from religion to language, the problem of non-Bengali Muslims (usually referred to as Bihari Muslims whose mother tongue is Hindi) remains unresolved till this day. But curiously enough, even the aspirations of Bengali Hindus and Chakma[1] Buddhists could not be fully accommodated in Bangladesh. This is, the state of Bangladesh having temporarily rejected religion as the basis of 'national' identity in favour of linguistic identity to wrest freedom from their co-religionists in Pakistan, had to re-claim its religious identity to gain authenticity as a 'nation' (see Chakravorty and Narain, eds., 1986).

In Pakistan, the saliency of the religious factor took a more virulent form (see Weiss, ed., 1986). Not only were the aspirations of religious minorities such as Hindus and Christians not fully accommodated but even Muslim protestant sects such as Ahmedias[2] were labelled heretics and apostates and declared non-Muslims. The case of Muslim refugee migrants from India to Pakistan, usually referred to as Mohajirs, is equally problematic in that they are treated as outsiders and their nativity claims within the territory under the jurisdiction of the state of Pakistan is contested. Thus, both in Bangladesh and Pakistan, the rupture between insiders and outsiders is clear and vivid.

The case of Sri Lanka illustrates even more acutely the rupture between insiders and outsiders in South Asia. While the original inhabitants[3] of the island state are rendered marginal and reduced to a microscopic minority, all the contending groups—Sinhala Buddhists, Tamil Hindus and Tamil Muslims—are migrants from India. But this common 'regional' background does not in any way dilute the religio-linguistic identity conflicts. The current turmoil in Sri Lanka is geared not simply to reinforce these identities within the framework of the polity. At least a section of the Tamil Hindus are aspiring for and demanding a sovereign state.[4] Even if they succeed in achieving their objective in a distant future the problem of religio-linguistic identity cannot be solved as there will be Tamil Hindus in the

Sinhala Buddhist areas and vice-versa. To complicate matters, both Christians and Muslims are dispersed throughout the territory of Sri Lanka and the former are drawn from both Sinhalas and Tamils (see Tambiah, 1986).

The case of India is admittedly more complex not only because of India's stupendous size but also because of her staggering cultural pluralism. Although 83 per cent of Indians are Hindus, the Muslim population is over 13 per cent and India is the third biggest Muslim country in the world. Christians constitute only 3 per cent of the total population but they count over 25 million. The followers of Sikhism, the youngest of the religions of Indian origin, currently asserting their religious identity vehemently, number about 15 million. Several migrant religions have made India their home. In fact, 80 per cent of the world's Zoroastrians live in India. Indian religious pluralism makes it extremely difficult to declare Hinduism as the sole religion of India. However, those who profess 'alien religions' are viewed as outsiders by Hindu nationalists (see Oommen, 1990: 43–66).

The situation in regard to the three remaining South Asian states—Bhutan, Burma and Nepal—is somewhat less complicating although all of them are multi-religious as is evident from Table 1. For one thing, inter-religious conflicts have been less virulent in these states in the past and an ethos of harmonious relationship between religious groups still persists. For another, their linguistic diversity is limited as compared to other South Asian states. Finally, the democratic tradition which permits an open expression of interests based on primordial loyalties is not strong in these polities.

The general point that emerges from the foregoing description is that state formation in post-colonial South Asia is based on religion. Even in those cases where it is not explicit, religion has great potency in moulding the societal ethos. The fact that religious identity is often bolstered through linguistic identity invariably reinforces the insider-outsider wedge as is evident from the following points:

First, the tendency to identify specific languages exclusively with particular religions. For example, Sanskrit is identified with Aryan Hinduism, Tamil with Dravidian Hinduism, Urdu with North Indian Islam, Pali with Sinhala Buddhism, Punjabi written in Gurumukhi with Sikhism. The coupling of religion with language meant the crystallization of a series of complex and competing identities.

Second, the above often leads to particular religio-linguistic groups staking their claim on a specific territory as their exclusive homeland, often ignoring the equally legitimate claims of other groups. Such are the claims of Sikhs in the Punjab and Muslims in the Kashmir Valley (India), Tamil Hindus in Jaffna (Sri Lanka), Sindhi Muslims in Sind (Pakistan), Chakma Buddhists in the Chittagong Hill Tracts (Bangladesh). These claims are invariably defined as anti-national and perceived as threats to the 'nation', that is the state. Admittedly, state policy towards these religio-linguistic collectivities would be coercive, even downright oppressive. Understandably, such a state policy would draw its legitimacy from the majority of the population, particularly those belonging to the dominant religious collectivity.

Third, for South Asian states, the cut-off points of history vary, notwithstanding their common civilizational history, depending upon which religious collectivity constitutes their dominant population. Pursuantly, 'national' reconstruction is neither a New Beginning nor a New Revolution but the Re-conquest or the re-discovery of an *appropriate past* depending upon who constitutes the 'national mainstream'. Thus, if for India and Nepal the re-conquest dates back to the era of Aryan Hindu advent some five thousand years ago, to Sri Lanka, Burma and Bhutan the nodal points of history vary, depending upon the time at which Buddhism (or its dormant form) became the 'national' religion.[5] For Pakistan and Bangladesh, the cut-off point of history is more recent, the medieval period, when Muslim rule was firmly established in the Indian sub-continent. The differing layers of history invoked by the different states for 'national reconstruction' influence their policies towards religious collectivities. These policies in turn legitimize the cognitions about insiders and outsiders to the discussion of which I shall turn now.

I have noted above that the seven South Asian countries are populated by people drawn mainly from three religions. But one cannot find any pattern based on religious composition and the nature of state policies. This point contradicts the familiar stereotype that some religions (e.g., Hinduism) are catholic and tolerant and some others (e.g., Islam) are fundamentalist and rigid.

Pakistan and Bangladesh are the two Muslim majority states of the region relevant for our discussion. Pakistan is an Islamic state in that it is a state with Islamic laws but not a theocratic state, because the ordained priests (*Ulema*) are not given the responsibility for running the state although their opinion is often sought in the formation, interpretation and application of state laws. The state in Pakistan, however, is expected to enable the Muslims to order their lives "... in accord with the teachings and requirements of Islam as set out in Holy Quran and Sunnah ..." The objective of the state in Pakistan is clearly laid down in her constitutions[6] (see Ahmed, 1983: 127–46; Raza, 1983: 1–15).

The first constitution of Pakistan promulgated in 1956 explicitly referred to it as an Islamic Republic. Although this reference was omitted from the constitution of 1962, after eleven years the 1973 constitution declared Islam as the state religion and prescribed that (a) the President and Prime Minister ought to be Muslims, and (b) that all laws should be brought in conformity with the values of Islam. In fact, in 1981, President Zia-ul-Haq stated that the purpose of the state of Pakistan is to promote the ideology of Islam (see Wolf-Philips, 1983: 16–23). Subsequent governments of Pakistan have reiterated this position and reinforced this orientation.

The state of Pakistan emerged in 1947 with the explicit intention of protecting the interests of Muslims. Therefore, it should surprise none that the Islamic orientation of the state of Pakistan persists. In contrast, Bangladesh emerged to safeguard the interests of a linguistic category—the Bengalis. Given this thrust, adequate assurance to safeguard the interests of the Hindu and Christian Bengalis in Bangladesh too was given in the constitution. In fact, the constitution of Bangladesh adopted in 1972, soon after its emergence as an independent state, describes it as a secular and socialist state. But from 1975 onwards the military regime of Bangladesh has been taking definite steps towards Islamization.[7] This trend culminated in May 1988 when the Bill to declare Islam as the state religion of Bangladesh was passed. Thus the eroded saliency of religion in the context of the conflict between the two wings of Pakistan was gradually recovered by the new state of Bangladesh. The point to be noted is that although Bangladesh started as a secular state, right from the beginning the Islamic ethos persisted and finally got institutionalized.

The constitutions of Pakistan as well as Bangladesh guarantee to every citizen the right to profess, practise and propagate his religion. But, in Bangladesh, complaints of discrimination by the state are voiced by religious minorities. The situation in Pakistan is more problematic in that not only do non-Muslim religious minorities complain about discrimination based on religion but revolts against even Muslim sects are not unknown.[8] Thus constitutional guarantees and social praxis are at wide variance and the latter is determined by the compulsions of state craft which cannot ignore the pressure exerted by the dominant religious collectivity.

The three Buddhist majority states of South Asia too vary in regard to the official status accorded to religion. Thus, while Buddhism is the official religion of Bhutan right from the beginning, its official status has been shifting in Burma. In 1948, although several legislations supporting Buddhism were introduced, only in 1961 was it declared the state religion. But, in 1962, this recognition to Buddhism was withdrawn and equal respect to all religions was adopted as the state policy. However, Buddhism was declared as state religion subsequently. If the official status of Buddhism in Burma fluctuated, in post-colonial Sri Lanka it was more or less stable in that no explicit official recognition was given to Buddhism.[9] However, the predominant tendency is to identify Sinhala Buddhism as the 'national' religion. As one commentator puts it, Buddhism is "for all practical purposes the official religion" (Obeyesekere, 1970: 62) of Sri Lanka. The general point is that although Buddhism occupies the place of dominance in all the three states, it has differing official statuses in them. But, the state policy facilitates the process of dominance by the majority religious collectivity irrespective of its nature—monarchy (Bhutan), military dictatorship (Burma) and democracy (Sri Lanka).

The two Hindu majority South Asian states too vary drastically in regard to official status accorded to religion. Nepal is a monarchical Hindu state wherein the monarch must be an adherent of Aryan culture and Hindu religion. In contrast, India has no state religion and the maxim, "equal respect to all religion" is a constitutional refrain. It is clear that South Asian states, with the exception of India, have either explicitly adopted a state religion or have accorded the pride of place to the religion of the majority/dominant religious collectivity. Does the Indian exceptionalism make any difference in actual practice?

III

India emerged as a result of the division of territory to create Pakistan based on religion as noted earlier. The communal riots, which followed uprooted around 15 million people, perhaps the biggest of its kind in human history. Between 1946 and 1951, 6 million Muslims left Indian territory for Pakistan and 9 million Hindus came to India from Pakistan. And, Pakistan eventually became an Islamic state. Given this background, it goes to the credit of emerging free India that no constitutional recognition was accorded to Hinduism, the religion of its overwhelming majority. And yet, Hinduism occupies a commanding position in India.

Secularism of the Indian state can only mean one of the following or both: (a) equal respect to all religions, and (b) equal distance from all religions. In what follows I shall examine whether or not the Indian state has adhered to this announced obligation. In pursuing this task I shall confine my attention to *four* different but related spheres. The *first* of these is how religious collectivities are defined for official purposes. An understanding of the state's definition of religious collectivities gives a clue to the nature of state policy towards them. The *second* point I want to examine is how far the constitutionally guaranteed freedom of conscience and the freedom of propagation of religion are allowed to be practised in reality. *Thirdly*, I propose to examine the implications of the state policy of protective discrimination for different religious collectivities. *Finally*, the role of the state as a religious reformer will be analyzed, so as to unfold how state intervention reinforces or militates against the constitutional spirit.

The Indian Constitution and the Hindu Code Bill define Hindus in such a way as to include Jains, Buddhists and Sikhs—the three Indian protestant religious groups. That is, all those who profess religions of Indian origin are Hindus from whom those who follow religions of 'alien' origin are differentiated. This constitutional expansionism denies the identity of minority religions of Indian origin. Further, the constitutional exclusionism has created an abysmal wedge between 'Hindus', the accredited inhabitants of India, and the rest who do not belong there. There is another context in which the official definition of the religious collectivities is problematic. From 1871 to 1931 British Indian Census invoked terms such as 'primitive', 'tribal' or 'animist' to describe the religion of Scheduled Tribes (STs) and to a limited extent those of Scheduled Castes (SCs). The first census enumeration of independent India was undertaken in 1951 and those tribals who were not converts to other 'world religions'—Christianity, Islam, Buddhism—were automatically categorized as Hindus. Thus, through a mere definitional twist, the census authority of free India seems to deny the authentic religious identity of millions of Indians and thrust upon them an identity which they disown (see Oommen, 1990: 43–66).

Some sociologists and social anthropologists argue that the Hindu mode of absorption is a very long-drawn one and there are several Hinduized tribes, particularly in Central India, who may be legitimately designated as Hindus (e.g., Bose, 1967; Ghurye, 1943). The argument is not without substance. But, the census authorities of India do not make any distinction between the Hinduized and non-Hindu tribes and automatically categorize all tribes which have not converted into other religions as Hindus. This is a denial of the authentic religious identity of the non-Hindu tribes and amounts to forceful imposition of an identity which they often strongly deny.

It is also pertinent to recall here that there have been a large number of movements in India through which the SCs have declared that they are not Hindus. At any rate, it is a well-known sociological fact that the STs which do not profess one of the world religions—Hinduism, Buddhism, Islam, Christianity—are usually animists. Even, the SCs practise a mixture of animism and Hinduism. The religion of pre-Aryan people of India is quite different from sophisticated Hinduism. And yet, the census authorities categorize all of them as Hindus, thereby using the census as a political instrument to augment the count of the

Hindu population. Such a device admittedly finds favour with the dominant religious collectivity, viz., the Hindus. Clearly, the Indian state defines Hinduism expansively to include all religions of Indian origin. This category (insiders) thus gets juxtaposed against the rest (outsiders) which reinforces the plural society ethos in India.

My *second* point relates to freedom of conscience and propagation of religion. Article 25 of the Indian Constitution assures not only freedom of conscience but also the right to propagate one's religion. Propagation of religion may lead to conversion. Therefore, if the spirit of the Indian Constitution is adhered to, the state should not intervene when people convert from one religion to another. While the state in India has never prevented conversion as such (as in Nepal for example), it has intervened in the process of conversion alleging that fraudulent means have been used.

But what is important for the present discussion is to underline that the state intervention occurs only with regard to conversion to Islam and Christianity because these religions are perceived and defined as products of conquest and colonization. (However, if one goes by the available historical evidence, such a characterization is unsustainable. Pre-conquest Islam and pre-colonial Christianity existed in India). In contrast, one does not come across any popular protest or state intervention even when substantial number of persons convert from one of the religions of Indian origin to another of them. Therefore, it is clear that the state intervention is selective which erodes the meaning of secularism as is defined in the Indian Constitution. Differential response to conversions by the state depending upon the religion to which it takes place reinforces India's plural society and prevents the development of pluralism.

Let me now turn to the policy of protective discrimination—the *third* area which I want to invoke in order to demonstrate the insider-outsider dichotomy. Notwithstanding the assurance given in the Constitution vide Article 15, there are contexts in which the state in India discriminates between citizens based on religion. The assumption behind the policy of protective discrimination is that there are groups in India which are culturally, socially and economically backward and therefore specific efforts should be made to uplift them. But, the problem arises when the state policy differentiates between religious groups.

The genesis of the discrimination may be traced to the Constitution (Scheduled Castes) Order, 1950, which declared "no person who professes a religion different from Hinduism shall be deemed to be a member of a scheduled caste", denying non-Hindus the statutory benefits that are given to SC Hindus. In the beginning the order applied to all religious collectivities except Hindus.[10] However, in 1956, the government extended the same benefits to the Sikhs and in 1990 to the Buddhists. The argument which is usually advanced in pursuing this differential application is that Islam and Christianity do not recognize the caste system and hence it would be anomalous to extend the policy of protective discrimination to these religious collectivities. But this argument is equally valid in the case of Buddhism and Sikhism. In fact, they are products of protest movements against the oppressive Hindu caste system. Therefore, the discrimination based on those who profess religions of Indian origin and those who profess religions of alien origin creates and perpetuates the distinction between insiders and outsiders.

The *last* point, I want to discuss is the role that the state plays as s social reformer. The state in India has been playing a positive, although limited, role in changing several of the traditional inhuman practices directly or indirectly associated with, or attributed to, Hinduism. The more obnoxious of these practices are human sacrifice, temple prostitution, *sati* and untouchability. The state has also intervened to change the personal laws and make them uniform for Hindus, Jains, Buddhists and Sikhs, through the Hindu Code Bill, as noted already. In contrast, the state is hesitant to change the personal laws of minority religions of alien origin although the Indian Constitution is committed to bring about a Uniform Civil Code. This in spite of the fact that in the personal laws of these religions there are several unjust and oppressive practices particularly against women.

The arguments frequently advanced against the non-intervention in minority religious affairs by the state, are two. *First*, the Indian state being secular should not interfere in the internal affairs of minority religious communities. The initiative for reform and change should come from within. But, this argument is, and should be, equally applicable to all religions if the secularity of the state is the basis of non-intervention. But, this is not adhered to because the state did intervene in the case of religions of Indian origin. *Second,* the minority religions resist state intervention. This argument is also specious because (a) the state has already intervened in the minority religions of Indian origin, and (b) the conservative elements within Hinduism did resist tooth and nail the reformist policy of the state. The point is, all religious communities have their share of obscurantists, conservatives and progressives. The state need not and perhaps cannot wait till such time everybody endorses all the desirable changes. Therefore, if a state assumes the role of reformer, it should play the role vis-à-vis all the religious collectivities. On the other hand, if the state policy is one of non-interference in the affairs of religious collectivities it should scrupulously adhere to this principle vis-à-vis all religious groups.

It appears that the Indian state is more confident to play the role of reformer with regard to Hinduism as the Hindu majority closely identifies itself with the state. On the other hand, the state cautiously distances itself from the minority religions of alien origin which creates a wedge between these religious collectivities and the state. In turn, the state policy also reinforces the wedge between the two sets of religious communities—insiders and outsiders.

IV

I have tried to demonstrate that the notion of plural society as adumbrated by cultural pluralists based on the degree of participation of populace in a polity in different types of institutions is not a sustainable one. Further, the distinction that they have made between different types of societies have two basic problems. *First,* the *differentia specifica* of these types is not identified; in fact, they are not identifiable in terms of the criteria they use. *Second,* their categorization cannot account for the hierarchical type of society. These reasons prompted the proposing of an extended categorization of societies—homogeneous, heterogeneous, hierarchical and plural.

The first three types are viewed as additive and plural society is conceptualized as an entity in which the internality of some of the elements are questioned. According to this conceptualization, all societies are stratified; in heterogeneous societies different racial, cultural and social segments co-exist but need not be unequal. If institutionalized inequality exists in a heterogeneous society, it becomes a hierarchical society. Finally, while the inhabitants of plural society are polarized between insiders and outsiders, pluralism is conceptualized as a positive attitude to heterogeneity which attests the dignified co-existence of these desperate elements and the celebration of diversity.

South Asian polities are hierarchical and plural. Both equality and identity are fundamental issues in establishing a just and equitous social order in South Asia. Of the two problems, the issue of identity, that is, the issue of internality of some of the collectivities in the system, is discussed in this paper. While both religion and language contribute to the making of plural polities in South Asia, the former is more problematic. It has been demonstrated that the polarization which persists between the dominant/majority religious collectivity, the insiders, and the religious collectivities which are perceived as outsiders to the system is reinforced by the state. Therefore, the first necessary step to be taken to consolidate South Asian polities is to (a) accept the internality of all the elements in the system, and (b) ensure their dignified co-existence. This value orientation to diversity/heterogeneity is designated as pluralism.

Notes

1. Although the population of all tribes in Bangladesh is distributed into more than one religion, the Chakmas and the Marwas are predominantly Buddhists inhabiting the Chittagong Hill Tracts bordering India and Bangladesh (see Hussain, 1986: 196–211; Phadnis, 1989).
2. Ahmedias do not accept the Islamic belief that Mohammed is the last prophet and uphold that Ghulam Ahmed, who lived just a century ago, was a prophet. According to unofficial estimates, the Ahmedias constitute around three per cent of the population of Pakistan and are mainly drawn from the Sunnis, the Muslim sect which accounts for about eighty per cent of Pakistan's population.

3. The Veddas, the original inhabitants of Sri Lanka, counted 3,971 in 1907 but shrunk to a mere 800 by mid-1960s.
4. However, the possibility of the Tamils getting their Eelam (homeland) has substantially diminished with the Sri Lankan army capturing Jaffna, the bulwark of LTTE at the time of writing.
5. If for Sri Lanka this nodal point is around the 3rd century BC (see Rahula, 1956: 62–77), for Bhutan it is the 7th century AD (see Hasrat, 1980: 34–45) and for Burma it is the 11th century AD when Thervada Buddhism got firmly entrenched there (see Smith, 1965: 3–11).
6. The Pakistan Constitution was re-written several times. For an account of this, see Raza (1983: 1–15).
7. For a discussion of the shift from 'secular' to Islamic thrust of the state in Bangladesh, see Talukdar (1986: 47–73) and Mohsin (1986: 28–41).
8. In 1953, Pakistan Punjab witnessed widespread anti-Ahmediya riots. For an account of the same, see Report of the Court of Enquiry (Munior Commission) Constituted under the Punjab Act 11 of 1954 to Enquire into the Punjab Disturbance of 1953. Punjab: Supdt. of Government Printing, 1954.
9. This is a recent development in that from 3rd century BC to the 19th century AD only a Buddhist had the legitimate right to be the king of Sri Lanka (see Rahula, 1956: 62–77).
10. This incidentally unfolds the ambiguity of definition of the Hindu by the Indian state. For purposes of Hindu Code Bill, the definition is expansive and for the application of Constitution (Scheduled Caste) Order, 1950 it is exclusionary.

References

Ahmed, Munir D., 1983, "Conflicting Definitions of the Islamic State in Pakistan", in Wolfgang-Peter Zingal (ed.), *Pakistan in its Fourth Decade*, Hamburg: Des Deutschen Orient Institutes, pp. 127–46.

Bose, N.K., 1967, *Culture and Society in India*, Bombay: Asia Publishing House.

Braithwaite, L., 1960, "Social Stratification and Cultural Pluralism", *New York Academy of Sciences*, 83:816–31.

Bryce, J., 1910, *The American Commonwealth* (2 vols.), New York: The MacMillan and Co.

Chakravarty, S.R. and Narain Virendra (eds.), 1986, *Bangladesh: History and Culture*, New Delhi: South Asian Publishers.

Dahl, R.A., 1961, *Who Governs*? New Haven: Yale University Press.

Despres, L.A., 1967, *Cultural Pluralism and Nationalist Politics in British Guiana*, Chicago: Rand McNally and Co.

Furnivall, J.S., 1939, *Netherlands India: A Study in Plural Economy*, London: Cambridge University Press.

——, 1948, *Colonial Policy and Practice*, London: Cambridge University Press.

Ghurye, G.S., 1943, *The Aborigines So-called and their Future*, Poona: Gokhale Institute of Economics and Politics.

Hasrat, B.J., 1980, *History of Bhutan*, Thumphu: Education Department, Government of Bhutan.

Hsu, F.K.L. 1963, *Clan, Caste and Club*, Princeton: D. Van Worstand and Co.

Hussain, H., 1986, "Problem of National Integration in Bangladesh", in S.K. Chakravarty and Virendra Narain (eds.), op. cit., pp. 196–211.

Kuper, Leo, 1971, "Ethnic and Racial Pluralism: Some Aspects of Polarisation and De-pluralisation", in L., Kuper and M.G. Smith (eds.), 1971: *Pluralism in Africa*, Berkeley and Los Angeles: University of California Press, pp. 459–87.

Mohsin, K.M., 1986, "Trends of Islam in Bangladesh", in ibid., pp. 28–41.

Obeyesekere, Gananath, 1970, "Religion Symbolism and Political Change in Ceylon", *Modern Ceylon Studies*, Vol. 1(1), pp. 43–63.

Oommen, T.K., 1990, *State and Society in India: Studies in Nation-building*, New Delhi: Sage Publications.

——, 1992, "Reconciling Equality and Pluralism: The dilemma of 'Advanced' Societies", *International Review of Sociology* (N.S.), Vol. 1(1), (Centenary Celebration Volume), pp. 141–72.

Phadnis, Urmila, 1989, *Ethnicity and Nation-building in South Asia*, New Delhi: Sage Publications.

Rahula, Walpola, 1956, "Buddhism as State Religion" in Walpola Rahula, *History of Buddhism in Ceylon*, Colombo: M.D. Gunasena and Co., Ltd.

Raza, Rafi, 1983, "The Continuous Process of Re-writing the Constitution", in Wolfgang-Peter Zingel (ed.), op. cit., pp. 1–15.

Rogers, D., 1964, "Monolithic and Pluralistic Community Power structure", in K.L., Simpson and I.H., Simpson (eds.), *Social Organization and Behaviour*, New York: Wiley.

Sayre, W.S. and Kaufman, H., 1960, *Governing the New York City: Politics in Metropolis*, New York: Russell Sage Foundation.

Simpson, R.L. and Simpson, I.H. (eds.), 1964, *Social Organisation and Behaviour*, New York: Wiley.

Smith, D.E., 1965, *Religion and Politics in Burma*, New Jersey: Princeton University Press.

Smith, M.G., 1960, "Social and Cultural Pluralism", *Annals of the New York Academy of Sciences*, 83: 763–77.

——, 1965, *The Plural Society in British West Indies*, Berkeley and Los Angels: University of California Press.

——, 1971, "Some Developments in the Analytic Framework of Pluralism" in L., Kuper and M.G. Smith (eds.), op. cit., pp. 415–58.

Tambiah, S.J., 1986, *Sri Lanka: Ethnic Fratricide and the Dismantling of Democracy*, New Delhi: Oxford University Press.

Talukdar, Maniruzzaman, 1986, "Bangladesh Politics: Secular and Islamic Trends", in S.K. Chakravarty and Virendra Narain, op. cit., pp. 42–73.

Tocqueville, Alexis de, 1956, *Democracy in America* (2 vols.) New York: Knopf (originals 1835 and 1840).

Van den Berghe, P.L., 1971, "Pluralism and Polity: A Theoretical Explanation" in L., Kuper and M.G. Smith (eds.), op. cit., pp. 67–81.

Varma, S.P. and Narain, Virendra (eds.), 1972, *Pakistan: Political System in Crisis: Emergence of Bangladesh*, Jaipur: South Asian Studies Centre.

Weiss, Anita M., 1986, *Islamic Reassertion in Pakistan: The Application of Islamic Laws in a Modern State*, New York: Syracuse University Press.

3

Floating Identities

Some Thoughts on the Construction and Manipulation of Cultural Similarity and Difference

APARNA RAO

> "Who are you?" "And who are you?"
> "What is the evidence that you are who you say you are?"
> "Kill him, kill him."
>
> —Saadat Hasan Manto in *Mistake Removed*

In the mad search for 'the real' identity which was part and parcel of the horrors of the partition of the subcontinent name was no evidence, religious knowledge no evidence; the body itself represented no evidence of the person. In this attempt to completely reduce the subject-agent to the clear-cut, objectified categories of being-and-belonging, the exercise of choice and the importance of context at the levels of both the individual and the group had to be negated. In so doing the very essence of the phenomenon of identity was violated and reduced to that of identification. Like all acts of irrationality, it also brought into tragic focus the potentially disruptive and destructive interface between subjectivity and objectivity, between the perceived and the perceiver, between intrinsic emotions and their cultural manipulation for political ends.

Most social scientists would now tend to agree with Ruddock (1969: 104*ff*) that "... the sense of identity is tentative and mobile ... perhaps 'labile' ..." (but see Kakar in Engineer, 1987: 541). This is hardly surprising if we think of identity as "... a system of conceptions and related actions for the purpose of delimiting oneself from other identities" (Orywal, 1988: 35). In spite of what some of the founding fathers of our disciplines, such as Durkheim (1914) and Mauss (1938) suggested, in all societies sets of identities are chosen by or imposed upon individuals along their gender-specific life-spans. Such choices and impositions may be long-lasting or only short-term, as observable in the phenomenon of passing, wherein long-term, mutually incompatible identities are exchanged briefly for more mutually compatible ones. Identity—or rather multiple identities, be these concurrent and/or consecutive—are never static; the formation of identity(ies) is a process which lasts as long as life lasts. At any given moment identity exists both singly and in groups. Whereas modern Western society takes for granted and at least ideologically encourages the former, the latter is spoken of disparagingly. Perhaps, the one exception to this is the discourse on class-identity. In non-Western societies, by and large, ideology focuses on identity-in-groups, individual identity often being considered with some ambivalence. Just as in the latter societies the assertion of individual identity is often spoken of as disruptive to social cohesion, in Western contexts it is group identity—often classified as 'ethnicity'—that is construed as destructive for the social fabric of democratic societies. This view is based primarily on two assumptions: first, that the individual is swamped by the group and second, that ethnicity operates only to exclude. Group identities can naturally be of many kinds, and like all these too can be either ascribed, achieved or both—and usually multiple. As Berreman (1972) found in Dehradun, there exists great variability in ascription, depending on who is conversing with whom, when. The ascriptive categories—religion, region, language, caste, class, etc.—people mentioned all had to do with group identity. Now group identity is also a processual phenomenon observable in all human societies. It consists of the dynamic cognitive model of one's own group,[1] of 'us', as different from (though not necessarily opposed to) a corresponding and equally dynamic model of 'them'[2] (cf. Rao and Schneider, 1994 for a brief discussion of Muslim societies). As Cohen (1978: 387) observed:

> The division into exclusive groupings is always done in relation to significant others whose exclusion at any particular level of scale creates the we/they dichotomy.

It should be stressed that equally, the mechanisms that lead to exclusion of some simultaneously also lead to the inclusion of others. Heterogeneity requires homogeneity and *vice versa*. The choice of both sets of persons is moulded by a variety of factors, few of which are constant. Both group and identity are fluid phenomena, and both subjective and objective criteria contribute to their existence, to the way they are perceived, hence also to their 'significance', and to the use of both ascription and achievement as means of inclusion and exclusion. These usually subjective (e.g., race, ethnic group) and often objective (language, religion, though these also are more often than not fuzzy sets) criteria can lead to what Wallman (1979: 9) termed "... the recognition of significant difference between 'them' and 'us'", between the 'they-group' and the 'we-group', the degree of significance again, being context-specific. These criteria can also serve as a basis for the "... dialectical tension existing between homologous affiliation and heterologous contraposition" (Lopreato, 1984: 332), and they are often used "... symbolic system(s) which may be activated ... in the pursuit of ... goals" (Levy, 1975: 28).

The result of such potential recognition, tension and pursuit—the practice and intensity of all of which vary contextually—is what is generally termed 'ethnicity', although the term has beyond doubt been much misused and misunderstood. Here, ethnicity will be considered not as an inert 'thing', but as a cognitive "system of relations and representations" (Melucci, 1982 in Schlesinger, 1987: 237). It is seen as a specific kind of relationship between groups—call them 'ethnic groups' if you like—or their institutional representatives (such as the state) operating within the same wider resource-context and considering themselves 'culturally' distinct at any given moment. (The contents of 'cultural' distinctiveness, I should add, are also far from static, and can be both objective and subjective; the importance accorded to them always varies according to ideological and political perspective.) The specificity of the relationship lies in the ideologization of the innate, and hence universal, capacity to recognize and differentiate within the framework of the diachronic and synchronic process of interaction at various levels of social, economic and political organization. It is this interaction that enables the construction of cognitive models of 'us' and 'them'—models which vary among individuals, overlap depending on context, are always fuzzy, and are by no means necessarily conflictual. Even when they do actually become laden with conflict, they lead to violence only under specific circumstances, as Orywal (1996) has shown in his perceptive analysis. The ideologization referred to above will primarily use a non-class-based discourse, although the issues discussed may well be class-oriented. It may also tend to use an implicit or explicit 'blood'-based discourse, wherein 'blood' and 'cultural values' are seen to concur—even though at times only for a short while. In the course of this interaction the various groups of individuals involved in the pursuit of their respective goals may make use of their models of 'us' and 'them', and this in turn can lead to modifications in either or both of these models. These eventual modifications in these cognitive models combined with the diachronic process of change in the patterns of group interaction can be considered a form of adaptation in so far as they consist of a continuous process of assimilation and accommodation. Clearly, this process of interaction has to be considered in the wider framework of the relations of production and appropriation, of securing resources (be these material or symbolic) and the practical consequences of ethnicity cannot be understood while disregarding relations of power, dependence and dominance at various levels of social organization. As Rao (1939: 38) observed:

> ... the presence of ethnic ties does not necessarily mean that they are ethnic formations. The latter are the result of political action. Hence, it is essential to analyse the situational contexts of ethnicity and ethnic formations.

The concept of ethnicity put forward above binds together elements of the three main theoretical approaches to the study of the phenomenon, none of which alone appears to be satisfactory in practice (see Sokolovskii and Tishkov, 1996: 192 for touching very briefly on such an integrative approach). Such a composite and dynamic view of ethnicity allows for a better, and 'rational' understanding both of 'imagined communities' (Anderson, 1983) and of the much debated 'resurgence of ethnicity'. Also, proceeding contrary to widespread norms of current political discourse (e.g., the US President's 1993 statement before the United Nations in which he distinguished between "ethnic, religious and civil wars") the inclusion at the analytical level of parameters such as language, religion, territory, caste, clan, etc. enables a broader and more comparative approach cutting across specific historical and cultural configurations. It also enables analysis of phenomena which are more often than not overlapping. Finally, it would be misleading to always view ethnicity in opposition to "... class-based forms of social identification and conflict" (Glazer and Moynihan, 1975: 7). Together with, and often inseparable from class, ethnicity can become a parameter of social interaction (Van den Berghe, 1975), though equally often it may be used to suppress class-based movements. The recent history of large parts of Asia and Africa has provided ample examples of a "... class conflict (which) tends to irrupt into revolution only if it can conceptualize itself in ethnic ... terms" (Gellner, 1981: 66).

'Ethnic' conflict in South Asia too has many components, including in certain cases class; common to them all is the question of a more perceptually equitable sharing of access to things that are perceived as resources. This paper will briefly describe the process by which in one particular case individuals and groups have over several generations come to conceptualize in different degrees their cultural, socio-economic and political problems in 'ethnic terms'. It will illustrate how problematic it is to speak of 'ethnic groups' as automatic units of identity, without considering:

> ... the possibility that a variety of answers will differentiate not only the people concerned from those who have observed or written about them, but also different categories, such as classes, among the population. (Tapper, 1988: 85)

On the other hand, as Talbot (1995: 694) remarks, "… modern identities do not spring fully fashioned out of nowhere". Indeed, this essay will also show that 'ethnicity'—understood as the relationship discussed above—can and has existed in pre-colonial, 'tribal' situations, just as much as it has in colonial-cum-feudal contexts and does in the framework of post-colonial nation-states. However, the forms this relationship took changed according to the broader political setting. For, as Thapar (1989: 222) notes, even in ancient India "the notion of community was not absent but there were multiple communities identified by locality, language, caste, occupation …". And within each community identity could also be multiple, depending on what was at stake, for whom. It was only with the crisis of the modern nation-state that attempts were made to reduce this multiplicity to maleable, discrete units. But even here it must be remembered that, whether colonial or post-colonial, the state is never "an independent actor"; it is for ever "interrogating and having to accommodate (local) conditions …" (Robb, 1997: 246).

Paraphrasing Cohen's (1974) classic conclusions, the anthropological analysis presented here will make use of "… sociology … political science … history" to explain the changing forms of identity and ethnicity. The paradigmatic case dealt with here is that of the Bakkarwal and Gujar of Jammu and Kashmir—Muslim communities in a demographically majority Muslim region, and yet in many other cultural aspects very different from the majority community of Kashmiri Muslims. In this sense, this case presents a unique example of the functioning of minority-majority relations within the contemporary framework of the Indian state. In particular, it illustrates that in areas "where non-Hindu minorities have constituted a majority in the federating unit, the operation of 'hegemonic control' has been exercised …" (Singh, 1995: 482) not only through Hindu minorities, but equally through non-Hindu minorities. The data presented here draw largely on ethnographic fieldwork among the Bakkarwal and certain Gujar communities in various parts of Jammu and Kashmir.[3]

The Context of Enquiry

Communities known as and/or referring to themselves as Gujar (or dialect variants thereof) live scattered across a large portion of southern Asia ranging from pockets as far west as Central Afghanistan (e.g., Balland, 1988) right across large areas of Pakistan to wide belts in northern India. Their contemporary economic strategies in rural areas range from sedentary agriculture to largely mobile pastoralism; similarly, their religious affiliations vary regionally between Islam, Hinduism and Sikhism. Even within Jammu and Kashmir where all Gujar are Muslims, there are several types of Gujar communities (Gupta, 1981: 74; Rao and Casimir, 1985).

The Gujar are generally held to have first entered Jammu and Kashmir from the Punjab and the North West Frontier Province (cf. Census of India, 1941: 1/9–11). It is hard to determine the precise dates of these migrations, but during the period of Sikh rule they appear to have fanned out in all directions from the area of Poonch. In 1848, there were in the whole of Kashmir 3,656 buffaloes, whose owners were Gujar, and one of their sub-groups, the 'Sheer Gujri', specialized in supplying Sringar city with cow's milk (Sharma, 1983: 142, 141). It is likely that different waves of migration and the various phases of displacement followed by attempts at adapting to the new ecological and socio-economic contexts led to the emergence of several, at first primarily professionally specialized and preferentially endogamous, sub-groups in Jammu and Kashmir. When research was begun in 1980 there were three such preferentially and *de facto* overwhelmingly endogamous communities, all of whose exonym was 'Gujar'. One of these lived the year through primarily in the region between Jammu, Reasi and Rajouri as sedentary agriculturists while practising a limited degree of sedentary or transhumant cattle breeding; the second spending the whole year in the Kashmir valley and in the mountains surrounding it as primarily transhumant cow and buffalo breeders, with wealthier families increasingly investing in agriculture; and the third community was composed of mainly nomadic buffalo breeders who spent the winters in Punjab and the summers in the upper reaches of the vale of Kashmir, though a few of the wealthier also had land. While the first community was known additionally as Kandi Gujar (from the Kandi zone in which they lived); the second, who have been referred to elsewhere as the Valley Gujar (Rao and Casimir, 1985, 1987, 1990) were known only by the term Gujar; the third group often referred to itself, and was also known to some as the Banihara or Dodhi Gujar.[4] In addition to these three groups, there were two other communities—those of the Bakkarwal and the Gujar-Bakkarwal. The former were overwhelmingly endogamous nomadic goat and sheep breeders who migrated twice annually between the high altitude pastures of the Kashmir valley and the colline belt stretching from Poonch in the west to Kathua in the east (Casimir and Rao, 1985); increasingly, the very wealthy were also taking to a little agriculture. The Gujar-Bakkarwal (whom Khatana, 1992 does not distinguish from the Bakkarwal) spent most of the time in the region surrounding Poonch and were predominantly wealthy agro-pastoralists with transhumant sheep and cattle breeding. To the south of the Kashmir valley in the area between Poonch in the west and Kathua in the east, the three terms—Gujar, Bakkarwal and Gujar-Bakkarwal—lie on a multidimensional socio-economic scale, and that the classification of any family in one of these three groups appears determined by eventual land ownership and the type of livestock. A combination of these factors, whose proportions can vary over the years for each family also determines an individual's social status and weight in local politics. While each of these groups has specific economic features and varying, though overlapping, geographical distribution, they are all Sunni Muslims. There are also distinct dialectical differences in the speech of each community, major differences in social organization (e.g., while the Banihara are clan—*got*—exogamous, the others are preferentially clan—*zat/khel*—endogamous), and certain mutually recognizable differences also in dress, jewellery, hairstyles and general appearance. These differences notwithstanding, all except the Bakkarwal claimed to be Gujar, and also recognized the claims of the others to this common appellation. Also, perhaps, since in comparison to most of the surrounding populations in Jammu and Kashmir all these Gujar groups inhabit and use ecologically marginal spaces and have been traditionally more pastoral—with cattle unlike the Bakkarwal who herd small-stock—than agrarian, they tend to be lumped together by non-Gujar as one larger community. In official population censuses of the area too, only the Bakkarwal were listed separately and distinguished from the Gujar on the basis of language difference. Administrative policies also resort to a certain ethnic pigeonholing and do not distinguish between them, although the needs and problems of each group are specific to their ecological and economic context.

Though Gujar in Jammu and Kashmir are attested for long, the first explicit documentary mention of the Bakkarwal ("*bakarwan*") in Jammu and Kashmir is dated 1899 (McDonell, 1899: 15). To begin with, the term was used literally, i.e., to designate a professional category of 'people with goats'—as opposed to say, those with cattle. It was only around 1912 that in official documents this professional category turned into an 'ethnic' category, whereby two types were distinguished: 'locals', who had lived and migrated within the state borders for at least one generation, and 'foreigners' who were considered undesirable new migrants (C.S., 1914 a, b, c). Since then, the borders of the area have been delineated afresh. Today, there are Bakkarwal on both sides of the ceasefire line between India and Pakistan; few data are available on those living west of this line, but it can be stated that the specific corporate group now living to the east of it emerged as a community only in the early years of this century. In the following pages I shall deal with five rough phases in the history of the Bakkarwal and Gujar. These phases reflect various aspects and stages in the processes of the recognition of difference, of dialectical tension, and of the pursuit of specific goals referred to earlier. They also illustrate how the perception of what a resource is can change over time.

Phase 1 ca. 1830–1910: Creating Community

Among all the shrines and *pir* venerated by the Bakkarwal and Gujar perhaps, the most interesting ethnographic case is that of the shrine of Wangat Sharif, which is also referred to as a *dargah*. This is the resting place of Ubaid Allah Bijran of the Naqshbandi order. A medium-sized shrine in the 1980s, with a few servants (*khadim*) attached to it, this place developed into a sacred site with the arrival there of Ubaid Allah from Hazara (in present-day Pakistan) with a small group of followers. Indeed, this immigration can be considered a decisive event in the transformation of the Bakkarwal from the occupational category (*pesha*) they were to one single ethnic group (*kaum*). The individuals and families who accompanied Ubaid Allah formed the nucleus for the ethnogenesis of the Bakkarwal community as it exists in Jammu and Kashmir today. Here, today, the community is a conglomerate of Sunni families of several 'ethnic groups'—the numerically strongest of these being the Gujar (if we are to go by *zat* names)—whose ancestors hail from the valleys of Allai and Kunhar, in Pakistan. The following is the essence of the story of this migration and its spiritual leader, who is seldom referred to by his name, but rather as *Ji Sab, Lar ka Baba, Babaji Larvi, Hazrat Bab Sab, Babaji*, etc. It is my endeavour here to try and reproduce as far as possible the essence of the narratives as I received them—as a story of this man and of the Bakkarwal and not *about* him, or this community. For, as Mayaram (1997: 157) reminds us, "the narration of a story of the past has a meaning in terms of cultural memory and the attempt to structure a present".

Mohammad Ubaid Allah, a Gujar of the Bijran *zat*, was born around the middle of the 19th century in Sanjura, Hazara, as the son of a poor Gujar named Phul Gul. His father died young leaving behind a widow and three orphans, of whom Ubaid Allah was the youngest. His youth was full of hardship, but since he was born as a *wali*, he had a deeply religious bent of mind and developed ascetic tendencies very early in life. His mother encouraged him and gave him much support, while his mother's brother cared for him and brought him up. When Ubaid Allah was hardly twenty, he sought spiritual guidance from several preceptors, of whom the two most important were Qazi Rahim Dad and his pupil Khwaja Shah Hazrat Nizam-ud-Din *Mushkil-Kush* of Kaiyan Sharif, in Muzaffarabad district. The former had himself been a pupil of Shah Wali'ullah Dehlvi, and was a member of the Naqshbandi order as well.

In the meantime, Ubaid Allah had grown up into a strikingly handsome youth, and was married to his mother's brother's daughter, who, however, had no interest in religious matters. Within two years of his marriage, his mother passed away, and since the young couple had no children, Ubaid Allah sought and obtained a divorce in order to dedicate himself entirely to spiritual matters. Only several years later did he remarry; his second wife was the devout sister of two Gujar friends and companions.

In the last decade of the century Ubaid Allah migrated to Kashmir with a group of roughly sixteen *murid* and *khidmatgar* and their families said to belong mostly to the Gujar, but also to the Awan, Gakkhar and Swati communities, primarily from the valleys of Allai and Kunhar. He settled in the area of Lar, a pasture area above the Sind valley, not far from Wangat, in northern Kashmir. In the years that followed the numbers of his disciples swelled, and it is said that "although they belonged to so many different groups, they all felt that as *Babaji's murid* they were all one". The area of the shrine came to be known as Babanagri.

Babaji Larvi's concerns are portrayed as being of a purely spiritual nature,[5] but his narrative is not perceived by the Bakkarwal in a vacuum. It is set in the wider politico-religious framework of a conscious break with the past in British held Hazara for the creation of a new, morally and economically acceptable future in the Dogra kingdom of Jammu and Kashmir. Many describe their ancestors as *muhajirin*, and Babaji's migration into Kashmir as a *hijra*. The oppressors in his case were not the wealthy merchants of Mecca but the rich, mostly Sayyed, landlords of Hazara,[6] and nearly one hundred years later informants remembered the saying, "*jiya chalen Munnawar Shah, sade nilo ka*" (the grass gets singed wherever Munnawar Shah[7] treads).

But for the break with the oppressive past to be really successful, for the future to be stable it was essential to weld together these bands of newcomers and provide them with a clear corporal identity. Such a corpus required territorial location, and this in turn meant the creation of a centre of meaning for the new community. This is how this creation of space out of place is described:

> In Lar, a pasture area above the Sind valley, not far from Wangat in northern Kashmir, Ubaid Allah offered prayers on a huge rock on which he had spread a woollen shawl. After the prayers it was found that his genealogy within the Naqshbandi order as well as the seal of a village *patwari* were stamped on the shawl. It was washed, but the more it was washed the

brighter shone the insignia. So, the shawl was taken to Hazara and shown to Ubaid Allah's *murshid* there; he recognized in these insignia the indication that Ubaid Allah was pre-destined to be the *wali* of the entire land around Wangat. This whole area was a wilderness covered with forest, so the small band of followers started to clear and cultivate the land: "Unused and unusable land was now transformed by them into useful land, in order to feed so many people".

These 'many people' were probably mostly Gujar who are described as having come in several waves, as individuals or in small amorphous groups of nuclear and extended families of goat and/or buffalo breeders (Rao, 1990); but it should not be forgotten that acephalous groups often "tend to display an ethnic homogeneity which masks their actual history of recruitment". (Lancaster, 1974: 707). Be that as it may, driven by a variety of economic, ecological and political reasons (Rao, 1988a), these migrants to Kashmir slowly came to form several sodalities which were economically far from homogeneous (Rao, 1988b). Marriage also took place overwhelmingly within sub-groups (*zat* or *khel*) among the Gujar and within each of the groups such as Awan, etc.

The picture that emerges on the whole is that of a period of economic expansion in which pasture lands and grazing areas were perceived as principal resources, peaceful and non-exploitative access to which was a major goal. In such circumstances, 'ethnic salience' (Cross, 1978) of each of the component units (i.e., various Gujar *zat*, Awan, etc.) was minimal, since there was relative equity and little competition for resources within these units. The difference in livestock composition—i.e., usually goats or buffaloes, rather than both goats and buffaloes—and hence in the kind of pasture required at different altitudes and different zones led to a certain niche specialization (cf. Barth, 1956) and certainly contributed to diminishing eventual competition. Furthermore, forests and pastures in Kashmir had only recently been taken under official purview,[8] and restrictions were few. The low degree of ethnic salience, in its turn, enabled the formation of a new composite community—that of the almost entirely goat-herding Bakkarwal as increasingly distinct from, though similar to, the overwhelmingly buffalo-herding Gujar. The common interests of each group lay in finding adequate grazing for the main source of subsistence of all families—their goat or buffalo herds. Babaji Larvi provided these units with the moral force and authority to seek out new terrain and establish themselves as pioneers in a new land. It was thus also the period of a new ethnogenesis, a phase classified by Brass (1985: 1) in general terms as the first phase in the building of ethnic identity. It was a phase in which the position of each component unit and its respective members had to be clarified; hence also, the outer edges of the composite community had to be defined—not perhaps to be made water tight for individuals or small families, but certainly for larger groups. The question of belonging, for example, of who is a Bakkarwal and who is not, and of who had automatic access to specific resources and who not, had now to be negotiated and settled.

Among the Bakkarwal this negotiation became the task of elderly men widely respected for their personal qualities, notably wisdom and bravery, and generally considered exemplary. Known as *mukaddam*, they were men of influence in several ways: they were certainly old enough to have large extended households, but not 'too old' and vigorous enough to often function as migration leaders as well. They were wealthy, though not necessarily always the wealthiest, and finally, as men of understanding they acted as middlemen between their unit and other similar units. It is said that these men 'could control the best'; on the other hand, they are also said to have best understood the requirements of their respective units and helped generously in times of need. Although there was no formal system of elections, a *mukaddam* was chosen "because he told the truth, wasn't corrupt, was the most fair minded" Indeed, when Bakkarwal speak of having chosen a man as *mukaddam*, they use a religious analogy—that of following (literally, "holding on to the seat of": "*takya pakarna*") a saintly man. These were, then, the men who had proved their control over pasture and people and on whom it was now incumbent to clarify and defend the contours of this new composite community.

Phase 2 ca. 1910–1925: Heterologous Contraposition

The next phase followed closely on the first firm occupations of land and pasture and with these the first confrontations with the

Kashmiri took place. Several Bakkarwal and Kashmiri men and women recalled that conflicts often took place between Bakkarwal and local Kashmiri shepherds in particular (cf. Scott O'Connor, 1920: 152–62). Although no precise data are available about the numbers of the latter at the time, it is known that as early as 1847 some 5,27,300 sheep and goats were in their care in the Kashmir valley (Sharma, 1983: 143). For the year 1921, Kak (1924: 6), himself a Kashmiri Hindu, reports how Bakkarwal and Kashmiri were involved in disputes over access to land:

> ... practically every land dispute in which both parties are not Bakarwals is taken up as a communal question by them, and they spare no efforts in fighting to the bitter end often spending enormous sums of money, to which the whole tribe subscribes, in following the case from tribunal to tribunal ... the Bakarwals ... live severely apart, their hands being against everybody and everybody's hands against them.

Following the general model proposed by Brass (1985: 1), this period constituted the second phase of identity formation in which struggles between 'ethnic groups' took place in order to clarify rights, privileges and the distribution of resources.

Such a delineation of the outer boundaries of the community paired favourably with the fact that within it little competition existed, especially since the relative influence of the various men of influence (*mukaddam*) was apparently of little consequence. *Zat* exogamous marriage alliances further helped stem eventual rivalry among them, and Babaji Larvi's family played a major role by marrying into economically influential families such as those of the Khatana and the Kohli, lending the latter moral force while thwarting political rivalry. Since, however, most marriages continued to be arranged within *zat/khel* boundaries, community cohesion could have been brittled. Indeed, even the horizontal solidarity among men of influence was to change slowly as a response to the system of indirect rule, the Bakkarwal and Gujar were soon subjected to. But precisely these new extraneous political factors which on the face of it encouraged this brittleness combined with a mobilization of community-specific cultural factors to favour cohesion.

Following the agrarian model of collecting land revenue in North India, each larger grouping of Bakkarwal was assigned a *lambardar* from among the existing *mukaddam*; some of these were designated by the administration, others were chosen by their respective groupings, still others simply declared themselves to be *lambardar*. Thus, a fairly large number of more or less informal men of influence was officially reduced to a few formal leaders, and from among the *mukaddam*, whose relative importance had until then been negligible, a select few were elevated to higher positions of formal power. It was the beginning of the end of perceived equity in access to resources. The *lambardar* were paid a small salary and were held responsible for law and order within their respective units. They were also in charge of procuring animals on the hoof for the kitchens of the British Indian army. Thus, for example, in 1914, British officers in Gilgit ordered a certain 'Abdul Karim Goatman' and his people to sell them 500 goats at half price, failing which they would be refused the right to graze their herds in the Kalapani valley (C.S., 1914d). Till about 1932 the primary task of these *lambardar* was, however, to collect grazing taxes from the herdsmen of their groups and submit these to the government. Hence, the larger a grouping, and the greater the revenue forthcoming, the more important it became. The *lambardar* of the largest groupings thus also automatically became—or at least were confirmed officially in their roles as—the most important men, politically. Also, since a *lambardar* got 5 per cent of every unit of tax collected, and since the entire economy was monetarizing, it was in his interest to expand the size of his group. This led to the emergence of the system of *sakawat*, through which a reasonably wealthy and politically ambitious man could accrue both power and wealth. By binding himself to poorer men with little or no stock in relationships of apparent socio-economic mutually, a wealthy and pious man gifted surplus, taxable stock, food and clothing to poor families who helped in herding and obtained at least temporary access to pastures controlled by the former. Distribution of livestock created social reciprocity and also acted to minimize the socio-economic risk of each individual through dependence on the others within each *sakawat* network (Rao, 1995). And yet, access to cash and to influential persons beyond the community also came to be perceived as new resources. This started becoming increasingly important after 1924 with a committee consisting of the Settlement Commissioner and the Conservator of Forests being appointed to draw up a complete programme of forest demarcation. Perhaps more than before, political and economic status became interconnected; one of the goals that could now be attained consisted in the clear conjunction of wealth, power and piety. Competition also emerged among *lambardar* and among *mukaddam* who wanted to become *lambardar*. To become *lambardar* the aspiring *mukaddam* had to effectively coordinate their old, internal, factional roles and the new external, extra-factional ones (cf. Sahlins, 1963: 290ff.).

Internal political changes were a response to changes in the larger context and thus the likelihood of ethnic salience (Cross, 1978: 40) increased. Existing elements of culture—such as kinship obligations within each corporate group (*biradari*) and feelings of Islamic duty and piety within *sakawat* networks—were mobilized to provide structure to concurring groups, while also rendering the perception of access to resources within each of these groups fairly equitable. This very mobilization served then, to dampen potential ill-will between the poor and the rich, and was used by the mobilizers themselves to build and extend marriage-cum-political alliances increasingly required in a world where the very nature of resources was changing. This phase can be regarded as the seminal stage of a process which took shape in the next phase and "... by which ... distinct groups of people or ethnic groups acquire subjective self-consciousness and political significance ..." (Brass, 1974: 403)—a phase which according to him could lead to 'nationality formation'.

Phase 3: ca. 1926–1947: The Ideologization of Identity

Babaji Larvi passed away in 1926 (15 *Shaban*, 1347 A.H.), at the age of 63, and was buried in Babanagri. He was followed on the *gaddi* by his biological son Hazrat Bab Mian Nizam-ud-Din Larvi (1901–1972). "Wangat Sharif, in the Lar Pargana", it is said, "became an important shrine of the Nizamiya Naqshbandiya order". Among the numerous political personalities who are said to have visited the shrine at some point of time are the Maharajas of Kashmir, Lord Mountbatten, later Sheikh Mohammad Abdullah in his capacity as Prime Minister of Kashmir, and the Indian Prime Ministers Nehru and Indira Gandhi. Yet, as mentioned earlier, Babaji Larvi is projected by the Bakkarwal as an essentially apolitical figure. In this respect he differs from his son Mian Nizam-ud-Din and grandson Mian Bashir, the present incumbent. This difference between the three generations was related by several Bakkarwal to the changing position of the entire community. Whereas Babaji Larvi took care only of spiritual matters (*piri*), his son and grandson were perceived of by many as having no way out but to manage both spiritual and temporal (*miri*) affairs.

"History", Levi-Strauss (1966: 91) once advised, "should admit that it never completely escapes from the nature of myth". The early years of Mian Nizam-ud-Din as *sajjadeh nishin* of Wangat (1926–1972) coincided with several new political developments which affected the Bakkarwal and Gujar. It also coincided in Kashmir as a whole with the period in which tensions between Maharaja Hari Singh (1925–1952) and the local majority (Muslim) population, as also between him and nationalists of all religions who were fighting simultaneously British colonial power and local feudalism, reached a peak. As far as the Bakkarwal and Gujar are concerned, from various administrative records of the second decade of this century, it appears that increasingly non-Kashmiri herdsmen were perceived both by rural Kashmiris as well as by Dogra and British official as being excessively aggressive and predatory in their herding strategies. Thus, for example, it was observed that:

> In the summer of 1918, while working on this alp with which I had been well acquainted for some 24 years past, I was so much impressed by the excessive damage its vegetation had suffered through overgrazing by shepherds and Gujars ... through a series of new Gujar settlements ... having overrun with increasingly large herds ... . In ... 1919 ... the Maharaja ... decided that the Mohand, Lar and Kanydalo Margs should be closed to grazing for three years in the first instance. (Stein, 1923)

Already in 1912 the government had started closing selected grazing areas to migratory herds owned by non-Kashmiri (C.S., 1914f), pleas from local Gujar (Desi Gujar) notwithstanding (e.g.,

Imam Din, 1924). These measures were accompanied by a steep rise in taxation (C.S., 1914e). When this was considered inadequate to restrict herd-growth and curb further migration into Kashm from the west, a formal notification was passed, in 1920, prohibiting the entry of 'foreign' Bakarwal and Gujar into the state's territories (C.S., 1914f). From about the mid-1920s the government was considering declaring all these communities as 'Criminal Tribes' (Anon, 1926); finally, on 15 August 1928, a notification was signed declaring the Bakkarwal, but not the Gujar, as a criminal tribe (Banerji, 1928; C.S., 1914g). Based primarily on a professional difference—the nature of livestock herded and the alleged effects of overgrazing—this categorization was formulated clearly in 'ethnic' terms; it was presented as a result of cultural difference. When considering these types of "paternalistic economic intervention" in the realm of 'public interest' in general and forest conservancy in particular, one should keep in mind the political goals and the 'ideological trappings' of the rulers, but also the by now established colonial view that:

> ... the state not only had a duty to protect established interests but also that it should advance the economic and social well-being of its subjects. (Robb, 1997: 277)

It should, indeed, be remembered that measures taken by the colonial-cum-feudal powers and discussed above reflected both the status of the emerging community of 'goat herders' as well as the rather tense interaction between them and other populations using similar local resources.

Meanwhile, in the 1920s, a movement had begun in Jammu and Kashmir as a whole for the improvement of the conditions of Muslims and for greater religious freedom. This movement can again be seen in the larger perspective of the subcontinental struggle for freedom. Several local Gujar had joined this movement; among these the most important were Maulvi Mohd. Abdullah Seakhvi (Fazil-e-Deoband) and Maulvi Abdul Karim, both from Mirpur, and Chaudhri Ilahi Bakhsh of Jhelum district. Somewhat as in Punjab earlier (between 1906—formation of the Indian Muslims League—and 1918—the *Khilafat* movement), now, in Jammu and Kashmir political consciousness among

Muslims as Muslims started growing, and Muslim society began to form and consolidate itself as a power factor in the political life of the area. But parallel to this stream of Muslim identity ran another, representing economic (land-based) and 'ethnic' identity; the latter's concerns were voiced by the Gujar-Jat Conference, an important organization, which succeeded as early as 1927 in getting all sedentary Gujar in Jammu and Kashmir recognized as 'State Subjects'.[9] Four years later, all nomadic Gujar of the area also achieved this status (Gupta, 1981: 74). In 1929–30 the anti-British organization 'Majlis-e-Ahrar-e-Islam-e-Hind' was founded in Lahore; again, several Gujar (Qureshi, 1979: 46) and Bakkarwal, including Mian Nizam-ud-Din became members. It is in this capacity, for example, that he disguised the communist muhajir Abd-Allah Safdar (cf. Ansari, 1986: 532, 536) as a Bakkarwal herdsman, gave him a herd of goats and helped him cross the border and flee British Indian territory (pers. comm. Ch. Mohammad Shafi Qizlbash 1986, who introduced Safdar to Nizam-ud-Din on Nehru's request). The *Majlis* began sending *jathas* into Kashmir (Page, 1982: 248–49), and also requested the Maharaja to improve the conditions of local Muslims, but the latter took little notice. On *Id* 1931 when the mufti-e-'*azam* of the Jammu *idgah* was prevented by the police from delivering the sermon, violence broke out, and the 'Kashmir Agitation' began. This started with a series of demonstrations which were to last several weeks. They ended in November 1931 with the Maharaja setting up the Glancy Commission, one of whose most important findings was that the system of grazing taxes, especially for nomadic pastoralists, was prohibitive (Kashmir Riots Commission, 1932: 29–30):

> One of the main planks of the Muslims Agitation was the heavy rate and unequal incidence of the grazing-tax. As recommended by the Glancy Commission the demand for this tax has been suspended in the seven … tehsils of Jammu, Samba, Akhnoor, Kathua, Jasmergarh, Mirpur and Bhimber and a special officer has been appointed … moreover orders have been issued that no additional fee should be charged when cattle … migrate to cooler uplands in summer … A further relief … is the exemption from payment of Kahcharai on sheep and goats brought within

Municipal limits for the purpose of slaughter. (Administrative Note, 1932: App. A)

The system of taxation had, indeed, by now, reached cruel proportions. But this unduly heavy taxation did not affect all equally and even strengthened the position of the wealthy. By about the mid-1902s what had become important was not to maximize the number of animals in one's own herd, but the number of herd owners over whom one had control, thereby gaining direct or indirect access to their animals. This control and access enhanced power and wealth as explained above. The heavy taxes levied on livestock meant that it was to no one's advantage to officially multiply stock much. On the contrary, it was much more rational to distribute taxable stock and thus minimize the tax burden of each household. This economic stratification was toned down by the social network of *sakawat* referred to earlier. Simultaneously, however, since the gifts were never very generous, there was little if any chance of a client building up his own herd and becoming an independent herdsman. Heavy taxation thus ultimately favoured stratification and the wealthy, and when we remember that money-lending also took place largely within the community, we realize to what extent access to resources were controlled and limited. The closing of pastures, however, affected all equally—the rich and the poor, the Bakkarwal and the Gujar. For the former the declaration as a criminal tribe also cut across nascent economic stratification and closed all avenues to new resources. In the political protest actions that followed the very men who had formerly collected taxes and were wealthy could come forward as political leaders. They could agitate on behalf of the poor against oppression from without the community and hence be perceived by them as friends and benefactors—as 'big men' desiring equity. The time was perhaps ripe then, or concerted action against the powers that be, but for such action to be effective allies from beyond the community were increasingly required.

In the early 1930s when Sheikh Abdullah formed the 'Muslim Conference', Haji Israel Khatana, a Gujar, became one of its first members. Several other Gujar also joined and a tendency towards affiliation along communal lines developed, with several Hindus in the valley and in Jammu forming their respective associations.

In 1932 Srinagar witnessed riots between Kashmiri Muslims and Kashmiri Hindus, and it was reported that "many pandit families ... migrated to Srinagar from the villages" (*Times of India*, 26 September 1932). During one of the hearings of the Glancy Commission, a Gujar had also testified that when he went to sell milk in a Hindu home he had been attacked; another witness said how he had seen three Gujar being dragged to a temple by Hindus and then killed (Kashmir Riots Commission, 1932: 43, 46). In 1936, as a reaction to this religious polarization, a regional Congress Party was organized in Jammu and *Pir* Mian Nizam-ud-Din became one of the first members. As we have already seen, religious identity and identity based on other cultural factors ran parallel and were represented by different organizations, which taken together reflected the "patchwork of multiple loyalties" (Reetz, 1997: 288) that was so typical of the entire nationalist movement. It may well be that Mian Nizam-ud-Din's decision to join the Congress was based on the second line of non-religious identity. Be this as it may, in 1937 at a political gathering in Jammu the title of *amir-e-qaum* was bestowed on him for his services towards the poor. In 1936–37, when the first people's representation, the *Praja Sabha* was inaugurated by the Maharaja, in addition to Mian Nizam-ud-Din and Haji Israel Khatana, the sons of several *hijrat*—companions of Babaji Larvi found themselves involved. In 1944, when partial elections to the *Praja Sabha* took place, Mian Nizam-ud-Din was elected. In the meantime, another political organization had come up—the *Anjuman-e-Mashaekh*. It was a religious organization, many of whose members were *pirs* in the region and Mian Nizam-ud-Din became its president in Jammu and Kashmir. In all these years the influence of the Muslim League in Jammu and Kashmir was limited; indeed, Mian Nizam-ud-Din and his followers are credited with having largely contributed to the success of its rival—the Indian National Congress.

Phase 4: ca. 1947–1990: The 'Ethnic Game'

It is interesting to note that in spite of this, when the first border conflict arose between India and Pakistan, Mian Nizam-ud-Din was accused by the local government of having supported Pakistan. He defended himself in 1948–49 in a pamphlet entitled

Ailan-e-Haq and was declared innocent. In the first local elections in 1951 he won unopposed on a Congress ticket and remained a member of the local assembly till 1965. Mian Nizam-ud-Din passed away in 1972, but his son Mian Bashir Ahmad remained active in electoral politics. However, unlike his father, he switched back and forth between political parties. This switching is another element in the interplay of individual and group identity. While in the course of his political trajectory Mian Bashir no doubt changed parties out of personal ambition, he clearly also did so in the framework of a broader search for identity which the Gujar and allied communities in Jammu and Kashmir east of the ceasefire line were forced by political circumstances to pursue after 1947.

Even prior to 1947 the situation of the Bakkarwal and the Guajr in terms of ethnicity had varied slightly according to whether they lived in the Kashmir valley or to the south of it. Linguistically, and in many other cultural respects, they were closer to the Hindu Dogra who dominated the Jammu region. In terms of religion, however, they were obviously closer to the Muslims (mostly Kashmiri—who formed the majority in the valley—but also 'Pahari') who were relatively bereft of political power throughout the area. From the perspective of the centre-periphery theory, prior to 1947, all Hindus of the area taken together could be considered as constituting the political centre, and all Muslims likewise the periphery. Religion, and not language, was the prime factor in determining political power and identity. After 1947, in the Kashmir valley, all Kashmiri, whether Muslim or Hindu, considered themselves for a variety of reasons, as representing the political centre; for them all non-Kashmiri, irrespective of religion, were peripheral. It is then not hard to realize that for the Bakkarwal and Gujar two mutually conflictual streams of identity—one based on religion, the other on non-religious cultural factors—which had always existed began to take more concrete shape, depending on the context of alliance locally and temporally relevant. As opposed to other parts of North India where perhaps language was less important than religion in the process of socio-political differentiation (cf. Brass, 1974: 404), in Jammu and Kashmir, religion, language and a variety of other cultural traditions must be taken into account when analyzing the process of identity formation and ethnicity.

However, their importance can be fully grasped only against the now unfolding backdrop of intensifying competition for resources in an increasingly capitalistic economy.

With the cessation of colonial rule in 1947 the system of *lambardar* among the Bakkarwal changed somewhat. While salaries were no longer paid, the privileged social and economic positions in the families of these *lambardar* had in the meantime acquired, survived. The terms *lambardar* and *mukaddam* continued to be used, with the *mukaddam* from the ex-*lambardar* families still being known as *lambardar*. There remained, however, little difference if any in the duties of a *mukaddam* and those of a *lambardar*, each of these men being primarily responsible for settling quarrels within his respective group. With increasing police intervention in case of disputes, even these jural responsibilities were reduced, and yet in many other respects they became "even more important than before, because we have more and more problems, and new ones too, and we can't cope with them". Neither the *lambardar* nor the *mukaddam* were now formally elected, and "what prevails is either might or money". A fairly clear segmentary structure still obtained, with a sort of hierarchy of patron-client structures in every grazing and browsing locality. Each of these patron-client structures formed a sub-faction, with patrons at every level often being related by birth or marriage to the patrons of the levels above them. This overall pattern largely supports Oldenburg's hypothesis (1992: 2659) for northern India that "patrons also ... value as many males as possible in their dependent clients". Each client is bound by loyalty to the leader of his sub-faction for a variety of reasons, both historical and contemporary, but all crucial to subsistence. Access to land—to pasture in particular—and to cash are two major reasons.

With the drawing of the ceasefire line between India and Pakistan and the wars between the two countries, high-altitude pastures available to the Bakkarwal and Gujar shrank drastically after 1947. In the period immediately prior to, during, and after 1947, the pasture areas of the Bakkarwal were cut through; so was the Bakkarwal population itself. For those remaining to the east and south of the ceasefire line, in Indian-held territory, summer pastures in the Gilgit area grew out of bounds. Similarly, in winter, the areas of Mirpur, Muzaffarabad and two-thirds of Poonch were cut off for many of them. Although the population was also reduced, a considerably higher population density than before can be postulated in the remaining pastures. Land thus became a scarce resource. This scarcity applied not just to grazing areas, but also to agricultural land. In several areas government lands were encroached upon (cf. Bhadarwah W.P., 1954: 9; Kishtwar W.P., 1961: 46), and semi-permanent dwellings built on these *nautor* lands; two laws passed in 1958 and 1977 gave proprietory rights to all such encroachers, and as many Bakkarwal and Gujar commented, "the richer among us have taken the forest by force, the poorer have to find a way out to survive". Land scarcity increased over the years, not only due to population growth (for the Bakkarwal ca 29.6% for the 1960s and 1970s, cf. S.A., 1984: Table 5), but also due to various government measures. Primary among these were the building of roads (cf. Ramban W.P., 1961: 11) and the extension of urban settlements. All these factors led to summer pastures being heavily curtailed and much of the fallow and wasteland formerly used for winter grazing no longer being available (for details, see Rao, 1992).

After 1947 taxation was reduced even further and the need for cash rose—to buy food from government ration shops, to pay for winter grazing, to pay for veterinary services, and so on. This cash could be acquired either by selling animals on the hoof or by engaging in wage labour, or both. With the sharp rise in demand for meat in the Kashmir valley meat prices rose and over the years it became extremely profitable to own large herds. But, to maintain these one needed labour and access to grazing. Till the late 1970s wage labour outside the pastoral sector was minimal and the poor had little choice but to work as hired shepherds (*ajri*) for the rich, entering thereby into a system of quasi-bondsmanship (Rao, 1995). In the 1970s availability of alternative employment opportunities outside the pastoral sector grew. This promoted prosperity among the poorest and led no doubt to a certain loosening of the ties of direct dependency on patrons built up over generations. It did not, however, lead to its demise. First of all, wage labour to which the poor had access was seasonal and temporary. Secondly, increasingly wealthy Bakkarwal and Gujar were well acquainted with the new agencies of employment—be these governmental or private—and used these ties to their own benefit in various ways. One of these was to get only men of their choice employed. Thus, the system of brokerage implicit in the entire system could not be broken. In fact, poor men working for pilgrims and tourists as porters and 'horsemen' partially entered into a new system of bondage. Pack horses had to be registered with local government authorities, who gave preference to men offering several pack animals at a time. Wealthy men monopolized access to these authorities, but were rarely willing to send their own horses on these rather hazardous trips. So, they requisitioned animals from several poor men in their clientele, who then went along with their beasts of burden. But, since each lot of horses was registered under a rich middleman's name, he received the official cash earnings. The men who went with their horses received only a fraction of these earnings, since each middleman kept large chunks as 'commission'.

Thus, there remained numerous vertical chains of loyalty based primarily on the patron-client tradition. But, there came into being increasingly also a structure of loyalty which ran horizontally, was based on wealth, and cut across factions. This structure was evident among the families of men of influence who tended to stick together and intermarry (Rao, 1993b). It became apparent in 1983 when the government decided to abolish the institution of *lambardar;* on 20 September, 1984, after a protest meeting in Srinagar, the decision was reversed and the post restituted (Sharma, 1984). Till 1947 such influential men acted as mediators and middlemen between their units and other larger units at various levels of the socio-political hierarchy. Hence, each localized unit had some degree of control over its own middlemen. After 1947, with the advent of the electoral system, these middlemen became the leaders of the vote banks and group control over them all but disappeared; it came to be replaced by 'brokerage networks' (Bailey, 1963), composed of local leaders, local party bosses, politicians and a variety of 'contractors' (cf. Srinivas and Beteille, 1964: 167). 'Goats are votes', a veterinary doctor once commented in Kashmir. In other words, each vertical chain of loyalty between patrons and clients functioned as a vote bank. Indeed, the old *sakawat* system helped the development of vote banks because they followed existing structures. As elsewhere in India, here too, men of influence usurped the right of specific persons under their power to exercise electoral choice and thus imposed their political decisions on them. "The only one to vote here was *Haji*, since the names of the others do not figure in the (voters') lists ... but then he voted for us too ...", said Karim, a distant relative of the *Haji* who voted. Whereas in this rather extreme case this *Haji* voted for several men and women of many households belonging to his sphere of influence, usually only the heads of households exercised franchise for themselves and all the adult members of their respective households. As Makhni explained, "The other men—the sons, shepherds and others—are with the animals and we women are busy at home or fetching firewood ... so Sifo's father went and put his mark (thumb impression as a voter) for us all". Cognitively alien structures further reinforce these intra-community relations of dependence and surrogate decision-making, since for almost every action in the public sphere beyond the community—be it the rare opening of a bank account, the periodic process of getting oneself registered as a voter, or even the basic question of obtaining a ration card—an average Bakkarwal or Gujar must request some man of substance to testify to the veracity of his/her identity. Thus, state structures turn the assertion of identity into mechanical acts of identification.

Increasingly among the Bakkarwal and the Gujar, these we-groups of the wealthy and politically ambitious and influential could function only on a broader platform. The question then arose of whom to build such a platform with—of whom to include or exclude. 'One mechanism', Seneviratne (1997: 5) rightly observes, "by which ... a group awakens to a consciousness of identity is the perception of a threat to the group by a force external to it." But even perceptions can be introduced and stimulated through external catalysts. That the British constructed and created group identities to then manipulate them in the political sphere is by now firmly established, but even in post-colonial India such manipulation is as old as the Indian state. As Rao and Rao (1974: 454–55) point out, during Nehru's era as Prime Minister not only did "... caste form an important criterion in the selection of candidates ...", but Congress candidates openly appealed to caste-consciousness; in Bihar villagers were told "the daughter and the vote are never given to one outside the caste", while in Rajasthan one slogan went "not a single Jat vote should go to a Rajput". Similarly, though constitutionally "the secular settlement ..." may well have theoretically "deprived the politicization or religious identities of legitimacy" (Madan, 1987: 747), in reality religious groups were also manipulated, and following the colonial strategy, "Nehru who swore by secularism took care to select Muslim candidates for constituencies where Muslims formed a considerable section of the electorate" (Rao and Rao, 1974: 455). One outcome was that till the Babri Masjid episode Muslims largely voted for the Congress. From the late 1960s when politics in India came to be conceived of "... as essentially an electoral game" (Kothari, 1985: 5) increasingly in this game issues and ideologies gave way to strategies to keep oneself in power and "... the numbers game essentially became an ethnic game" (Kothari, 1985: 7). In this 'ethnic game' among the Bakkarwal and Gujar both religious feelings and non-religious cultural traditions have been used to make and break the rules, and almost all political parties have tried to determine the players. While the Congress and the National Conference chose Mian Bashir and Chaudhri Mohammad Shafi Khatana, Hajji Israel's son, another Khatana was a Gujar was also exploited by all concerned. For many individuals this 'ethnic game' paid dividends: Mian Bashir was once again the Congress candidate in the Jammu elections and his brother-in-law became finance minister in the interim government of 1986–87.

In the 1970s and 1980s there were numerous attempts by the Indian government to encourage and de-emphasize the cultural differences among these various groups of Gujar and emphasize those between the Kashmiri—the majority population of the valley on the one hand—and the entire minority-cluster of Bakkarwal, Gujar, and 'Pahari' on the other. Through this construction of what Cross (1978) terms 'ethnic allegiance'—a situation in which several ethnic groups join together because they feel that they share economic and political interests—influential Bakkarwal and Gujar came to perceive that they were discriminated and exploited against by the Kashmiri. This, in its turn, led to opposition towards the local Kashmiri-dominated provincial government. Puri (1987: 836) went as far as to remark that "... the politico-cultural aspirations of non-Kashmiri Muslims are not exactly similar to those of Kashmiri Muslims", and that in large parts of Jammu "the votes were broadly divided on caste lines, viz., Gujar and non-Gujar". Partly for these reasons, and partly in the hope of building a wider regional political platform, many of the influential and hence politically aware members of each of these communities stressed that they all belong to a greater Gujar community conceived of in terms of what Kaviraj (1997: 329) has called "a global geography of identities and their territorial distribution ..."—one that includes all Gujar, whether Muslim, Hindu, or Sikh. In 1978, for example, the Akhil Bharatiya Gujar Sudhar Sabha compiled and presented a catalogue of demands concerning 'the Gujar' of Jammu and Kashmir to the Central Government (ABG, 1978). Five years later, Mian Bashir declared that all non-Kashmiri in the valley (in other words, irrespective of religion) suffered similar disabilities (Bashir Ahmad, 1983: 1). In the 1980s one could, indeed, observe the emergence of a new implication of the old term *biradari*—glossed earlier as a kind of solidarity group—among certain literate Bakkarwal, Gujar and Gujar-Bakkarwal. While talking on non-Bakkarwal and non-Gujar these men often referred to one another as belonging to 'our Gujar biradari'; however, the vast majority of Bakkarwal I spoke to felt that there were too many differences between Gujar and Bakkarwal to warrant their being considered one single community (*kaum*), and I was often asked, "I am a Bakkarwal—why should I call myself a Gujar?"

The numbers' game was hence translated by means of at least three ideologically contradictory systems, all of which already existed—namely, Islamic identity, language identity, and *zat* structures—into the structure of vote banks mentioned above. No wonder then that the quest for identity and the concomitant conflict between mutually competing loyalties sharpened.

Phase 5 ca. 1990–?: A Watershed Period

Attempts at 'ethnic' mobilization attained paramount importance against the background of political events in Jammu & Kashmir, which have culminated in civil war, great state repression, and much brutality from various quarters on all local communities in the last few years (Rao, 1996). It is beyond the scope of this paper to discuss these here, but for the comprehension of our topic, one must keep in mind the ubiquitous presence throughout the Kashmir valley—and since late 1992 also to the south of it—of armed men belonging either to the Indian army or paramilitary forces, or to one of the numerous militant organizations fighting for the separation of the area from India in one form or another. The Bakkarwal who migrate twice annually had to face and deal with these various outfits; so did most of the Gujar. The militant organizations obviously tried to get their help to cross the ceasefire line amidst difficult mountain terrain (e.g., Vinayak, 1996), and although profit probably was a major motivation, the question of identity now became more crucial than ever before. The two streams of 'ethnic' consciousness mentioned earlier now became more complex. One of these led to the formation of the Gujar Liberation Tigers, a small organization which in alliance with certain Kashmiri groups briefly fought Indian forces (Asia Watch, 1991: 144). The kidnapping in Srinagar of the Gujar Assistant Director of Radio Kashmir on March 7, 1992 was a fallout of this. Yet another, older stream was based on religious sentiments; as Khatana (1991: 2), himself a Hindu Gujar from Haryana, put it:

> The Muslim Gujar community of Jammu and Kashmir at present is faced by two different phenomena, Gujar consciousness and Muslim consciousness. The Gujar voluntary organisations are making the Gujjars conscious of their ethnic identity while the Islamic organisations and institutions are endeavouring to promote Muslim consciousness.

From the perspective of the Indian state the danger now arose of the Bakkarwal and Gujar as Muslims beginning to fraternize with the Kashmiri against India. The central government's long pending decision in 1991 to declare both communities scheduled tribes was a strategic move in the expectation of preventing such solidarity and indeed driving the wedge deeper still between Kashmiri on the one hand and Gujar and Bakkarwal on the other. This was followed by attempts to recruit members of the Gujar, Bakkarwal, 'Pahari', and other non-Kashmiri speaking communities—especially those living near the ceasefire line—into working either as informers or as members of armed counter-gangs (e.g., Vinayak, 1994; Sidhva, 1995). Simultaneously, however, the government also tried to prevent an eventual alliance between the Gujar and Bakkarwal on the one hand and the so-called Muslim 'Pahari' population of the area. Though "… . Paharies have never been defined in the living history of Jammu and Kashmir …" (DE, 1992), the term used to be applied to certain non-Kashmiri speaking Muslims and Hindus on either side of the border, and certain Gujar and Bakkarwal living in border areas had entered 'Pahari' as their mother tongue in the census of 1981. An official 'Pahari Board' was now formed, which included no Gujar or Bakkarwal, nor any Hindu 'Pahari'.

The emphasis on ethnic differentiation between Bakkarwal (together with Gujar) and Kashmiri, simultaneously, highlighted the alleged similarities of all populations akin to the Gujar, irrespective of locality and religious faith. Thus, Hakla Poonchi (1991: 1–2), a Gujar journalist from Poonch, wrote:

> Gujjar community comprises of two main tribes, one is Gujjar and the other is Bakerwal. … Apart from our Jammu and Kashmir State, Gujjars are scattered in other Indian states … Gujjars are living example of integrity and prosperity, which is required by our country at this critical situation. Gujjars are Muslims, Gujjars are Hindus, Gujjars are … Sikh and after all Gujjars are one.

But, the apparent unity even among the Bakkarwal had been badly shaken as early as 1987. Two major events took place that year. First, the elections which took place to the State Assembly of Jammu and Kashmir in March were received by the vast majority of the local population as having been thoroughly rigged; popular discontent which may have had a chance of democratic expression was thus entirely crushed. Secondly, during the Bakkarwal spring migration that year, shortly after these elections, the entire area was severely affected by very heavy rain, hailstorms and landslides. Thousands of Bakkarwal animals perished while crossing the steep and narrow passes. Fairly rapidly, the Central Government ordered monetary compensation to be paid to the affected families; however, this money had not reached the poor among them even by spring 1992. The rich, on the other hand, received their compensation immediately, and it was widely held among less well to do Bakkarwal that these wealthy men had pocketed their shares.[10] This was not considered surprising, since it was equally widely opined that "any way these people have been eating our money for years". In May 1989, in one of several 'reshuffles' of the state cabinet, a son of Mian Bashir was appointed minister and in August his uncle, Mohammad Aslam Kohli became speaker of the state assembly. There could now be little doubt that the wealthy among the Bakkarwal and Gujar were perceivable as actively supporting a government which was increasingly being considered illegitimate and thus anti-people. Many of them now came to be considered as part of a much wider network, which was conceived of largely in terms of what is generally known as dependency theory. Scarce economic resources originating from outside Jammu and Kashmir—primarily Delhi—were controlled there and local access to these resources was monopolized by a clientele group on behalf of the central powers. Rich Bakkarwal and Gujar were seen as part of just this clientele group.

Nearly two and a half years after the inclement weather had wrought havoc, shortly before the autumn migration in 1989, several of these wealthy men were asked by Kashmiri militants for large sums of money as contribution towards their campaign to fight the Indian state; most refused to pay and were beaten up. Those who demanded the money mentioned explicitly the compensatory amounts issued in 1987, and felt that "since that was anyway not their own money, they should now hand it over". On the face of it at least, these demands for money were thus being made—perhaps by new would-be patrons—on behalf of the poor who felt cheated of their dues. In spring 1990 and summer 1991 again some men of influence were beaten up—this time both by Kashmiri militants and by Indian army or paramilitary personnel. The latter suspected them of aiding the militants by accepting them as part of their migrating units (*tola*). Hence identity and migration permits were made compulsory for each household in a *tola*—something which had, incidentally, been suggested as far back as 1913 to control overgrazing and immigration (Beadon-Bryant, 1913); to obtain a permit each household head had to request (and often bribe) his faction leader, and these men in turn had to bribe local officials, such as *tehsildars*. Those who failed to obtain permits had to bribe their way through the military checkposts either with cash or livestock. The wealthier the herd-owner, the larger the bribe, and the greater the humiliation vis-à-vis his traditional clients and followers. Large bribes also had to be paid to the Indian forces posted in and near some of the choicest summer pasture areas of Talel, Gurez and Bandipora, close to the Indo-Pakistan ceasefire line and used primarily by the rich. Grazing was now curtailed in many of these areas, flocks straying over army lines of control were confiscated, and their owners penalized. In other areas, such as Rangdum, where grazing pressure had increased, I was told:

> Everybody behaves badly with us—the Border Security Force, the Army (in this particular case the Gurkha Regiment), and the militants. They all demand money or animals, or both, and when we refuse they often take them by force. Often, if you refuse you can be arrested as a militant; but you can also be kidnapped by a militant, or forced to give one of your young men temporarily to smuggle arms.

The wealthier the owner identified, the heavier the penalty. The richer the herd-owner, the greater his chances of being black-mailed and the more he had at stake. For a variety of reasons, therefore, the wealthiest ceased to migrate as they had before, and gradually even those slightly below them in the socio-economic hierarchy kept to their respective winter areas. Since to survive, their flocks must however migrate, these men of wealth and influence grew more dependent than ever on the labour of the poorer. Many of the latter gave vent to their pent up feelings of submission by openly refusing for the first time to pay their traditional patrons dues of various kinds, which (they now said) they had always found excessive, if not illegitimate. For the first time, resentment and identity based on economic status were expressed.

The final blow to existing ideologies and structures came in 1990 when the shrine of Wangat Sharif was attacked. This attack demonstrated the violability of a space which is by definition inviolable, since the divine grace with which such a space is imbued implies that ... "conflict informing the modes of ordinary existence has to be forsaken" (Das and Nandy, 1985: 180). The, especially sudden, transformation of a space from one that has always been perceived of a inviolable to one that is demonstrably violable can entail the de-sacralization of a sacred place, and this in turn would imply that the spiritual power that had turned this anonymous space into holy place has forsaken it. The power associated with Wangat Sharif was, however, symbolized not just by the shrine, the tomb, and other insignia, but also by the descendants of the saint. Indeed, it seems that the attack on the shrine symbolized an attack on its politically and morally discredited *sajjadeh nishin*. Not that Mian Bashir was the only politically discredited *pir* in Jammu and Kashmir, there were many others, of whom some were attacked in person. But their shrines were not attacked, as far as I know. It is commonly held that Wangat Sharif was attacked because it was linked to the present incumbent not just spiritually, but also in terms of biological kinship; in other words, the shrine stood for the family of a politician-cum-*pir* and it was this particular combination of *piri* and *miri* that was being targeted. Politically and morally, Mian Bashir had earned himself a bad reputation much earlier by switching parties: "Who can trust a man—and a *pir* at that—who gives his word to one and then goes off to another, one who changes his party?"

Were Wangat Sharif then, to be bereft of its power, so too would these descendants. This would jeopardize the entire system of *piri-muridi*, since the loyalty of a *murid* is by definition everlasting. It would, by extension, endanger the existing political structures among the Gujar and Bakkarwal. On the other hand, were the descendants capable of demonstrating their continuing power—for example, by executing wonders wrought through divine grace for the benefit of people—no one would doubt them, or their source of power, Wangat Sharif. Since to see these wonders few or none could go to the shrine in this period of threat and uncertainty, the only way out was for the *gaddi* to come to them at appointed places—and this is precisely what Mian Bashir did by leaving (his detractors said by fleeing) the valley and staying to the south of it. Like numerous other political and spiritual leaders, both Kashmiri and non-Kashmiri, Mian Bashir too decided to leave the Kashmir valley, which is inhabited primarily by Kashmiri. He spent his days south of the Pir Panjal range, in a region where various Gujar communities and the Bakkarwal comprise a large proportion of the population. This translocation was legitimized by couching it on the one hand in the terminology of another *hijra*: those who attack a shrine can, following certain interpretations, be portrayed as 'not real Muslims', and in this conscious moment of transforming space into place, the *sajjadeh nishin* drew upon the doctrinal obligation to emigrate from a 'House of War' to a (real) 'House of Islam' as an expression of the identity of the Muslim community (e.g., Masud, 1990). By doing so, he retained the faithful core, to whom he remained *nisf-e-Khuda* (half God). Out of the 'array of cultural distinction' (Brass, 1979: 42) available to him, Mian Bashir thus tried to use both religious and non-religious factors to conserve, and eventually build upon individual and group political identity.

The shrine of Wangat Sharif is now functioning once again, though one of Mian Bashir's sons was attacked in 1995. Individual Gujar and Bakkarwal were recruited to help the government plan the elections of 1996; one such important figure is that of Bahadur Khan of Kangan, who is said to be "... the creation of Mian Basheer ..." (Sidhva, 1995: 22). Mian Bashir, the chairman of the Pradesh Congress election campaign committee, tried to get himself nominated as the president of the local wing of the Congress party, against a Kashmiri rival, Ghulam Rasool Kar. Adapting Pastner's study among the Zikri of Baluchistan one could say that here too, albeit in a very different manner, "... feuding in the realm of the spirit becomes a surrogate for secular competition ..." (Pastner, 1984: 308). After the elections, the feuding continued, with the All India Gujar Parishad's state unit chief Shamsher Hakla Poonchi condemning the new government for failing to grant the Gujar and Bakkarwal the benefits due to them as Scheduled Tribes, and for not including any member of these groups in the new ministry (*Times of India*, 18 November 1996). The struggle in the process of identity formation appears thus, not to have reached the third phase postulated by Brass (1985: 1), but instead have remained—or returned to—the second phase.

Conclusion

In a recent study Banks (1996) addresses the question of whether the phenomenon of ethnicity is observable among 'majorities'.

Since ethnicity is a process, it can, I suggest, be observable among all types of groups. Furthermore, 'majority' is only a concept based on the demographic selection of specific variables. Since this selection has to be context-specific and problem-oriented, the perception—self and/or other—of a group as a majority (or minority) is no way a static given. It is the choice of the variables—language, religion, etc.—that one can often observe the distinction between identity and identification, between achievement and ascription and further between self-ascription and other-ascription. For were identity only the Other of Others (Dumont, 1972: 78), then it would "... involve a displacement of self-representation by the Other" (Mayaram, 1997), and be purely ascriptive. There would then be no place for achievement and emotion. And yet we must not forget that the 'Other' can be manipulated by the 'I'; even ascription can be either acquiesced to or rejected by the subaltern voice—or both depending on context. The case discussed above reflects changing ascriptions and achievements which suited the different subjects. Majorities, like minorities, are created by such subjects according to circumstances and choices, depending on the goals pursued. In this case religion or other cultural features were just such variables chosen according to the needs of the hour as perceived by a variety of participants in a broad regional system of power. These variables helped mould inclusiveness just as much as exclusivity. The alternate or even concurrent use of both sets of variables was perhaps, facilitated by the broader framework of an at least formally secular state.

This paper has attempted to illustrate the dynamic relationship between individual and group identities, as well as their floating natures which adapt, assimilate and accommodate to specific situations. The five phases discussed here are partly comparable with the three phases in the formation of the Sikh community identified by for example, Singh (1996); the major difference lies in Singh's and my understanding of the term 'ethnic group'—whereas he appears to consider such an entity a discrete and given unit, my understanding is what Madan (1972: 84) has called 'generative'; that is of an entity which is perpetually trying to define itself—and is being defined—by a delineation of borders.

The study has also tried to show that one cannot talk of group identity without talking of politics. In doing so, it has exemplified Glazer and Moynihan's (1975: 9) observation that ethnicity pairs well with democratic systems; however, it has shown that this 'relatively easy involvement' of the two is not as 'obvious' as Saiyed (1995: 271) seems to suggest it is. It requires a state that not only abdicates its democratic responsibility towards conflict management (also see Phadnis, 1989), but even creates and encourages conflict. In the Indian context it has needed a conscious and determined policy of constructing vote banks on the basis of 'cultural difference', and this is turn has been possible only when individual opportunism and ambition at various levels of the polity have led to the manipulation of 'cultural difference' for personal political ends.

In the example cited in this paper, the ethnographer has, with all the subjectivity her profession entails, simply been lucky enough to be a witness to the flow of identity through various political phases of interaction between sets of we-groups and they-groups, created from within or without. Over the years here she could observe numerous, at times mutually conflicting "... discourses that (were) try(ing) to establish their authority in changing societal configurations" (Van der Veen, 1996: 197). A closer look at other communities and 'ethnic' groups may yield similar results, and afford us more insight into the manipulation of identity and the production and development of processes whereby "... putative homogeneity (is created) out of heterogeneity" (Williams, 1989: 439)—and, I would add, *vice versa*, for collective identities everywhere are a result of both primordial ties and specific historical processes.

Notes

1. This unit must be larger than the nuclear family, but its outer limit is hard to fix, since even a large extended family can operate as a sub-clan.
2. This could bring us tantalisingly close to the much debated questions of the 'Other' and the orientalist discourse, but it is beyond the scope of this paper to discuss these points here.

3. In addition to several weeks spent in the region collecting secondary data, a little over 28 months were spent, partly along with my husband, staying intermittently in the field between 1980 and 1985, and then again in 1991 and 1992 (for details, see Rao, 1997). A brief trip to Jammu and Srinagar in 1994 helped supplement and check on press reports and other information received after 1992. Research between 1982 and 1985 was generously funded by the German Research Council (DFG); the rest was financed by the author herself.
4. A brief survey conducted in 1985 among 20 children (11 F, 9 M) in two private secondary schools in Jammu town showed that these milk-selling Gujar and the Bakkarwal are differentiated by all, though both groups are ranked low in social status. Between them the children mentioned 30 local communities; while all mentioned the Dogras and Brahmins, all but two mentioned the Gujar and six mentioned the Bakkarwal.
5. It is said that around 1891, when he was going through great trouble, Maharaja Pratap Singh sought Babaji Larvi's blessings; he obtained them and things improved, but when he offered Babaji a *jagir* the latter declined.
6. The Sayyed owned the village of Kaghan and all the pastures above it (Hutchinson, 1893; Mason & Paget, n.d.: 6). Following the land settlements of 1869–70, five villages in Kaghan valley belonged to the Sayyed, and five to the Swati (Rev. Hazara, 1876: 153). The latter are originally probably Pashtuns from Swat who in the 16th century fled the in-coming Yusufzai Pashtuns and went to Hazara (McMahon and Ramsey, 1981: 60–63; Barth, 1985: 22–23, 159); their influx into Hazara continued through the 17th and 18th centuries (Ahmed, 1973: 19). At the turn of this century several families belonging to various communities left Hazara for Kashmir; many of their descendants are still influential in Srinagar (cf. e.g., Princes List, 1925: 13).
7. Munnawar Shah was actually a Sayyed landlord in Kanela, near Balakot.
8. Although from 1857 onwards attempts were made by the state to administer these through the office of the *Mahal Nawara*, it was only in 1883 that the first forest laws (*ain-e-janglat*) were passed (K.W.P., 1983: 34). In 1891 the official demarcation of forests began and three years later the *First Forest Regulation for Forest Conservation* was drawn up.
9. The question of 'state subjects' and non-state subjects (*mulki* and non-*mulki* respectively) was raised in the 1920s primarily by Kashmiri *pandits*, in the face of increasing competition from Punjabis who were largely favoured by Maharaja Pratap Singh.

10. The Jammu and Kashmir government's version is that all those who actually lost stock were compensated *via* the local District Magistrates; those (especially from the winter regions of Rajouri and Poonch) who suffered no losses because they had not yet migrated also claimed compensation but were not given any, pending proof of actual losses (pers. comm. District Magistrate, Jammu, March, 1992). Blaming the government and threatening the state was one way of still trying to maintain solidarity within these communities; hence Mohammad Yunus, leader of the Gujjar Students' Federation could tell a reporter "We refuse to be taken for granted as a vote bank any more. There is a lot of anger in our community that the money that is supposed to be spent on rehabilitating our nomads is being stolen by the government. So far we have not joined the angry youth of Kashmir. But, the time isn't far off" (Badhwar, 1989: 43).

References

ABG, 1978, "Representation from the Akhil Bharatiya Gujar Samaj Sudhar Sabha to the Ministry of Home Affairs", Delhi: Government of India, No. BC. 11026/4/78-SCT-IV.

Admn. Note, 1932, "A Brief Note on the Administration of the Jammu and Kashmir State for the Year 1932". London: India Office Records: Official Publications, Administrative Records Jammu and Kashmir V/10/1266.

Ahmed, Akbar S., 1973, *Mansehra: A Journey*, Lahore: Ferozesons Ltd.

Anderson, Benedict, 1983, *Imagined Communities, Reflections on the Origins and Spread of Nationalism*, London: Verson Eds. & NLB.

Anon, 1926, Appendix I to Notes, Newspaper Cutting from "Kashmir", Lahore, 7th April, 1926, London: India Office Records, File No. 264 of 1923 (R/2 Crown Rep's Records Indian States Pt. 1 – Kashmir). R/2 (1067/90).

Ansari, K.H., 1986, "Pan-Islam and the Making of the Early Indian Muslim Socialists", *Modern Asian Studies*, 20(3): 509–37.

Asia Watch, 1991, *Kashmir Under Siege*, New York: Human Rights Watch.

Badhwar, Inderjit, 1989, "Kashmir: Valley of Tears", *India Today*, May 31.

Bailey, F.G., 1963, "Politics and Society in Contemporary Orissa", In C.H. Philipps (ed.) *Politics and Society in India*, London.

Balland, Daniel, 1988, "Nomadic Pastoralists and Sedentary Hosts in the Central and Western Hindukush Mountains, Afghanistan". In, Nigel J.R. Allan, Gregory W. Knapp and Christoph Stadel (eds.), *Human Impact on Mountains*. Totowa: Rowman & Littlefield Publishers.

Banerji, Albion, 1928, Extract from the Jammu and Kashmir Government Gazette, Jammu, Thursday the 15th Bhadon 1985. Appendix II to Notes. London: India Office Records, File No. 264 of 1923 (R/2 Crown Rep's Records Indian States Pt. 1 – Kashmir). R/2 (1067/90).

Banks, Marcus, 1996, *Ethnicity: An Anthropological Construction*, London: Routledge.

Barth, Frederik, 1956, "Ecologic Relationships of Ethnic Groups in Swat, North Pakistan", *American Anthropologist*, 58(6): 1079–89.

——, 1985, *The Last Wali of Swat*. Oslo: Universitetsforlaget AS.

Bashir Ahmad, Mian, 1983, "Mian Bashir Alleges Criminal Callousness towards Hill People", *Kashmir Times*, January 7, 1983.

Beadon-Bryant, F., 1913, *Note on a Tour of Inspection of Some of the Forests of the Kashmir State*, Calcutta: Government of India.

Berreman, Gerald, 1972, "Social Categories and Social Interaction in Urban India", *American Anthropologist*, 74: 567–86.

Bhadarwah, W.P., 1954, Bhadarwah Forest Division, 4th Working Plan 1954/55–1973/74. Government of Jammu and Kashmir.

—— Brass, Paul R., 1974, *Language, Religion, and Politics in North India*. Cambridge: Cambridge University Press.

——, 1979, "Elite Groups, Symbol Manipulation and Ethnic Identity among the Muslims of South Asia". In, David Taylor and Malcolm Yapp (eds.), *Political Identity in South Asia*. London: Curzon Press.

——, 1985, "Ethnic Groups and the State". In, Paul R. Brass (ed.), *Ethnic Groups and the State*. London: Croom Helm.

Casimir, Michael, J., 1991, *Flocks and Food: A Biocultural Approach to the Study of Pastoral Foodways*, Cologne: Bohlau Verlag.

—— and Aparna Rao, 1985, "Vertical Control in the Western Himalayas: Some Notes on the Pastoral Ecology of the Nomadic Bakarwal of Jammu and Kashmir", *Mountain Research and Development* 5(2): 221–232.

——, 1995, "Prestige, Possessions, and Progeny. Cultural Goals and Reproductive Success among the Bakkarwal", *Human Nature*, 6(3): 241–72.

—— forthcoming. Sustainable Herd Management and the Tragedy of No Man's Land: An Analysis of West Himalayan Pastures, Using Remote Sensing Techniques, *Human Ecology*.

Census of India, 1941, *Jammu and Kashmir*. Parts I and II, Vol. XXII. Jammu, 1943.

Cohen, Abner, 1974, "The Lesson of Ethnicity". In, Abner Cohen (ed.), *Urban Ethnicity*. London: Tavistock.

Cohen, Ronald, 1978, "Ethnicity: Problem and Focus in Anthropology", *Annual Review of Anthropology*, 7: 379–403.

Cross, Malcolm, 1978, "Colonialism and Ethnicity: A Theory and Comparative Case Study", *Ethnic and Racial Studies*, 1(1): 37–60.

C.S., 1914a, Letter from the Revenue Minister, His Highness, the Maharaja Sahib Bahadur, Jammu and Kashmir State, Srinagar to the Chief Minister, Jammu and Kashmir State, Srinagar, dated, the 10th of September, 1914 (Liability of Bakarwals crossing over to Gilgit to sell sheep and goats to the Supply and Transport Dept., Gilgit). Jammu: Jammu Archives, C.S. Old Records, File No. 221/A-9 of 1914.

——, 1914b, Letter from the Revenue Minister, Jammu and Kashmir State, Jammu to the Chief Minister Jammu and Kashmir State, Jammu, dated, the 21st June, 1916 (Exclusion of Foreign Bakarwals from Frontier Districts). Jammu: Jammu Archives, C.S. Old Records, File No. 221/A-9 of 1914.

——, 1914c, Copy of a Letter No. 306, dated Jammu, the 21st January, 1916, from the Settlement Commissioner Jammu and Kashmir State to the Revenue Minister, Jammu and Kashmir State (Bakarwals). Jammu: Jammu Archives, C.S. Old Records, File No. 221/A-9 of 1914.

——, 1914d, Telegramm from Abdul Karim Goatman, Bandipura with H.H.'s Order No. 359/m of 126.14 endorsed thereon. Jammu: Jammu Archives, C.S. Old Records, File No. 221/A-9 of 1914.

——, 1914e, Copy of a letter No. 1618, dated 7th December, 1915, from the Wazir Wazarat, Gilgit, to the Settlement Commissioner Jammu and Kashmir State, Jammu. Jammu: Jammu Archives, C.S. Old Records, File No. 221/A-9 of 1914.

——, 1914f, Letter from the Chief Minister Jammu and Kashmir State to the First Assistant to the Resident in Kashmir, Srinagar, dated, Jammu, 21.4.1920. Jammu: Jammu Archives, C.S. Old Records, File No. 221/A-9 of 1914.

——, 1914g, Notification dated, Srinagar, 29th October 1931 and signed by Hari Kishan Kaul, Prime Minister. Jammu: Jammu Archives, C.S. Old Records, File No. 221/A-9 of 1914.

Das, Veena and Nandy, Ashis, 1985, "Violence, Victimhood, and the Language of Silence", *Contributions to Indian Sociology,* 19(1): 177–95.

DE, 1992, "Pahari Board for Whom?" *Daily Excelsior*, March 29, 1992: 3.

Durkheim, Emile, 1914, Le dualisme de la nature humaine et ses conditions sociales, *Scientia*, XV: 206–21.

Engineer, Asghar Ali, 1987, "Ethnic Conflict in South Asia", *Economic and Political Weekly*, XXII(13): 540–42.

Gellner, Ernest, 1981, *Muslim Society*. Cambridge: Cambridge University Press.

Glazer, Nathan and Moynihan, D.P., 1975, "Introduction". In, N. Glazer and D.P. Moynihan (eds.), *Ethnicity: Theory and Experience*. Cambridge: Harvard University Press.

Gupta, Kishori Lal, 1981, Social History of Jammu Province from 1901 to 1961. Jammu: Unpublished PhD Thesis, Jammu University.

Hakla Poonchi, Shamsheer, 1991, Gujjars of the Himalayas. Some Reflections. Paper presented at the Symposium on the Himalayas, Delhi: Jawaharlal Nehru University, December 1991.

Hutchinson, Lt. Col. J.B., 1893, Note No. 105/Camp (14.11.1893) from Officer on Special Duty Kaghan Valley to the Commissioner and Superintendent Peshawar Division. Delhi: Indian National Archives.

Imam Din, 1924, Appeal to the Resident, Kashmir by Imam Din and other Gujar. London: India Office Records, File No. 264 of 1923 (R/2 Crow Rep's Records Indian States Pt. 1 – Kashmir). R/2 (1067/90).

Kaviraj, Sudipta, 1997, "Religion and Identity in India", *Ethnic and Racial Studies,* 20(2): 325–344.

Khatana, Ram Parshad, 1991. Dilemma of the Gujars in Jammu and Kashmir, Paper Presented at the Symposium on the Himalayas, Delhi: Jawaharlal Nehru University, December 1991.

——, 1992. *Tribal Migration in Himalayan Frontiers*. Gurgaon: Vintage Books.

Kishtwar W.P., 1961, Revised Working Plan for Kishtwar Forest Division from S. 2018 to S. 2044 (1961/62–1987/88). Government of Jammu and Kashmir.

Kothari, Rajni, 1985, "Communalism in India: The New Face of Democracy", *Lokayan Bulletin*, 3(3): 3–21.

KWP, 1983, "Revised Working Plan for the Kashmir Forest Division, 1982–83 to 1991–92". Srinagar: Government Press.

Lancaster, C.S., 1974, "Ethnic Identity, History, and 'Tribe' in the Middle Zambezi Valley", *American Ethnologist*, 1(4): 707–30.

Levi-Strauss, Claude, 1966, *The Savage Mind*. Chicago: The Chicago University Press.

Levy, Sydelle Brooks, 1975, "Shifting Patterns of Ethnic Identification among the Hassidim". In, John Bennett (ed.), *The New Ethnicity: Perspectives from Ethnology*, New York: West Published Co.

Loperato, Joseph, 1984. *Human Nature and Biocultural Evolution*. Boston: Allen & Unwin.

Madan, T.N., 1972, "Two Faces of Bengali Ethnicity: Muslim Bengali or Bengali Muslim", *The Developing Economies,* 10(1): 74–85.

——, 1987, "Secularism in its Place", *The Journal of Asian Studies,* 46(4): 747–59.

Manto, Saadat Hasan, 1991, *Partition, Sketches and Stories* (translated from the Urdu by Khalid Hussain). Delhi: Viking.

Mason, A.H. and Paget W.H., n.d. Record of the Expedition against the Tribes of the North-Western Frontier since the Annexation of the Punjab. Delhi: Indian National Archives.

Masud, Muhammad Khalid, 1990, "The Obligation to Migrate: The Doctrine of Hijra in Islamic Law", In, Dale F. Eickelman and James Piscatori (eds.), *Muslim Travellers: Pilgrimage, Migration, and the Religious Imagination*. London: Routledge.

Mauss, Marcel, 1938. Une categorie de l'esprit humain: la notion de Personne, celle de Moi, *Journal of the Royal Anthropological Institute,* 68: 263–82.

Mayaram, Shail, 1997. *Resisting Regimes, Myth, Memory and the Shaping of a Muslim Identity*. Delhi: Oxford University Press.

McMahon, A.H. and Ramsey A.D.G., 1981, Report on the Tribes of Dir, Swat and Bajour together with the Utman-Khel and Sam Ranizai. Peshawar: Saeed Book Bank.

Orywal, Erwin, 1988, "Ethnicity: Conceptual and Methodological Considerations". In, *Le fait ethnique en Iran et en* Afghanistan. Paris: (eds.) Due CNRS.

——, 1996, Krieg als Konfliktaustragungsstrategie – zur Plausibilitat von Kriegsursachentheorien aus kognitionsethnologischer Sicht, *Zeitschrift fur Ethnologie*, 121: 1–48.

Page, David, 1982, *Prelude to Partition. The Indian Muslims and the Imperial System of Control 1920–1932*. Delhi: Oxford University Press.

Pastner, Stephen L., 1984, "Feuding with the Spirit Among the Zikri Baluch: The Saint as Champion of the Despised", In Akbar S. Ahmed and David M. Hart (eds.), *Islam in Tribal Societies. From the Atlas to the Indus*. London: Routledge.

Phadnis, Urmila, 1989, *Ethnicity and Nation-Building in South Asia*. Delhi: SAGE.

Princes List, 1925, List of Ruling Princes, Chiefs and Leading Personages. London: India Office Records L/P & S/20 – B. 275 – Jammu and Kashmir State.

Puri, Balraj, 1987, "Fundamentalism in Kashmir, Fragmentation in Jammu", *Economic and Political Weekly*, XXII(22): 835–37.

Qureshi, M. Naeem, 1979, "The "Ulama" of British India and the Hijrat of 1920", *Modern Asian Studies,* 13(1): 41–59.

Ramban, W.P., 1961, Revised Working Plan for the Ramban Forest Division AD 1961/62–1971/72. Government of Jammu and Kashmir.

Rao, Amiya and Rao, B.G., 1974, *Six Thousand Days. Jawaharlal Nehru, Prime Minister*, Delhi: Sterling Publishers.

Rao, Aparna, 1988a, Entstehung und Entwicklung ethnischer Identitat bei einer islamischen Minderheit in Sudasien. Bemerkungen zur Geschichte der Bakkarwal im Westlichen Himalaya. Berlin: Das arabische Buch (Occasional Paper 18).

——, 1988b, "Levels and Boundaries in Native Models: Social Groupings among the Bakkarwal of the Western Himalayas", *Contributions to Indian Sociology*, 22(2): 195–227.

——, 1990, "Reflections on Self and Person in a Pastoral Community in Kashmir", *Social Analysis. Journal of Social and Cultural Practice* (Special Issue, Person, Myth and Society in South Asian Islam (ed.) Pnina Werbner, 28: 11–25.

——, 1992, "The Constraints of Nature or of Culture? Pastoral Resources and Territorial Behaviour in the western Himalayas". In, M.J. Casimir and A. Rao (eds.), *Mobility and Territoriality: Social and Spatial Boundaries among Foragers, Fishers, Pastoralists and Peripatetics*. Oxford: Berg Publs.

——, 1995, "From Bondsmen to Middlemen: Hired Shepherds and Pastoral Politics", *Anthropos*, 90(1–3): 149–67.

——, 1996, "Die Konstruktion von Schande. Gedanken zur Eskalation eines Konflikts". In, Orywal, Erwin, Aparna Rao, and Michael Bollig (eds.) *Krieg und Kampf: die Gewalt in unseren Kopfen*. Berlin: Reimer Verlag.

——, 1997a, *Autonomy: Life Cycle, Gender, and Status among Himalayan Pastoralists*. Oxford/New York: Berghahn Books.

——, 1997b, "Prestations and Progeny: the Consolidation of Well-being". In, Thomas Schweizer and Douglas R. White (eds.), *Kinship, Networks, and Exchange*. Cambridge: Cambridge University Press.

——, forthcoming. "Blood, Milk, and Mountains: A Native Model of Procreation", In Monika Bock and Aparna Rao (eds.), *Culture, Creation, and Procreation: Concepts of Kinship in South Asian Practice*. Oxford/New York: Berghahn Books (1998).

——, and Michael J. Casimir 1985. "Pastoral Niches in the Western Himalayas (Jammu and Kashmir)", *Himalayan Research Bulletin* IV(2): 6–23.

——, 1987, "Explorations in Man-Environment Interaction in the western Himalayas". In, V.S. Datye, J. Diddee, S.R. Jog, C. Patil (eds.), *Explorations in the Tropics*. Pune: Department of Geography, University of Pune.

——, 1990, "Perspectives on Pastoral Economy and Ecology in the Western Himalayas". In, N.K. Sah, S.D. Bhatt, R.K. Pande (eds.), *Himalaya: Environment, Resources and Development*. Almora: University of Kumaon.

——, forthcoming, "Movements of Peoples: Nomads". In, Veena Das et al. (eds.), *The Oxford Encyclopaedia of Sociology and Social Anthropology*. Delhi: Oxford University Press.

——, and Schneider Irene 1994, Zum Stellenwert von Individuum and Gruppe im Islam. In, Reinhard Kirste et al. (eds.), *Interreligioser Dialog zwishen Tradition und Moderne*. Balve: Zimmermann Druck.

Rao, M.S.A., 1989, "Some Conceptual Issues in the Study of Caste, Class, Ethnicity and Dominance". In, Francine R. Frankel and M.S.A. Rao (eds.), *Dominance and State Power in Modern India. Decline of a Social Order*, Vol. I.: 21–45. Delhi: Oxford University Press.

Reetz, Dietrich, 1997, "In Search of the Collective Self: How Ethnic Group Concepts were Cast through Conflict in Colonial India", *Modern Asian Studies*, 31(2): 285–315.

Rev. Hazara, 1876, Report of the Land Revenue Settlement of the Hazara District of the Punjab 1868–1874, by Capt. E.G. Wace. Lahore: Central Jail Press. London: India Office Records, V/27/314/516.

Robb, Peter, 1997, "The Colonial State and Construction of Indian Identity: An Example on the Northeast Frontier in the 1880s", *Modern Asian Studies*, 31(2): 245–83.

Ruddock, Ralph, 1969, *Roles and Relationship*. London.

SA, 1984, *Statistical Abstracts*. Government of India, N.S. No. 27.

Saiyed, A.R., 1995, *Religion and Ethnicity among Muslims*. Jaipur: Rawat Publication.

Schlesinger, Philip, 1987, "On National Identity: Some Conceptions and Misconceptions Criticized", *Social Science Information*, 26(2): 219–64.

Seneviratne, H.L., 1997, "Identity and the Conflation of Past and Present". In, H.L. Seneviratne (ed.), *Identity, Consciousness and the Past: Forging of Caste and Community in India and Sri Lanka*. Delhi: Oxford University Press.

Sharma, D.C., 1983, *Kashmir under the Sikhs*. Delhi: Seema Publication.

Sharma, N.D., 1984, "Unsigned "Ordinance" irks Jagmohan", *The Indian Express*, 1 October 1984.

Sidhva, Shiraz, 1995, "The Bogeyman", *Frontline*, November 3.

Singh, Gopal, 1996, "Multiculturalism and Ethnic Movements in India: A Study of Sikhs in the Punjab". In, Satish K. Sharma (ed.), *Multi-Culturalism and Ethnicity in Global Context*. Jaipur/Delhi: Rawat Publications.

Singh, Gurharpal, 1995, "The Punjab Crisis since 1984: A Reassessment", *Ethnic and Racial Studies*, 18(3): 476–93.

Sokolovskii, Sergey and Tishkov, Valery, 1996, "Ethnicity". In Alan Barnard and Jonathan Friedman (eds.), *Encyclopedia of Social and Cultural Anthropology*. London: Routledge.

Stein, Aurel (Sir), 1923, Letter, dated August 17, 1923, Mohand Marg, P.O. ganderbal from Sir Aurel Stein to A.C. Lothian 1st Assistant to the Resident in Kashmir. Correspondence Regarding Proposed Removal of Pathan Settlement from Sind Valley. London: India Office Records, File No. 264 of 1923 (R/2 Crown Rep's Records Indian States Pt. 1 – Kashmir). R/2/(1067/90).

Talbot, Cynthia, 1995, "Inscribing the Other, Inscribing the Self: Hindu-Muslim Identities in Pre-Colonial India", *Comparative Study of Society and History*, 37(4): 692–722.

Tapper, Richard L., 1988, "History and Identity among the Shahsevan", *Iranian Studies*, XXI(3–4): 84–108.

Thapar, Romila, 1989, "Imagined Religious Communities", *Modern Asian Studies*, 23(2): 209–31.

Van den Berghe, Pierre, 1975, "Ethnicity and Class in Highland Peru". In, L.A. Despres (ed.), *Ethnicity and Resource Competition in Plural Societies*. Den Hague: Mouton.

Van der Veen, Peter, 1996, *Religious Nationalism. Hindus and Muslims in India*. Delhi: Oxford University Press.

Vinayak, Ramesh, 1994, "The Gujars: Resisting Militancy", *India Today*, June 30.

——, 1996, "Kashmir: Flowing Pipeline", *India Today*, February 15.

Wallman, Sandra (ed.), 1979, *Ethnicity at Work*. London: Macmillan.

Williams, Brackette, 1989, "A Class Act: Anthropology and the Race to Nation across Ethnic Terrain", *Annual Review of Anthropology*, 18: 201–444.

4

Cultural Plurality and Ethnic Closure

Anglo-Indians in Urban South India

LIONEL CAPLAN

The notion of ethnicity has of late generated such an abundance of theorizing that in a recent survey of the literature Banks describes it as a collection of "rather simplistic and obvious statements about boundaries, otherness, goals and achievements, being and identity, descent and classification ... constructed as much by the anthropologist as by the subject" (Banks, 1996: 190). He concludes that the term itself 'stubbornly resists definition' and that it is 'of increasingly limited utility' (Banks, 1996: 10). Moreover, an exclusive concern with ethnicity can overlook other ways in which people may choose to distinguish themselves or others (Banks: 189; see also Fardon, 1987: 171).

In the Indian context, ethnicity—with few notable exceptions (e.g., Brass, 1974)—seems to have attracted comparatively slight attention. This undoubtedly has to do in part with the long-standing emphasis on caste, with its implication of fixed boundaries and internal cultural homogeneity, the very antithesis of ethnicity as a process. Indeed, while the concept of cultural pluralism suggests tolerance for an celebration of diversity,[1] it also presupposes a view of cultures as autonomous and bounded, so that each social unit is seen to possess its own discrete culture, which provides meaning, continuity and normative order to all its members.

The idea of cultures as demarcated and self-perpetuating systems is, of course, part of social anthropology's corpus of received truths, although it has now begun to make room for an image of cultures as diverse and interconnected—a realization sometimes attributed to post-colonial globalization, international migration and advances in communicative technologies. But, if social scientists have recently tended to notice and take account of cultural heterogeneity, it has been a feature of numerous ethnographic settings for a very long time (Friedman, 1991: 111), not least the one I consider in this paper.

Even before the idea of 'pure cultures' began seriously to be questioned, Drummond (1980) had suggested that polyethnic societies (of the kind found in the Caribbean) could better be understood in terms of an approach which eschews cultural fixity and insularity. He adopts a creole metaphor to argue for the notion of a 'cultural continuum' which highlights diversity and internal variation. While other scholars have since utilized the concept of coreolization in different ways, each encourages us to turn aside from the image of 'cultural islands' (Eriksen, 1993).

This paper examines the situation of the Anglo-Indians of Madras (now known as Chennai), South India, who are—like Anglo-Indians throughout the country—the descendants of unions between European males (colonial officials, traders, soldiers, etc.) and local, non-European women. When the focus of interest is a population of mixed racial or ethnic origin, a creolist image provides an appropriate analytical starting point in as much as it directs attention to the historical meeting of disparate social and cultural streams (Hannerz, 1987: 555), to the porosity of cultural as well as social boundaries, and to the heterogeneity of cultural practices within as well as across the lines dividing the constituent groups which comprise the urban social order. I argue that Anglo-Indians, as indeed other groups, may be viewed as a culturally and socially plural population which, at the same time, imagine themselves as discrete communities.

Evolution of an Anglo-Indian Population

The Anglo-Indian population of Chennai city—which today numbers 10,000–15,000—is descended from a medley of different ethnic and racial categories—Indian and European. There has been a Portuguese presence in Chennai (at San Thome) since the early part of the 16th century, making it the first European settlement in the city, and giving rise to a substantial mixed-race population. Some of the earliest marriages of English pastors and soldiers in Fort St. George, established in 1639, were with 'Portuguese' women (i.e., of mixed Portuguese-Indian descent) resident in the Fort after having left San Thome. Portuguese was for a time the lingua franca in the English factory, and the Portuguese influence in Chennai was enhanced by the arrival of kindred populations from Kerala and other parts of India's south-west coast. This legacy is still evident; numerous observers have pointed to the large numbers of Anglo-Indians in South India with Portuguese surnames (for example, Bower, 1939).

During the 17th and 18th centuries British officers and officials employed by the East India Company were much less concerned than were their 19th-century successors about maintaining social distance between themselves and the local populace. The majority are reckoned to have maintained local paramours, due largely to the official encouragement of concubinage through the restriction of access to the colonies by European women (Stoler, 1989). One result of this 'colonial desire' (Young, 1995) was the further enhancement of the existing Eurasian population.

Men belonging to other European communities (e.g., Armenian, Dutch, French, Flemish, Prussian, Spanish and Italian) also found their way to Chennai in a variety of capacities and, like the Portuguese and British, established liaisons with local women, or with the offspring of previous Euro-Indian unions. Contemporary Anglo-Indians thus stem from a diversity of European forebears on the paternal side and—we have to assume, since the literature is almost totally silent on the topic—from an even greater heterogeneity of Indian antecedents on the maternal side. In their few references to these Indian forebears Anglo-Indian leaders have tended to stress the legitimacy of the unions and the worthy, even distinguished family backgrounds of these women. When John Ricketts came to Britain in 1830 to plead the Anglo-Indian cause before parliament he was asked at one point about 'the native mothers of East Indians' (as the Anglo-Indians were then called) and replied that in Bengal "the greater proportion of them are Mohomedans of respectable families, but in reduced circumstances" (Ricketts, 1831: 53; see also Anthony, 1969: 12; Weston, 1939: 145).[2]

By contrast, the British who claimed to know the community were usually scornful to these female ancestresses and of the legality of their unions. One early observer referred to the 'unmatrimonial connections' in which they were involved, and insisted that they were "often sold to their masters by their needy relatives" (Bevan, 1839: 18–19). Others were disdainful of these women, as they were of the 'poor whites' who partnered them. For Penny "the British solider of bygone days was a rough, illiterate man, possessing his full share of animalism. He chose his mate from the lowest women ..." (1908: 143).

With the arrival in India of growing numbers of women from Britain during the course of the 19th century,[3] the frequency of unions involving men within the dominant sectors of colonial society and both Indian and Eurasian women dropped dramatically, although subsequent political developments which brought large waves of both official and non-official British personnel into the country encouraged a resumption of these contacts. A number of Anglo-Indians I know in Chennai are the children or grandchildren of British railwaymen or soldiers who came out to India and married or cohabited with Anglo-Indian women. Other kinds of population influx have added further to the social heterogeneity of the community. Thus, a small number of Chinese men who found their way to Chennai earlier this century married into the Anglo-Indian community, as have more recently arrived students from various parts of Africa. Though, officially, their offspring are not Anglo-Indians—only descendants in the male line of European men are so designated[4]—in everyday local settings they are readily absorbed into and regard as members of the community.

Some authors detect a hierarchy among Anglo-Indians based on colonial descent in the male line. Gist and Wright (1973: 87) report that families with English surnames 'achieve a modicum of prestige' vis-à-vis other Eurasians, and that it is not unusual therefore for Portuguese surnames to be anglicized.[5] This is not the case of Chennai. Although a few names are given an English pronunciation (e.g., 'Rodrigues' is spoken as 'Rodericks'), the great majority of those with non-English surnames have shown no inclination to alter them. Indeed, many if not a majority of the most prominent Anglo-Indians in the city today carry Portuguese or other non-English names. As one man, aware of the attempts on the part of some Anglo-Indian national leaders (see Anthony, 1969: 371) to imply a hierarchy, countered with his own:

> The Europeans (i.e., those with Portuguese or Spanish ancestry) were traders rather than soldiers. They were fairly well-to-do. They weren't 'Tommies'. Since Independence, the European-descended have been doing well.

Occasionally, a cultural difference between what one man referred to as 'West Coast' (i.e., Portuguese-descended) and 'Tomy' (British-descended) Anglo-Indians might be asserted: he described the former as conservative and successful, the latter as 'pleasure-seeking'. But whenever such distinctions were articulated—usually in response to some real or imagined insult addressed to those with non-English surnames—speakers would be quick to point out that in Chennai there is no antagonism between those descended from different originally male ancestors because "they're much too mixed up together", i.e., heavily inter-married. In such a setting the division can have no social reality, but remains rhetorical.

Infiltration and Evaporation

The Anglo-Indian community in Chennai, as elsewhere in India, thus originated from the unions of a variety of European progenitors and local women. Since its inception, moreover, Anglo-India's boundaries have remained permeable, as many people 'evaporated' from the community and others 'infiltrated' into it. On the one side, it is argued that thousands were lost during the colonial era as they passed themselves off as Europeans (see Thurston, 1898; Anthony, 1969: 170ff; Arnold, 1979: 106), while on the other, perhaps just as many—Goans, Indian

Christians, even, it was claimed, liberated slaves—by virtue of having a European name and donning European clothes, "were changed overnight from Indians ... into Eurasians" (Staines, 1986: 88; see also Stark, 1936: 128; Anthony, 1969: 116).

Such ingress is explained by the employment opportunities available to Anglo-Indians on the railways, telegraphs, customs and other areas of the economy from about the mid-19th century, and the benefits they enjoyed in educational and charitable institutions run for Anglo-Indians from the end of the century. The magazine of the Anglo-Indian Association of Southern India gave frequent coverage to the subject. In one editorial, entitled 'The Invasion' (27 June 1917), it suggested that 'entrances into the Anglo-Indian camp' were 'wide open': at least 50 per cent of the pupils of so-called European Orphanages and 'Poor Schools', it insisted, belonged to the lowest castes. The editorial urged the community to be vigilant. A few months later (31 October 1917), it returned to the subject, this time expressing the view that "infiltration is an evil more prevalent in the (Madras) Presidency than elsewhere, which has done more than anything to bring the community into disrepute". At one point, the magazine blamed the Missionaries who had "admitted thousands of children and adults to baptism under assumed names ..." (28 August 1918). many of Anglo-India's 'social ills' were ascribed to infiltration (Dover, 1937: 115).[6]

Official concern about infiltration is still occasionally expressed, although the employment privileges enjoyed by Anglo-Indians during colonial times are no longer available to members of the community. But, the recent decision of the Tamil Nadu government to grant 'free' education to Anglo-Indian pupils attending Anglo-Indian schools, and its decree that either parent can confer this identity on the child, which contradicts the existing constitutional definition stressing only paternal descent, has provided some opportunities for further 'incursions'. This becomes evident when the question of marriage outside the community is considered.

Despite their disparate ancestry, the descendants of the original Eurasian offspring inter-married mainly among themselves. Yet, even during the late 19th and early 20th centuries—as the line dividing European and Eurasian hardened—it was not unheard of for girls from better Anglo-Indian families to marry into British official and military hierarchies, as well as with men of the domiciled European population (Hawes, 1993: 77, 81; Naidis, 1963: 421; Arnold, 1983: 153).[7] At the other end of the Anglo-Indian class spectrum, girls frequently formed unions with European men who had come out to India to work on the railways or other sectors of the economy, as well as with ordinary British soldiers; indeed, many of the girls raised in orphanages were sought out as partners by British men in the ranks (Roberts, 1835/I: 109). Hawes (1993) has shown how widespread these relationships were in the early 19th century, and there is evidence that they persisted throughout the colonial period, despite official discouragement at the beginning of this century (Hyam, 1986). As already noted, there are numerous Anglo-Indian families in Chennai today which are descended from British railwaymen who came to India late 19th century or at the beginning of the 20th century, and others whose progenitors were soldiers brought to the country during or between the world wars; both categories married or cohabited with Anglo-Indian women.

With the end of the British rule, a number of Anglo-Indian women from elite families, well-educated and in secure jobs, have turned increasingly to better-off non-Anglo-Indians as marriage partners—mainly but not exclusively Indian Christians—whom they meet at work, in church, or at university. Girls from somewhat less affluent sections of the community, with a modicum of education and reasonable employment prospects, look for partners within the Anglo-Indian population who they deem can support a family. A high incidence of male joblessness and casual, low-paid employment among Anglo-Indians at this class level means that such men, with few prospects of marriage to better-educated and better-employed Anglo-Indian girls, are compelled to seek partners—legal or casual—with low caste non-Anglo-Indian women from equally impoverished households. Occasionally, though not nearly so frequently as the men, Anglo-Indian women from the poorest families marry or cohabit with non-Anglo-Indian men from the same social level—the 'rickshaw class', one Anglo-Indian leader scathingly termed it—whom these women invariable meet in the slum neighbourhoods they inhabit. The children of all such marriages are now deemed eligible for free education in Anglo-Indian schools by the Tamil Nadu government.

While the great majority of Anglo-Indians—especially within the middle or artisan class—have all along married among themselves, and continue to do so, the impression sometimes given by Anglo-Indian leaders today is that the practice in Chennai (and other urban centres of India) of marrying outside the community has reached crisis proportions, and after emigration is the single greatest cause of the community's gradual and inevitable 'disappearance'. My guess, based on the genealogies of households I visited, is that between one-third and one-half of poor Anglo-Indian families—and probably a similar range among the well-to-do have—at last one member who is married to or cohabits with someone outside the community.

Whatever the frequency of these unions, infiltrations and evaporations, what seems evident is that the boundaries separating Anglo-Indians from the British on the one side, and 'Indians' on the other, were and continue to be extremely porous and, at both ends of the class spectrum, easily and frequently traversed.

Cultural Pluralism

The permeability of borders is reflected in the cultural sphere as well. The diversity of Anglo-Indian backgrounds and the influences encroaching on the community from all sides— European and Indian—gave rise to a creolized culture. There were and are, to be sure, certain lifeways—usually exaggerated by stereotype—which the British in colonial days and other Indians today regard(ed) as quintessentially Anglo-Indian—English speech, European dress codes and food preferences, Christian religion, freedom of marriage choice, penchant for western music and dancing, etc. Even members of the community themselves, when asked what distinguishes them from other Indians, identify as specially Anglo-Indian some if not all of these very features as emblematic of their culture.

Without denying the salience of this perception of cultural specificity and closure, closer examination reveals, on the one hand, a considerable plurality of practice within the community itself, and, on the other, a greater or lesser degree of continuity with the practices found in other groups within the urban milieu. Distinctions of class and status within the Anglo-Indian fold provide a rough basis for these cultural distinctions, though not the only one. The Anglo-Indian population of Chennai today, as in the past, consists of a small elite (professionals, businessmen, civil servants), a large, struggling 'middle class' of skilled technicians and artisans formerly employed in the railways, telegraphs and customs, and, latterly, within the industrial labour force in the city, and a substantial category of unskilled and poorly educated people in low-paid, part-time employment or without work altogether.

The link between class position and cultural practice has certainly been acknowledged within the Anglo-Indian fold for some time. In a letter to the magazine of the Anglo-Indian Association of Southern Indian in April 1917, one correspondent suggested that the community is divided into those who, at one end (the well-to-do), "are practically European, or approximate the European standard in appearance, manners, customs" and, at the other end (the poor), "who practically or closely approximate to the (equally impoverished) Indian standard", and are, he suggested, "in the process of adaptation to the (local Tamil) environment". His third category, designated simply as 'between the two', implied those belonging to the middle or artisan class within the community whose practices were and are more quintessentially (or stereotypically) Anglo-Indian.

But at all levels of the Anglo-Indian community cultural influences from the wider society were present during the colonial era and have grown even more evident since independence. Take the matter of English, one of the 'resonant practices and characteristics' (Thomas, 1992: 215), through which Anglo-Indian distinctiveness, is perceived. The majority of Anglo-Indians usually differentiate themselves from other Indians and indeed from other 'mixed-race' populations in the country by insisting that only they speak English as a first language. Despite their diverse origins, English had early on become their mother tongue, the language in which they study, worship and communicate with one another. The high quality of their English is attested to, they insist, by the demand for Anglo-Indian women as secretaries and telephonists in the top companies.

Even my own linguistically untrained ear could detect a range of abilities, largely—though not entirely—coincident with the speaker's education and class position. Among those who had been to university and move in business and social circles where English is the language of communication, the standard and mode of expressions are little different from that ordinarily found at such levels anywhere in the country. This also points, of course, to the existence for over a century and a half of an English-speaking, westernized Indian elite outside the Anglo-Indian fold.

Anglo-Indians belonging to the artisan class, with only an average amount of schooling, spoke and still speak a distinctive kind of local Anglo-Indian English, with characteristic modes of expression, inflection, slang and humour. Indeed, it was this brand of English which the British in India came to stigmatize and to ridicule. Writing in the first half of the 19th century, Roberts found Anglo-Indian pronunciation 'short and disagreeable', though she conceded that it was not "so completely barbarized as in America" (1835: 42–43). It is this 'distinct variant' of English which Maher regards as an 'Indian language' (1962: 25).

Nearly ninety years ago, the magazine of the Anglo-Indian Association of Southern India (29 April 1918) commented on the poor standard of English spoken among impoverished Anglo-Indian children, and attributed this to the "influence of Indian associates and environment, as a result of which (the) vernacular idiom is translated literally into English speech". At the lower end of the class spectrum, where low-income Anglo-Indians still live alongside the poor of other ethnic groups, opportunities for learning and speaking English have, if anything, receded. Where Anglo-Indians have married outside the community the language of the household is almost invariably Tamil. In such neighbourhood contexts even verbal interactions between Anglo-Indians can be conduced largely in the vernacular. In the course of a long conversation (in English) with a poor Anglo-Indian woman (who had married a Tamilian), we were briefly interrupted by the arrival of her Anglo-Indian sister-in-law and neighbour. They proceeded to talk to one another in a mixture of Tamil and English, and when I pointed this out after the visitor had left, my hostess shrugged and said: "Tamil comes easier; I speak to my children in Tamil although they also know a little English". In such contexts, Anglo-Indian English vocabulary and syntax are extremely limited. In homes where the mother is Tamilian and the father Anglo-Indian, children have even fewer opportunities to learn English. I was told by several head teachers in Anglo-Indian schools in Madras that not a few of their pupils from such homes arrive unable to speak English at all. Indeed, I have visited a number of such families and met children with popular Anglo-Indian names like Royston, Christopher, Jennifer and Vanessa who speak only Tamil.

If other Anglo-Indian cultural practices are considered, a similar diversity of behaviour is evident among members of the community, as well as significant overlaps with those outside. Thus, for example, the 'stereotypical' Anglo-Indian diet based, it is often claimed, on 'traditional English fare', turns out in practice to be a medley of 'East' and 'West', custards and curries—as it has been for some time (see Bell, 1812: 100; Maher, 1962: 18; Caplan, 1995).

In matters of dress, too, there are influences from outside the community, and varieties of practice within. Many Anglo-Indians adopted European costume during colonial times, including the pith helmet by men in the employ of government, which was "powerful community symbol of the British in India" (DeCaro and Jordan, 1984: 239). On formal occasions, such as weddings and dances, men who can afford to do so still tend to wear western suits and ties—I felt very undressed when I showed up at one wedding in a 'safari suit'. But for everyday occasions in a modern city like Chennai they dress no differently from anyone else—in light trousers, shirts and sandals. At home it is not yet common but by no means unusual for Anglo-Indian men to wear a *lungi*, and when I came to people's homes I was sometimes asked to wait while my host changed into something more appropriate in which to receive a guest.

Anglo-Indian women also assumed European fashions in dress; in the official company history of Binny's Ltd., one of the largest employers of Anglo-Indian women in the city, we are told that Anglo-Indian secretaries wore "long dresses or skirts ... no sari was to be seen" (DeSouza, 1970: 217). Most older women in the artisan or middle class persist in wearing frocks even today, while younger women, if they are employed outside the home, now increasingly alternate between dress at home or in church and sari at work.

But at both ends of the class spectrum more permanent changes are occurring. Among the well-to-do, where women are more likely to have married out of the community, and/or to work and mix socially with non-Anglo-Indians, there is a greater tendency to adopt the sari as the primary mode of dress for most formal occasions, while *tikkas* (or *pottu* in Tamil) on the forehead, and flowers in the hair—once regarded as the preserve of Hindu women—are increasingly worn as well. Younger women from such families follow the fashions of their school or university peers, which include the *churidar* or *salwar kamiz* (matching trousers and long tunics popular in North India) or even the western 'maxi' rather than the kinds of calf-length, fitted frocks with short sleeves favoured by most older Anglo-Indian women.

Increasingly, too, Anglo-Indian women of all ages from well-to-do families have access to television and, especially, cable channels, which show popular soap operas from abroad, and make them aware of global fashions. As the proprietor of a tailoring establishment which caters to women of all communities put it, "there is only one fashion these days; everyone wants the same".

Among the poorest Anglo-Indians, resident in slum colonies, the sari is now quite commonly worn, and I would imagine was in evidence in colonial days as well. Since they interact principally with poor Tamilians, as neighbours, workmates and domestic partners, they adopt many of the everyday cultural practices of their surroundings, including the mode of apparel. Some also mentioned as a reason for eschewing dresses the wish to avoid the jibes and hostile comments often directed at women whose dress exposes their legs.

The increasing, though differentially experienced, influences from the wider Indian society on Anglo-Indian lifeways raise important questions about the 'authenticity' of practices found among the least well-off sections of the community. I was frequently told that "the poor have lost their culture", that they are not able "to live like real Anglo-Indians". Brennan quotes an Anglo-Indian leader in Chennai bemoaning the lost identity of the poor who have "no shoes, no shirts ... no furniture ... speaking Tamil ..." (1979: 108). The late president of the All-India Anglo-Indian Association viewed those occupying the lowest stratum as somehow "not assimilated to the way of life and the attributes of the community" (Anthony, 1969: 372–73). Remarks of this kind grow out of an assumption that there is an agreed set of practices together adding up to a coherent Anglo-Indian lifestyle, which the poor somehow fail to live up to. They cannot or do not speak, dress, eat, marry or otherwise behave in the manner regarded as appropriate for Anglo-Indians. They are, in effect, left with no 'culture', although they may "have in their mind the acceptable Anglo-Indian style of life" (Brennan, 1979: 133). Such a view seems to insist on the notion of cultural homogeneity within clearly defined ethnic units, and those who do not approximate this lifestyle are either deemed to be excluded from the group or to be less than full members of it. It may be that the poor 'have in their minds' a more agreeable lifestyle modelled on that of better-off Anglo-Indians, and if they were middle class might very well adhere to it; but they are not. Nonetheless, they are themselves not without particular lifeways, even if these are largely shaped by their poverty and more than superficially influenced by their non-Anglo-Indian surroundings (Caplan, *forthcoming*). Theoretically, it seems to me, we need an approach which allows for a heterogeneous range of cultural practices both within and across the lines dividing ostensibly distinct groups.

I have stressed the growing impression of the wider Indian social and cultural environment on Anglo-Indian practices, both during the colonial period, and especially after it. But influences have gone and continue to go the other way as well, mainly through the medium of Anglo-Indian schools. Very soon after the establishment of these institutions—then known as European schools—in the 1880s, for the benefit of European and Eurasian children, Indian parents outside these two communities came to value their high standards and the benefits of an English education. But, the numbers of non-Europeans and non-Eurasians admitted were severely restricted until well into the 20th century when, for reasons mainly to do with the precarious financial position of these schools, a growing proportion of pupils allowed to attend were from that part of the Indian public able to pay fees.

D'Souza (1976: 285) provides figures which suggest that, by 1937, 30–40 per cent of pupils in Anglo-Indian schools (they had been renamed in 1932) were from outside the target communities. After independence, these schools were only allowed to continue as a separate system if they agreed to admit up to 50 per cent of their children from other communities (Roy, 1974: 59). In Tamil Nadu, where there are over forty such schools, the average enrolment of Anglo-Indian pupils (as of 1990) was only 15–22 per cent, and in some schools the proportion was as low as 1–3 per cent (Ignatius, 1990). To the dismay of many Anglo-Indian educationists and leaders, many of these schools have, in effect, become institutions for the education of well-to-do members of the Indian public on whom their financial viability depends.

The impact of these schools on non-Anglo-Indians educated in them is not readily measurable. But, the combination of English language, a westernized ethos, instruction by European teachers in the pre-independence period and by Anglo-Indian teachers (at least in the lower grades) since, emphasis on competitive sport, etc., adds up to an educational environment which encourages a cosmopolitan outlook and serves, in the view of some observers, to "dismantle or modify some of the barriers that separate Anglo-Indians from (other) Indians" (Roy, 1974: 59). Meeting and talking to former pupils of such schools, it is apparent that they share (mostly pleasant) memories, along with certain speech habits and even kinds of humour. Many close friendships (some of which later became relationships of affinity) were forged across the ethnic divide, and often persist into adulthood. Members of other communities who attended such schools often describe themselves as 'Anglo-Indianized', a recognition of the profound influence on their lives and lifeways of exposure to many aspects of Anglo-Indian cultural values and practices.

Creation of Community

I have portrayed the social and cultural world in which the Anglo-Indians of Chennai have emerged and survived to this day as one best described as creolized; where metaphors of continuity and gradation more accurately reflect their urban environment than those of separation and immutability. Yet whatever the realities of their own hybridized society and culture,

Anglo-Indians have all along sought to delineate clear and unequivocal lines of community, although these have not always been consistent or universally agreed. Moreover, during the colonial period, to a significant extent they reflected and responded to the categorizations of the British rulers. This final section identifies some of the processes involved in asserting the integrity of community.

In the early period of East India Company rule, distinctions between British and Indians were ill-defined and of little apparent consequence. The British helped to create and, for a time, accommodated a population of Eurasians in their midst. For a complex of reasons this willingness on the part of many Europeans to disregard racial and ethnic barriers ceased in the early part of the 19th century. The British in India—taking their cue from metropolitan discourses—soon delineated a notion of racial purity which in no uncertain terms excluded hybrid groups like the Anglo-Indians.

The response of leading Anglo-Indians, which persisted throughout much of the colonial period, was to insist on continued identification—biological and cultural—with the dominant group. The campaign at the beginning of this century to alter the community's official designation from 'East Indian' or 'Eurasian' to 'Anglo-Indian'—the term by which the ruling British in India had previously been known—was largely meant to emphasize this affiliation (Anthony, 1969: 2).[8] The notion of 'British blood' running in Anglo-Indian veins was a recurrent theme in this rhetoric. "We are people with British blood, ideals, habits, sympathies ..." (Warden, 1915: 9). One of Anglo-India's foremost historians entitled one of his books, dealing with Anglo-Indian fidelity to the rulers during the Sepoy 'Mutiny', *Call of the Blood* (Stark, 1932), and a more recent account of that event continues to explain the community's loyalty to the British in terms of its "ties of blood, language, dress and habits ..." (Anthony, 1969: vi, 17). The magazine of the Anglo-Indian Association of Southern India constantly referred in its editorials during World War I to kinship with and so the inevitability of support for the British: as one editorial phrased it, "Anglo-Indians cannot help being loyal to Great Britain, simply because their blood is British". Indeed, marriages between Anglo-Indians and

British were regarded by some as 'endogamous' unions, to be distinguished from those outside the fold (Anthony, 1969: 8).

Even today occasional references about blood ties emanate from older members of the community, but there are also jokes told against the kind of Anglo-Indian who, when offered a life-saving transfusion in hospital, expresses concern about the dilution of his 'British blood'. Such attitudes were not *sui generis*, as Sir Henry Gidney, president of the All-India Anglo-Indian Association between the wars pointed out, in 'earlier days' the Anglo-Indians "were looked upon and treated (by the colonial government) in most matters as British ..." (1925: 66).[9]

The stress on British descent, of course, ignored the diversity of European paternal links and, even more significantly, the community's Indian 'roots' on the maternal side. The tendency among those who spoke for or about the community was to deny maternal ancestry and culture. Indian art, music, philosophy, literature and religion were disregarded by or at best 'of limited interest' to members of the community (Gist, 1967: 205; also Hawes, 1993: 265). Carsten has recently considered the significance of 'forgetting' in the construction of identity, and points to the 'negative significance' of knowledge which is not passed on—in this case, about female ancestral ties—thereby allowing "other images of shared identity ... to come to the fore" (1995: 317–18).

Part of the process of stressing kinship on only one side was reflected in Anglo-Indian attitudes to local languages. Since English as their first language in part defined them as Anglo-Indian, many would insist (sometimes with a hint of pride) that they have no aptitude for Tamil. Before independence there would have been less incentive to acquire more than a passing facility in the language; some Anglo-Indians who are old enough to remember pre-colonial times suggest that in those days they needed only enough Tamil to "communicate with servants, traders and rickshaw drivers", as one woman phrased it. Another recalled that during her childhood if she or her siblings were heard to speak in the vernacular at home her grandmother would shout "who's talking in Tamil?" On one occasion during fieldwork a native Tamil speaker recalled that before independence he was always bemused (and not a little amused) by the 'deliberately childish' Tamil cultivated by many Anglo-Indians precisely, he though, in order to underline who they were (and were not).[10]

Nowadays, Anglo-Indians—of all ages and classes—speak colloquial Tamil with increasing facility, can enjoy Tamil cinema and television, and employ the language more and more in everyday contexts outside the home. One couple laughingly told me that while they usually speak English to one another, they quarrel in Tamil! Young Anglo-Indians are nowadays more aware of the necessity of acquiring a solid foundation in the 'high' Tamil taught at school, and teachers report that school children are increasingly able to cope with the lofty standards demanded in the Tamil syllabus.

Despite these persistent attempts to claim kinship and cultural identity with the British, already by the end of the 18th century official attitudes and policies towards Eurasians, which had previously encouraged and accommodated their emergence, changed dramatically. A series of discriminatory orders by the East India Company restricted their educational opportunities and excluded them from all superior and covenanted offices in the civil and military services, as well as making them ineligible for most subordinate public employments. Anglo-Indian writers have unanimously identified these regulations as responsible for depriving their people of 'every honourable career' and of reducing them to the "status of a proscribed and down-trodden race" (Stark, 1936: 59; Weston, 1939: 103–4).

In course of time, other policies alternately favoured and patronized, or disadvantaged and discriminated against them, according as how the authorities gauged British political interests. Like other populations occupying 'contradictory colonial locations', the Anglo-Indians were "subject to a frequently shifting set of criteria that allowed them privilege at certain historical moments and pointedly excluded them at others" (Stoler, 1989: 154). In the case of the Anglo-Indians both sets of criteria seemed to operate simultaneously. As numerous writings by and about Anglo-Indians have pointed out, they were classified as both 'Statutory Natives of India' and 'European British Subjects'. The former was meant to deny them the occupational privileges of the Europeans, which they had for a time enjoyed, and to ensure that they only had access to the same occupational chances as were granted to other local peoples. The president of the All-India Anglo-Indian Association, however, was to complain that Anglo-Indians had been effectively excluded from the process of Indianization following the reforms of the 1920s, so that, in practice, for employment purposes they were still regarded as 'aliens to India' (Gidney, 1934: 33). The status of 'European British Subject', on the other hand, was conferred mainly to enable the ruling power to call on Anglo-Indians to provide additional internal security in times of need. They were recruited into the Indian Volunteer Force[11] and later, as a condition of employment on the railways, into its successor, the Auxiliary Force, from which other (non-European and non-Anglo-Indian) railway employees were excluded. Among other things, the Force was meant to help in any 'emergency or nationalist uprising' and, when called upon to do so, keep the railways running during strikes (Sanyal, 1930: 307; Heathcote, 1974: 74–75; Arnold, 1979: 112).

If official policies placed them in an ambiguous location between European and native Indian, unofficial British attitudes towards Anglo-Indians were, with few exceptions, unequivocally hostile. Nineteenth century journals and memoirs kept by British residents or visitors in India make evident the growth of social prejudice and intolerance towards Anglo-Indians (see Steuart, 1913; Dyson, 1978). While taught at first to consider themselves British, Anglo-Indian claims and attempts to be just that were apparently the "cause of mirth and scorn in European social gatherings throughout India" (Minto, 1974: 51; see also Clarke, 1878: 33). Narayanan (1986: 88) has also observed that in the novels written by British in India, the Eurasian's 'greatest fault' was his 'presumptuous efforts to appear like the English".

Such exclusionary policies and attitudes on the part of both official and unofficial British undoubtedly led to the realization by Anglo-Indian elites that they were regarded as a separate—and inferior—group, and encouraged them to think of themselves as a distinct social entity (see Goodrich, 1952; Grimshaw, 1958). But it is doubtful if Anglo-Indian self-awareness was due entirely to British rejection of their claims to be included in the European fold. The evolution of a largely intra-marrying population—despite the number of 'external' unions at both ends of the class spectrum—served to create primary, multiplex bonds within a restricted social universe, and to reinforce notions of a shard past and common lifeways. One very thoughtful and articulate member of the community, who had read some of the social science literature arguing that only British repudiation of Anglo-India compelled it to turn inward, insisted that "from the very beginning we've had to reflect on who we are, what we are. You had this debate going on, a group of people trying to make sense of their common experiences". From at least the early 19th century those who spoke for Anglo-India began to assert the existence of a discrete social body and demand acknowledgement of its claims. Thus, the anonymous author of a 'Petition of the Indo-Britons of Calcutta' (1829) prefaced it with a statement that "... the petitioners are members of a numerous, increasing and widely dispersed class (who) form a distinct class of society in British India, which dates from the time when the Company first formed permanent establishments on the continent ..." (1829: 471). At around the same time, John Ricketts, a leading Calcutta Eurasian, visited the UK to present a petition on behalf of the community in that city and appear before select committees of the British Parliament, which was enquiring into the affairs of the East India Company before renewing its charter in 1833. Ricketts drew attention to the status anomalies of Anglo-Indians, their legal and economic disabilities and the "invidious distinctions which mark them, in the land of their birth, as outcasts and aliens, bereft of all privileges ..." (1831: 34; also Skipton, 1912: 18).[12]

Growing self-awareness was not confined to Calcutta, which at the time had the largest population of Anglo-Indians. According to a report in *The Asiatic Journal*, a petition was also drawn up at a meeting of 'East Indians' in Madras held on 23rd December, 1831 "similar in effect to that prepared by the same class at Calcutta" and was "forwarded to the Calcutta East Indian Committee for transmission to England" (Madras Mail, 1886: 32).[13]

A few decades later (1848) the Anglo-Indians of Madras presented a 'Testimonial' to the outgoing Governor, Lord Tweddale, publicly thanking him for his efforts on their behalf, and especially for the fact that 'new sources of employment' had been opened to them in 'the uncovenanted and other branches of the service' under Tweddale's administration. The document was signed by just under 1,300 Anglo-Indians, a not inconsiderable sign of community organization.[14]

These and other similar activities suggest that already in the early 19th century Anglo-Indians were conscious of themselves as a distinctive group with particular interests, even if these were only articulated on an ad-hoc basis. Very soon, however, these concerns were to be formally addressed through the creation in 1876 of 'The Eurasian and Anglo-Indian Association' in Calcutta (later to become the All-India Anglo-Indian Association, based in Delhi), followed soon after (1879) by 'The Eurasian Association' (later the Anglo-Indian Association of Southern India), based in Madras. Indeed, as early as 1829, there were reports in the *Asiatic Journal* that arrangements were in hand to establish an 'East Indian Association' in Madras, and that a committee had already been appointed to frame rules for such an organization (Madras Mail, 1886: 5). While these two main Associations did not invariably see eye to eye on many matters (see Renford, 1979)—even today, they are divided on a range of issues—they were and can be seen to be representing the community's diverse interests to government and in the wider society. Thus, the campaigns to change the community's official designation from 'Eurasian' to 'Anglo-Indian', the efforts to mitigate the effects of the government's reform policies following World War I which encouraged 'Indianization' and was thus seen to threaten Anglo-Indian privileges in certain sectors of the employment market, and the attempts to secure for Anglo-Indians some measure of recognition and protection under the Constitution of independent India are all well known in the community and outside (see Gidney, 1934: 33; Anthony, 1969: 195ff; Grimshaw, 1958: 234).

In Chennai, both Associations[15] have for some time now been important channels of access to state benefits such as free or subsidized schooling, since they are frequently required by the authorities to attest to a person's Anglo-Indian credentials (which entitles them, for example, to education in Anglo-Indian schools). Nowadays, the Associations also have control of substantial funds to help community members in need. Indeed, the confinement of philanthropic efforts to Anglo-Indians by these and other organizations established for charitable purposes in the city may be viewed as a commitment to community, a means by which the limits of the 'moral universe' are set, and within which mutual trust between donor and recipient obtains (Werbner, 1990: 306).

Of late, the two Associations have been at loggerheads over the question of seeking 'backward' status for the community—with the All-India body opposed and the South Indian body in favour (see Caplan, *forthcoming*). Anglo-Indians who are not closely involved in these and other disputes sometimes despair at what they see as the irreparable divisions in the community and the constant squabbling of its leaders. All other communities, they sometimes insist, are united in their efforts to promote the interests of their members, but not the Anglo-Indians despite the fact that they are only a 'microscopic' group. Indeed, the joke they most commonly tell about themselves compares Anglo-Indians to a basket of crabs which, if one of their number seeks to climb out, is 'pulled down' by the others. However, these controversies seem to me to attest to active, vigorous community institutions which, if disparate in their aims and ambitions, nonetheless are equally focused on a common social entity over and within which they struggle, which serves ultimately to reinforce the notion of a coherent, identifiable community of Anglo-Indians.

Conclusion

Recent anthropological interest in creole societies and cultures suggests both a growing appreciation of ethnographic realities fostered by global interconnectedness, and an awareness that existing theoretical models which presuppose chaste cultures within clear ethnic boundaries are no longer adequate. An approach, such as that suggested by Glissant (1989), which allows us to regard as unexceptional the idea of cultures as heterogeneous and hybridized, seems a more appropriate starting point for considering India's rapidly changing urban milieux. With this in mind I have tried to indicate the complex cultural gradations to be found within the Anglo-Indian population of Chennai over the past two centuries, and the difficulty, to paraphrase one Anglo-Indian writer (Stark, quoted in Bower, 1939: 119–20), of knowing where the culture begins and where it ends. In this respect, 'cultural pluralism' denotes heterogeneity of beliefs and practices within as well as across the lines dividing the urban population. While the imprint of the dominant British group on Anglo-Indian lifeways was understandably paramount during the colonial period, cultural influences from the surrounding 'Indian' society were never absent, and have grown even more apparent since independence. But, the flow has not been only one way, as members of other communities inter-marry with Anglo-Indians and some of the relatively affluent educated in Anglo-Indian schools declare themselves 'Anglo-Indianized'.

Despite the social and cultural flux within and between these disparate groups, making their frontiers porous and traversable, assertions of ethnic closure and integrity have been a feature of Anglo-Indians since at least the early 19th century. Two principal ethnic strategies have been evident: one, pre-eminent during the colonial period, affirmed the boundary distinguishing Anglo-Indians from the generality of the Indian population, on the one side, and denied any such demarcation between themselves and the colonial rulers, on the other. In denying and contesting, unsuccessfully as it turned out, the borders erected by the colonizers, Anglo-Indians were involved in a process of ancestral and cultural amnesia on the maternal side, coupled with an insistence on biological and cultural affinity with the ruling group based on a different kind of forgetting, namely, the exclusion of paternal connections other than British ones.

The other ethnic strategy involved relations with the state. Though also pursued during much of the colonial period—the British, after all, were not only a cultural and social 'reference group', but represented the colonial state—it was even more exclusively prosecuted from the early part of the 20th century as the voices of Indian nationalism became more strident, and the emergence of an English-speaking, well-educated, urban elite within Indian society eroded what many leading Anglo-Indians had regarded as their monopoly on a westernized way of life. Thereafter, Anglo-Indian ethnic assertions focused less on the interactions between themselves and other Indian groups at the social and cultural interface, so to speak, and more on persuading the state, including the framers of the Republic's Constitution, of the legitimacy of their claims to a special protected minority status. In this, Anglo-Indians were somewhat more successful.

To sum up, then, my argument is that the 'realities' of porous social boundaries and plural cultures which characterize urban populations—within as well as across the lines which divide them—is not inconsistent with affirmations of ethnic integrity and closure. In India's urban centres today, both processes occur simultaneously, and while Anglo-Indians may constitute something of an 'extreme case' for the fluidity of their social and cultural borders, they may be far from unique.

This paper is based in part on fieldwork conducted in Chennai from November 1991–February 1992, and again during January-February 1996. I am beholden to the Nuffield Foundation for an award which supported the first research visit and to the British Academy which funded the second. Thanks are also due to Pat Caplan for her critical comments on an earlier draft of this text.

Notes

1. The social and political project termed 'multiculturalism' in the UK is, according to Rattansi, based on the notion of a 'harmonious', democratic cultural pluralism, a healthy cultural diversity' (1992: 24–25).
2. Williamson (1810: 413) reported that "nine in ten of the women domiciled by (European) gentlemen are Musulmans (or) Portuguese".
3. This migration, it has been argued, was encouraged to police the growing racial divide in British India.
4. Official definitions of 'Anglo-Indian' since the 1930s (and into the present) identify "a person whose father or any other male progenitors in the male line is or was of European descent but who is domiciled within the territory of India and is or was born in such territory of parents habitually resident therein, and not established there for temporary purposes".
5. Almost without exception, those with non-English surnames have English given or Christian names.
6. Dover, a prominent Anglo-Indian writer, also ridiculed the periodic protests of Anglo-Indian leaders against the assimilation of 'foreign elements'—a distinction, he remained them, not applied to 'equally foreign Europeans' (1937: 115).

7. Domiciled Europeans were people of European parentage on both sides who were born and lived in India. In the eyes of many British officials they were only a cut above the Anglo-Indians, as one Anglo-Indian put it, "because of too much association with India". There were numerous marriages between members of the two communities. Both groups were organizationally united in 1928 in the Anglo-Indian and Domiciled European Associations of Southern India, still the official name of the Anglo-Indian Association of Southern India, based in Madras.
8. 'Anglo-Indian' became the official designation of the community in 1911.
9. There were a few Anglo-Indian voices raised in support of the Indian Nationalist Movement, but this was not a popular stance, and at least one president of the Anglo-Indian Association of Southern India had to resign for his views.
10. This attitude to Indian languages was apparently a widespread feature of Anglo-India. Sen, writing about Anglo-Indians in Calcutta, remarks that the "desire ... to learn the local language has been lacking among them" (1988: 251). Similarly, Bayer notes how in the past Anglo-Indians in Mysore "did not take the existence (of the local language) into account" (1986: 114), while Bhattarcharya found that while 72 per cent of his sample in Bombay could speak the local Marathi and Hindusthani dialects, only 28 per cent could read and write these languages (1968: 169). Lobo, in a critical review of the Anglo-Indian educational system, has argued that the language policy of Anglo-Indian schools was structured to teach English as a second language to Indian students, not to teach Anglo-Indians an Indian language (1994: 16).
11. Clarke (1878: 55) mentions the raising of the 'Madras Volunteers' after the 'Mutiny'.
12. The 1833 Charter formally abolished these restrictions, but in practice change was slow to come for Anglo-Indians.
13. This petition was drawn up some nine months after Ricketts had returned from Britain. On his return he had disembarked at Madras and was feted by members of the Anglo-Indian community there.
14. The 'Testimonial' was transcribed from the original by Theon Wilkinson, Wynard R.T. Wilkinson and Christopher Hawes, July 1995.
15. The Anglo-Indian Association of Southern India has its headquarters in Chennai, while the All-India Anglo-Indian Association (with headquarters in Delhi) has a number of branches in the city. One of

these, located in north-central Chennai, has the largest membership of any branch in the country.

References

Anthony, F., 1969, *Britain's Betrayal in India*, Bombay: Allied.

Arnold, D., 1979, "European Orphans and Vagrants in India in the Nineteenth Century", *Journal of Imperial and Commonwealth History*, VII: 104–27.

——, 1983, "White Colonization and Labour in Nineteenth-century India", *Journal of Imperial and Commonwealth History*, 11: 133–158.

Ballhatchet, K., 1980, *Race, Sex and Class Under the Raj: Imperial Attitudes and Policies and their Critics, 1793–1905*, London: Weidenfeld and Nicolson.

Banks, M., 1996, *Ethnicity: Anthropological Constructions*, London: Routledge.

Bayer, J.M., 1986, *A Sociolinguistic Investigation of the English Spoken by the Anglo-Indians in Mysore City*, Mysore: Central Institute of Indian Languages.

Bell, Rev. A., 1812, *The Report of the Military Male Orphan Asylum at Madras*, London: John Murray.

Bevan, Major H., 1839, *Thirty Years in India: or, A Soldier's Reminiscences of Native and European Life in the Presidencies, from 1808 to 1838* (2 Vols.), London: Pelham Richardson, Cornhill.

Bhattacharya, D.K., 1968, "The Anglo-Indians in Bombay: An Introduction to their Socio-economic and Cultural Life", *Race*, 10: 163–72.

Bower, J.A.H., 1939, *Ambition Mocked our Useful Toil: Autobiographical Sketches and Musings on A-I Problems*, Madras, The author (Xeroxed).

Brass, P.R., 1974, *Language, Religion and Politics in North India*, London: Cambridge University Press.

Brennan, N.L., 1979, "The Anglo-Indians of Madras: An Ethnic Minority in Transition", Ph.D. Syracuse University.

Caplan, L., 1995, "Creole World, Purist Rhetoric: Anglo-Indian Cultural Debates in Colonial and Contemporary Madras", *Journal of the Royal Anthropological Institute*, 1.

——, forthcoming. "Dimensions of Urban Poverty: Anglo-Indian Poor and their Guardians in Madras".

Carsten, J., 1995, "The Politics of Forgetting: Migration, Kinship and Memory on the Periphery of the Southeast Asian State", *Journal of the Royal Anthropological Institute*, 1: 317–36.

Clarke, T.G., 1878, *The Fortunes of the Anglo-Indian Race: Considered Retrospectively and Prospectively by One of Fifty Years Knowledge and Experience*. (end ed.) Madras: Higginbotham.

De Caro, F. and Jordan, R.A., 1984, "The Wrong Topi: Personal Narratives, Ritual, and the Sun Helmet as a Symbol", *Western Folklore,* 43: 233–48.

De Souza, F., 1970, *The House of Binny*, Madras: Binny & Co.

Dover, C., 1937, *Half-Caste*, London: Martin Secker and Warburg.

Drummond, L., 1980, "The Cultural Continuum: A Theory of Intersystems", *Man*, 15: 352–74.

D'Souza, A.A., 1976, *Anglo-Indian Education: A Study of Its Origins and Growth in Bengal up to 1960,* Delhi: OUP.

Dyson, K.K., 1978, *A Various Universe: A Study of the Journals and Memoirs of British Men and Women in the Indian Subcontinent, 1765–1856*, Delhi: OUP.

Eriksen, T.H., 1993, "In Which Sense Do Cultural Islands Exist?", *Social Anthropology* 1, 1B: 133–48.

Fardon, R., 1987, "African Ethnogenesis: Limits to the Comparability of Ethnic Phenomena", In *Comparative Anthropology* (ed.) L. Holy, Oxford: Basil Blackwell.

Friedman, J., 1991, "Further Notes on the Adventures of Phallus in Blunderland". In *Constructing Knowledge: Authority and Critique in Social Science* (eds.) L. Nencel and P. Pels, London: Sage Publications.

Gidney, Lt-Col H., 1925, "The Status of the Anglo-Indian Community Under the Reforms Scheme in India", *The Asiatic Review*, XXI: 657–62.

——, 1934, "The Future of the Anglo-Indian Community", *Asiatic Review,* 30: 27–42.

Gist, N.P., 1967, "Conditions of Inter-group Relations: The Anglo-Indians", *International Journal of Comparative Sociology*, 8: 199–208.

Gist, N.P. and Wright, D., 1973, *Marginality and Identity: Anglo-Indians as a Racially Mixed Minority in India*, Leiden: Brill.

Glissant, E., 1989, *Caribbean Discourse: Selected Essays*, trans. J.M. Dash, Charlottesville: University of Virginia.

Goodrich, D., 1952, *The Making of an Ethnic Group: The Eurasian Community in India*, Berkeley: University of California Ph.D. thesis.

Grimshaw, A.D., 1958, "The Anglo-Indian Community: The Integration of a Marginal Group", *Journal of Asian Studies*, 18: 227–40.

Hannerz, U., 1987, "The World in Creolisation", *Africa*, 57: 546–59.

Hawes, C.J., 1993, *Eurasians in British India, 1773–1833: The Making of a Reluctant Community*, Ph.D. thesis, SOAS, University of London.

Heathcote, T.A., 1974, *The Indian Army: The Garrison of British Imperialism, 1822–1922*, Vancouver: David and Charles.

Hyam, R., 1986, "Concubinage and the Colonial Service: The Crewe Circular (1909)", *Journal of Imperial and Commonwealth History*, 14: 170–86.

Ignatius, C., 1990, "Care and Concern for the Anglo-Indian Child in School: A Report from Madras" (unpublished talk to the Association of Heads of Anglo-Indian Schools, Tamil Nadu).

Lobo, A.I.G., 1994, A Comparative Study of Educational Disadvantage in India within the Anglo-Indian Community: A Historical and Contemporary Analysis, Ph.D. thesis, Institute of Education, University of London.

Madras Mail, 1886, *References to Madras in 'The Asiatic Journal', 1829 to 1840*, reprinted from the Madras Mail.

Maher, R., 1962, *These are the Anglo-Indians*, Calcutta: Swallow Press.

Narayanan, G., 1986, *The Sahibs and the Natives: A Study of Guilt and Pride in Anglo-Indian and Indo-Anglican Novels*, Delhi: Chanakya.

Naidis, M., 1963, "British Attitudes Toward the Anglo-Indians", *South Atlantic Quarterly*, 62.

Penny, F.E., 1908, *On the Coromandel Coast*, London: Smith, Elder & Co.

Rattansi, A., 1992, "A Changing Subject? Racism, Culture and Education". In *'Race', Culture and Difference* (eds.) J. Donald and A. Rattansi, London.

Renford, R.K., 1979, *The Non-Official British in India, 1883–1920*, Ph.D. thesis, University of London.

Ricketts, J., 1831, Report of Proceedings Connected with The East Indians' Petition to Parliament, Read at a Public Meeting Held at the Town Hall, Calcutta, March 28, 1831, with an Appendix, Calcutta: Baptist Missionary Press.

Roberts, E., 1835, *Scenes and Characteristics of Hindostan, with Sketches of Anglo-Indian Society* (3 Vols.). London: Wm H. Allen.

Roy, W.T., 1974, "Hostages to Fortune: (a socio-political) Study of the Anglo-Indian Remnant in Indian", *Plural Societies* (summer): 55–63.

Sanyal, N., 1930, *Development of Indian Railways*, Calcutta: University of Calcutta.

Skipton, H.P.K., 1912, *Our Reproach in India*, London: Mowbray & Co.

Staines, J.R., 1986, *Country Born: One Man's Life in India, 1909–1947*, London: Croscombe Press.

Stark, H.A., 1932, *Call of the Blood or Anglo-Indians and the Sepoy Mutiny*, Rangoon: British Burma Press.

——, 1936, *Hostages to India or the Life-story of the Anglo-Indian Race*, Calcutta: The Author.

Steuart, A.F., 1913, "Some Notes on the Position of Early Eurasians", *The Asiatic Quarterly Review*, N.S. Vol. II, Nos. 3 and 4: 93–101.

Stoler, A.L., 1989, "Rethinking Colonial Categories: European Communities and the Boundaries of Rule", *Comparative Studies in Society and History*, 31: 134–61.

Thomas, N., 1992, "The Inversion of Tradition", *American Ethnologist*, 19: 213–32.

Thurston, E., 1898, *Eurasians of Madras*, Madras Presidency, Madras.

Warden, J.J. (ed.), 1915, *Problems of the Domiciled Community in Modern Light*, the Author.

Werbner, P., 1990, *The Migration Process: Capital, Gifts and Offerings among British Pakistanis*, Oxford: Berg.

Weston, C.N., 1939, *Anglo-Indian Revolutionaries of the Methodist Episcopal Church*, Bangalore: Scripture Literature Press.

Williamson, Capt. T., 1810, *The East India Vade-Mecum; or, Complete Guide to Gentlemen Intended for the Civil, Military, or Naval Service of the Hon. East India Company*, Vol. I, London: Black, Parry and Kingsbury.

5

Sinhala and Tamil Youth Violence in Sri Lanka

PETER KLOOS

One of the most dramatic aspects of the post-independence history of Sri Lanka is the increasing violence. Large-scale violence erupted for the first time in 1958. It culminated in the years between 1987 and 1990—the time of horror (*beeshanaha kala*, in Sinhala). Important actors in the escalation of violence, apart from the Sri Lankan government, were two youth movements, namely, the leftist, later patriotic, People's Liberation Front (Janatha Vimukhti Peramuna, or JVP) and the secessionist Liberation Tigers of Tamil Elam (LTTE).

Both movements emerged among dissatisfied young, often rural yet relatively well-educated people. In this paper I will compare these two youth movements that arose under similar conditions. What I want to do in this paper is to place the origins, careers and nature of both youth movements in the perspective of the post-independence history of Sri Lanka. I will do so in order to highlight similarities and differences between movements that both fought the Sri Lankan government yet never collaborated, not even in the years of island-wide civil war, namely, the years 1987–1989.

Origins and Context of Youth Violence in Sri Lanka

Political violence in Sri Lanka in the post-independence era is predicated on two basic struggles that surfaced during the early years of independence (1948). Both struggles are a concatenation of socio-economic and cultural differences and shifts therein during the colonial and the post-colonial period.

Ceylon on the eve of the colonial period was politically a divided island, with a Tamil kingdom in the north (Jaffna) and two Sinhala kingdoms, one in the south-west (Kotte), and the other in the inaccessible central mountains (present-day Kandy).

British colonial administration in 1831 united the island politically (after having occupied the last Kandyan kingdom in 1815). The consequences of unification were far-reaching: Jaffna Tamils in particular began to spread over the entire island. One reason was that, having earlier and better access to western education, they had a better command over English—the language of the colonial administration. This difference is due to the fact that when American missionaries came to Sri Lanka, the British did not allow them to work in Colombo. They began their work in Jaffna with the establishment of schools where English was taught. As a result, Tamils went earlier and in greater numbers than the Sinhala into the Ceylon Civil Service (and into the police and armed forces), and in the professions (medical and legal).

The Sinhala in their turn began to push into the northern and north-eastern areas of the island, close to and even into hitherto predominantly Tamil areas. At the beginning of the colonial era the area between Jaffna and the central mountains, nowadays the North Central Province, was a thinly populated, desolate area. In the 20th century large colonization schemes were implemented, not only in the south but also in the east and the north, resulting in massive migration of Sinhala into the north-central and north-eastern areas (see Farmer, 1957; Karunatilake, 1988). The Tamil population left these colonization projects, and the migration of Sinhala into the northern and north-eastern parts of the island, as a threat.

Both Sinhala and Tamil society are divided along caste lines. The Jaffna Tamil caste system resembles the South Indian, Hindu caste system. The *Vellala* form the highest caste, at least in Jaffna, the focus of Tamil society in Sri Lanka (see Banks, 1971). The Sinhala caste system is rather different from the Indian system (although it is derived from it). About half of the Sinhala belong to the highest caste—the *Govigama*—the caste of the cultivators. The other half consists of a variety of often quite small castes, which used to have special functions as servants, ritual servants, artisans, etc.

Colonial servants were predominantly recruited from the Vellala and Govigama castes. In the 19th century this resulted in the rise of a high caste, anglicized, often Christian colonial elite. To this elite eventually also belonged among the Tamils the academics, and among the Sinhala the new entrepreneurs who had become rich in liquor trading, plumbago mining and the exploitation of plantations (coconut in particular). This colonial elite began to take over the administration from the British already in the first half of the 20th century (Sri Lanka had universal franchise since 1931). It is this late colonial elite that finally took over the entire administration in 1947.

Both among the Sinhala and the Tamil there were and to some extent still are additional divisions. There are important differences between Jaffna Tamils and Tamils of the east coast, who were not subject to the king of Jaffna and who culturally differed in important respects from the Jaffna Tamils. Moreover, when the British began with coffee plantations in the central highlands in the 1830s, they brought in high numbers of South Indian migrant labourers (Bandarage, 1983). Many of these so-called Indian Tamils chose to stay in Sri Lanka. At independence in 1948, the total number of Indian Tamils was slightly higher than the number of Ceylon (Sri Lanka) Tamils. The Indian Tamils (in the 19th century often called Malabar coolies) belonged to far lower castes than the Jaffna Vellala and have been (and are) considered as a separate community.

The distinction between Sinhala and Tamil is by far the most important one. Still, it did not play an important role during the colonial time. Contrary to the situation in other colonies, the British in Sri Lanka did not follow a deliberate divide and rule policy (see Wickramasingha, 1991, 1995). And among the new elite, English and Christianity were more important than the native languages and Buddhism or Hinduism. Yet, the first political consequence of the old differences between Tamil and Sinhala surfaced already in 1948 and 1949, immediately after independence. It concerned the Indian Tamils rather than the Ceylon Tamils.

The first years after independence can be regarded as a period of continuation of the colonial period. After all, there had been no war of independence and there was no immediate necessity to completely overhaul the economic and political system. The national leaders of the day "became new drivers of the existing vehicle and all the contribution they made was to make the carriage go along" (Ivan, 1989: 6). Among these drivers were Sinhala politicians, like Senanayake, Jayewardena and Bandaranaike, but also Tamil politicians, like Ponnambalam and Chelvanayakam, at that time still organized in an explicitly Tamil political party, the Ceylon Tamil Congress (see Wilson, 1988). These national drivers were not quite continuing the path their vehicle was going. Among the earliest laws passed by the House of Representatives were the Citizen Act (1948), the Indian and Pakistani Residents (Citizenship) Act (1949), and the Parliamentary Elections Amendment Act (1949). The first two laws denied citizenship to the majority of the Indian Tamils, and the third one disenfranchised them. The political motive behind these enactments was the fear among Sinhala leaders of the electoral strength that could be exercised by the Tamil plantation workers, especially in the Central Province, where in several districts they outnumbered the Sinhala. Moreover, the Indian Tamils were suspected of sympathizing with the Trotskyist *Lanka Sama Party* (which in 1947, with 10 seats, was the second party in parliament, after the UNP with 42 seats). These Acts caused a split in the Tamil Congress. Some Tamil politicians accepted the Acts (see Wilson, 1988: 34ff). Others remained loyal to the Indian Tamils and opposed. As a result, the (Tamil) Federal Party was formed, led by Chelvanayakam (see Wilson, 1994).

The reaction against a still predominantly anglicized government and an equally anglicized civil (later public) service came soon afterwards, during the early 1950s. The 1956 elections were won by S.W.R.D. Bandaranaike on the waves of a massive anti-English, anti-Christian, Sinhala-Buddhist nationalism that was supported by the Sinhala speaking rural elites (village headmen, Sinhala teachers, ayurvedic physicians, etc.) and by the *sangha* (the Buddhist monastic order). The first felt discriminated by a civil service, a teaching system and a medical system that was still monopolized by the English-educated colonial elite. The *sangha* felt that Buddhism had suffered severely under Western rule and that it was time for redress.

Especially the issue of language set Bandaranaike on a collision course with the Tamil population. Teaching in native languages (*swabasha*) had been an issue in the early 1940s (see Dharmadasa, 1992), but the slogan which won the elections was not 'native languages' but 'Sinhala only'. Because Buddhism and Sinhala were so entwined, here for the first time Sri Lanka was explicitly conceived as a Sinhala-Buddhist state. In 1956, soon after the elections, the Official Language Act was introduced. It became known as the 'Sinhala Only' Act. Sinhala would be the official language of Sri Lanka. The 'Sinhala Only' Act was a direct attack on an essential element of Tamil identity, namely, language and literature. The Act also greatly reduced the possibilities for Tamils to compete with Sinhala for administrative jobs. This Act again brought together the Tamil politicians, who had split as a result of the Citizen Acts. As a result of fierce protests, Bandaranaike retraced his steps. He began negotiations with the (Tamil) Federal Party, and reached an agreement with its leader Chelvanayakam, in the form of a certain degree of devolution of power on a regional basis. Especially the *sangha*, however, was very much opposed to this, and due to its pressure the agreement (the so-called Bandaranaike-Chelvanayakam Pact) was unilaterally recalled by Bandaranaike. Tamil opposition to the 'Sinhala only' Act led to counter-demonstrations in the Sinhala areas. The prime objective of these demonstrations was to oppose any concessions to the Tamil minority (Warnapala, 1974: 244). Tension erupted in the May 1958 communal riots—the first of series of Sinhala-Tamil riots (Vittachi, 1958) and the first major violent conflict in Sri Lanka. The Federal Party was proscribed.

To understand the dynamics of conflict in the post-independence era in Sri Lanka, there is an important issue that should be considered before proceeding, namely, population growth after independence. At independence, Sri Lanka was economically relatively well-off. It had received independence without having to fight for it, and due to products such as tea, rubber and cocos it enjoyed a comfortable income in terms of foreign exchange. It was, in fact, one of the more affluent countries in Asia. Part of the available funds were pumped into island-wide free medical care and in equally island-wide free education. As a result of medical care, the population began to rise dramatically. The new generations went to school. As a consequence of the post-independence population growth, a relatively well-educated group of young people entered the labour market in the course of the 1960s, in search of jobs.

At the same time, however, world market prices for tea, rubber and cocos had begun to level off and even fall. Sri Lanka's economy began to stagnate (Abeyratne, 1998). As a result, there were no jobs for the ambitious young generation. The establishment tended to reserve economic and political opportunities for its own children. This led to the second major violent conflict in Sri Lanka, now among the Sinhala: the April 1971 insurgency. It was the left-wing *Janatha Vimukthi Peramuna* (JVP) that embodied youth dissatisfaction among Sinhala and blamed the government for it (see for early descriptions of the 1971 insurgency and its backgrounds, Obeyesekere, 1974; Alles, 1976).

The JVP was a Sinhala movement, but to understand political violence in Sri Lanka one should not isolate the 1971 insurgency. Two intersecting differentiations of Sri Lanka society set the scene for political violence:

Both the May 1958 riots and the April 1971 insurgency could—and have been—seen as unrelated events. With the knowledge we now have of a longer period, they should be seen as events in a pattern of growing tension, conflict and violence.

The Tamil equivalent of the JVP insurgency came only one year later. There are enough data to conclude that among Tamil youth too the unrest began in the late 1960s. In 1970 already young Tamils were experimenting with arms and explosives (Narayan Swamy, 1994: 244ff). In May 1972 a new constitution was adopted. This new constitution made Ceylon a republic, called Sri Lanka (one of the ancient names of the island). The new constitution guaranteed the supreme position in Sri Lanka of the Sinhala language and of Buddhism and consequently led to anti-government demonstrations in Jaffna and the raising of black flags. In the wake of these demonstrations secessionist youth groups were formed. The Tamil New Tigers, formed soon after the new constitution was adopted, was the first of them. These groups began to agitate not immediately against the government in Colombo but against the Tamil political establishment. The rise of these youth groups expressed a split in the Tamil community: between the established elite politicians who participated in the Sinhala dominated political process, and the radical and militant—often unemployed—youth. The former largely belonged to the old, English educated Vellala elite, the latter to Tamil educated castes. So, the same demographic-cum-social process that led to the 1971 insurgency among the Sinhala led in the late 1960s to the radicalization of Tamil youth. Unemployed youth were soon willing to use violence as a political means because the Tamil political establishment proved to be powerless, even in the face of discriminatory measures against Tamil students, for instance (De Silva, 1978). The situation in Jaffna gradually began to be more tense and in July 1975 the Tamil mayor of Jaffna, A. Duraiappah, a supporter of the Sri Lanka Freedom Party (SLFP), was assassinated by the New Tigers. This group in May 1976 split up in two groups: the Tamil Eelam Liberation Organization (TELO), and the Liberation Tigers of Tamil Eelam (LTTE).

The LTTE honoured its name by a programme of selective assassination of at first Tamil politicians, who were regarded as traitors, and later (Tamil) police officers. Because most of the killings concerned Tamils, the government tended to regard these killings as an intra-Tamil affair. Yet it strengthened army presence in Jaffna. This violent policy gained momentum from 1977 onwards.

The UNP (United National Party) government, after having won the 1977 elections, in May 1978 proscribed the LTTE and other Tamil youth groups, and began to fight them (the 1977 elections had been followed by widespread rioting against Tamils). Tamil separatist groups continued their guerrilla activities, now also targeting the armed forces. Police forces and the army retaliated. The official representatives of the Tamils, organized in the Tamil United Liberation Front (TULF), were losing support in Jaffna. Although they had managed to have District Development Councils introduced in 1981, these councils proved to be no real devolution of power and showed clearly that the parliamentary road was leading the Tamils nowhere.

The same year witnessed another step in the process towards civil war: after a number of political assassinations of UNP and TULF politicians in May 1981 in Jaffna the Sri Lankan police and military went berserk. Massive anti-Tamil riots took place in Jaffna and elsewhere. In Jaffna the public library with its invaluable Tamil manuscripts was burned down (Narayan Swamy, 1994: 73).

An important threshold in the Sinhala-Tamil relations after independence is July 1983. On 23 July the LTTE ambushed and killed thirteen soldiers (Narayan Swamy, 1994: 89f). The LTTE had ambushed and killed soldiers before. However, what happened after the bodies of the thirteen soldiers had been brought to Colombo was a violent reaction among urban Sinhala, amounting to a veritable pogrom. Although the pogrom has never been subject to systematic investigation, the available evidence points in the direction of a conscious move of certain members of the cabinet [see for early reports of the pogrom Dissanayaka, 1983 and Hyndman, 1985, and for an early analysis Meyer, 1986 (1984)].

July 1983 is usually regarded as the beginning of permanent civil war in Sri Lanka, but worse was still to come. The ambush of the LTTE, resulting in the July 1983 pogrom in Colombo and elsewhere, had unanticipated results because the Tamil militant groups greatly profited from it. The pogrom brought attention for them, also internationally; it brought support from Tamils abroad, it brought thousands of youth to become fighters, and it undermined even further the position of the parliamentary politicians. The radical LTTE eventually presented itself as the sole, and self-appointed, custodian of Tamil interests in Jaffna peninsula after it had systematically, violently and often treacherously wiped out its rivals (see Narayan Swami, 1994: 174–98).

The Sri Lankan army had no answer to the well-organized, ruthless war machine the LTTE had become. However, army operations against the LTTE in Jaffna in 1987 caused the Indian government to intervene. It forced a treaty upon the Sri Lankan president, who had to accept an Indian Peace Keeping Force (IPKF) in Sri Lanka. Far from keeping peace, the IPKF soon after its arrival in July 1987 found itself in a deadly struggle with the LTTE. The Indian army too had no answer to LTTE guerrilla strategies and tactics (Bose, 1994).

The arrival of the IPKF had an unexpected effect among the Sinhala: it estranged the Sinhala political elite from the Sinhala masses. The JVP returned to the political scene but now as a patriotic movement. It accused the governing elites of betraying the Sinhala motherland. Its armed wing began to attack politicians. The government retaliated. Despite the use of violence, there was at first much sympathy for the JVP among the Sinhala, even in circles of the armed forces—until JVP leaders made a—for them fatal—mistake: in 1989 they threatened to attack wives and children and other relatives of army and police men. This resulted in the creation of secret death squads bearing names such as black cats, red dragons, etc. This ushered in a total political crisis in Sri Lanka. The years 1987–1990 saw an almost complete breakdown of civil society. The government had to cope with a Tamil secessionist movement, fought in the north by the IPKF in Sri Lanka, and with the (second) JVP insurrection among the Sinhala in the south. Official and unofficial government violence, LTTE and JVP violence, and violence perpetrated to settle private quarrels or for material gain became indistinguishable: it was no longer quite clear who killed who and for what reason. Due to methods of killing and tire-burning of victims it was often not even clear who had been killed. Tens of thousands just disappeared, leaving no trace.

The ruthless persecution of the JVP led to the extra-judicial killing of its leadership in November 1989 (Chandraprema, 1991; Gunaratne, 1990). It was for the time being the end of this organized youth movement among the Sinhala. The elimination of the JVP leaders proved to be a turn towards a lessening of the political and moral crisis. The then president R. Premadasa forced the Indian army to leave the country (the last troops left in March 1990). As a result, the accusation against the government of unpatriotic behaviour subsided.

The government had to deal with the LTTE again. One of the manoeuvres of Premadasa already before the death of the JVP leadership had been to open negotiations with the LTTE. He used these negotiations to get rid of the IPKF. After more than a year of negotiation, however, the LTTE unilaterally terminated the discussions in June 1990 and began Eelam War II as it is usually called. The LTTE was so successful that within a short period it had carved out a *de facto* Tamil state in the north of Sri Lanka, where it was in charge and no one else.

There has been a war ever since. The People's Alliance Government (which in 1994 took over from the UNP that had ruled the country from 1977 onwards), did what it had promised during the electoral campaigns: it began peace negotiations. The LTTE showed some interest in peace talks. In June 1995, however, it broke off the discussion with a letter from LTTE leader Prabhakaran to the Sri Lankan government, and a surprise attack on Sri Lanka's navy in the harbour of Trincomalee even before the letter referred to had arrived. Thus began Eelam War III.

The Sri Lankan army resumed military activities and in 1995 occupied Jaffna. This did not bring peace. The LTTE remained a formidable foe.

The JVP too—although almost silent since the elimination of its top in November 1989—is not something of the past. The condition of its emergence in the late 1960s, a mismatch between ambitions and opportunities, is still very much there, and all that is needed is a charismatic leader to again mobilize dissatisfied youth. Ever since 1990 there are recurrent rumours that the JVP indeed is being reorganized.

Against the historical background of their emergence I turn now to similarities and differences between the LTTE and the JVP as violent political movements.

Similar Origins, Different Courses

JVP and LTTE share as common background—the dissatisfaction of youth. Because Tamil youth were also confronted with ethnic discrimination, their reaction and the proposed solutions were different from the reactions of Sinhala youth. The JVP was first of all a movement aiming at social revolution. The LTTE saw in a separate state—a *Tamil Eelam*—the beginning of social justice denied to them under Sinhala hegemony.

Neither revolution nor separation were solutions invented by JVP and LTTE. The necessity of fundamental changes in Sinhala society had already been voiced by several left-wing, Marxist political parties, like the Ceylon Communist Party (CCP) and the Trotskyist LSSP (see Gunaratne, 1990). The idea of a federal state of Sri Lanka was put forward by the Federal Party immediately after the 1948 and 1949 Acts regarding the legal status of the Indian Tamils (Navaratnam, 1995: 62f). These ideas, however, were drowned by the political monopoly of the UNP/SLFP combination. Yet there are direct connections between the insurgent movements and already existing parties. Rohan Wijeweera, the leader of the JVP, had been a member of the CCP (Gunaratne, 1990: 1–5) and derived part of his ideas from the CCP. Velupillai Prabhakaran, the leader of the LTTE, came from a politically-conscious family and had been a member of the Tamil Youth League, the youth wing of the Tamil United Front (Narayan Swamy, 1994: 53). The Tamil United Liberation Front (TULF) saw in the 1977 elections an opportunity to obtain a mandate of the Tamil nation "to re-establish the independence of the state of Tamil Eelam". The idea of re-establishing a Tamil state predates the rise of the LTTE (see Sivaraja, 1996).

Both Wijeweera and Prabhakaran thus applied already existing ideas to the situation in which they and their peers found themselves in the late 1960s in Sri Lanka and in which, they believed, only violent politics would work (Gunaratne, 1990: 1–25; Narayan Swamy, 1994: 49–59). But again, the outcome was not the same: the JVP became a revolutionary movement (Moore, 1993), the LTTE a secessionist one. Many characteristics of the JVP and the LTTE flow from this fundamental difference.

Given this difference it comes as no surprise that the ideologies legitimating revolution and separation, and the historical justifications, show little similarity. In the case of the JVP there was an extensive, Marxist and Maoist inspired ideology, backing its policies. The LTTE hardly needed an explicit ideology legitimating its cause: political reality of the day made it clear that decisions taken within the established democratic institutions of the Sri Lankan state would necessarily turn out to the disadvantage of the Tamil population. A 'homeland' of their own was therefore in their view for the Tamil people a *sine quo non* in order to survive. The LTTE did evolve a complex ideology but it was related to its violent methods.

Here again, there is an important difference that is related to the career of both movements but also to the personalities of the key leaders. The LTTE very early turned to the use of violence. Dates can be misleading but 1975 would be a reasonable choice to let violent politics begin: in May 1975 Prabhakaran killed the Tamil but also SLFP mayor of Jaffna (Narayan Swamy, 1994: 56). In the years to come there would be periods in which there was truce between the LTTE and its prime adversary, the Sri Lankan government, but in the end these truces proved to be ceasefires in an ongoing war. For the LTTE violent and non-violent tactics were legitimate alternatives from which to choose, depending on the perceived advantages.

The career of the JVP is more complicated. The movement attracted attention for the first time as a result of its abortive attempt in April 1971 to seize power. As a result, the JVP was proscribed. In 1978, the ban was lifted, and a reorganized JVP began to function in the democratic political arena as a recognized political party. It did even contest in local elections in June 1981, and its leader, Wijeweera, was put forward as presidential candidate in the October 1982 presidential elections. He received 4.19 per cent of the votes, third after UNP candidate J.R. Jayewardena (with 52.91%) and SEFP candidate H.S.R.B. Kobbekaduwa (with 39.07%). Wijeweera beat other, longer established left-wing candidates. Evidently, the JVP had become the most powerful leftist force in Sri Lanka, and visibly so. But, in 1983, after the July pogrom, the JVP, being accused by the government of instigating the pogrom, was proscribed again. There is not a shred of evidence that the JVP (or the other left-wing parties that were also proscribed) had been a factor in the July 1983 pogrom. It is more likely that it was its rising popular appeal that brought the government to proscribe the JVP (Gunaratne, 1990: 187). As underground movement, the JVP again turned to violent politics, especially after the treaty with the Indian government had been signed.

Yet, the JVP, for all its violence, was far less geared to warfare than the LTTE. This may also have to do with the personalities involved: Prabhakaran was and still is a fighting man himself (see Narayan Swamy, 1994: 52; Sahadevan, 1995: 259ff). Wijeweera was not. Violence, and to kill and be killed, is a far more basic element of the LTTE. Around being killed for the movement and for the Tamil cause a whole ritual complex of suicide and martyrdom has been built that is absent in the JVP (see O'balance, 1989; Schalk, 1997). As Chandraprema put it, "The JVP was only willing to kill for their cause; not to die for it" (1991: 307). The so-called 'Black Tigers' of the LTTE, however, were specifically trained for suicide operations. They were fully prepared to kill and to be killed. Scores of Black Tigers have died as suicide-killers.

The targets of JVP violence were first of all politicians both of the reigning UNP but, on first sight perhaps surprisingly, also of the left-wing SLFP. However, it would be better to say that JVP violence was directed at the political establishment of whatever political colour. The UNP was in power between 1977 and 1994, but with SLFP politicians the JVP had a bone to pick: it was the SLFP government that under Ms. Sirimavo Bandaranaike crushed the insurgency.

But JVP violence was also aimed at disturbing public life. The main method was to order a strike (a *hartal*, an Indian word that is often used in this context). Such a strike might be directed at a particular group or it might imply that everybody was to stay home. These hartals were backed up with threats to kill those who did not obey. Hartals were announced by pasting notices on trees. Mouth-to-mouth spreading and fear would do the rest.

A good deal of LTTE violence was also directed at individuals who were seen as enemies. But, the LTTE was also involved in guerrilla attacks, and in course of time in attacks coming close to those of a regular army. Under severe pressure, and no longer in power in Jaffna itself, the LTTE resorted to bomb attacks in Colombo and other centres. Fear for LTTE attacks is strong especially in Colombo, where the armed forces tend to see a suicide assassin in any young Tamil.

The LTTE does not confine its attacks to Sri Lanka. In all likelihood it was an LTTE suicide killer (a young woman) who assassinated Rajiv Gandhi in May 1991 (see BBC, 1991). LTTE cadres killed also Tamils abroad who were seen as traitors or as a risk for the movement.

Assassinations abroad and bomb attacks with predominantly civilians as victims resulted in a change in attitude towards the LTTE internationally. Especially in the years after the 1983 pogrom there was much sympathy abroad for the plight of the Tamil population in Sri Lanka and for the LTTE as the champion of the Tamils. Because the JVP never spread its field of action abroad, it never was subject of international attention.

How were the JVP and LTTE organized? For obvious reasons not much is known in any detail about their internal organization, and it is unlikely that much will be known. The top of the JVP is with one or two exceptions dead. Many top leaders of the LTTE have perished, and the surviving leaders are taciturn about it: it is in the nature of insurgent movements to be secretive about themselves.

In line with the basic difference in policy—revolution and separation—I would argue that the JVP resembles a loosely organized political party. It had a Central Committee at the top. The LTTE resembles a small army, led by a war leader. Gunaratne (1990) gives an extensive description of the structure of the JVP at different stages. The JVP had a politburo, appointed by the Central Committee and a number of District Committees. Special committees were in charge of the universities, the trade unions, propaganda, etc. Moreover, there were cover organizations, and the JVP infiltrated in existing organizations, students' organizations in particular. For the rest the movement was built on local cells that did not know much about each other and about the links between various parts of the JVP.

Propaganda was very important for the JVP. Reference should be made to the *panthi paha*, the 'five lectures'. These were lectures, to a large extent, drawn up by Wijeweera, on topics such as the crisis of the capitalist system, how to solve the crisis, the role of the revolution, the history of the JVP, etc. In the 1960s and later classes were held throughout the country in order to enlist support. A smaller number of people were invited to participate in educational camps. In this way, the JVP acquired sympathy and support especially among the rural youth. It is probably not possible to say with any degree of precision how many members the JVP actually had at any time but evidently the aim was to become a mass movement.

The LTTE proper never really aimed at becoming a mass movement; it preferred a fairly small number of absolutely loyal and trained cadres. The word 'cadre' was a special meaning here because it applies first of all to a militarily trained person. The boundary between who does and who does not belong to the LTTE is probably far sharper than is the case with the JVP. Of course, in the case of the LTTE too, there is a belt of sympathizers. The difference between a trained cadre and a sympathizer lies probably in the wearing of a cyanide capsule cadres who are expected to bite when running the risk of being caught. LTTE cadres live in the expectation of dying for the movement.

As far as I know, there are no detailed descriptions of the internal structure of the LTTE, although Gunaratne (1997) gives a general blueprint of the organization. The LTTE is secretive about how even its Central Committee is manned. The LTTE is more rigidly and autocratically top-down organized than the JVP, with Prabhakaran (often called *supremo*—a word that was rarely if ever used for Wijeweera) at the top. From the literature and other sources I gather that Prabhakaran is surrounded by a small group of cadres utterly loyal to him and that he does not accept any ambitious second in command who might threaten his position as absolute leader: those who did have been eliminated. According to the authors of *The Broken Palmyra*, Prabhakaran resembles "some kind of subcontinental cult god whose mighty will commands the rise of devotees and later sends them obediently to their destruction" (Hoole et al., 1990: 183). The JVP had a more participatory nature. Discussion was important.

When the LTTE publishes names of Tigers killed in action, the dead are often given ranks, such as major, captain, lieutenant, etc. From this one may infer that the LTTE indeed closely resembles an army. The ranks are rarely given in case of living persons, perhaps in order to avoid insight in the internal hierarchy.

Within the LTTE there are special 'tigers', like the Black Tigers, trained for suicide attacks, the Sea Tigers (and since 1998 also Air Tigers), but also Women Fighters. Here again is a difference between JVP and LTTE. In the JVP a few women did participate, but in the case of the LTTE there are full-fledged women regiments. The first women received their training in Tamil Nadu, in India, in 1984. Later training took (and still takes) place in Sri Lanka. In 1986 women fighters for the first time took part in an attack (Ann, 1993) Women fighters too wear a cyanide capsule (see the BBC documentary of 1991).

In the case of the JVP I pointed out that in the period 1978–1983 the movement acted as a legitimate political party, contesting official elections. The LTTE too has had an interesting interlude, namely, between 1990 (the departure of the IPKF) and 1995 (the occupation of Jaffna by the Sri Lankan army). In these five years Jaffna and surroundings were *de facto* an independent Tamil state where the LTTE was in charge. In the years 1997–1990 the LTTE had not only managed to keep an Indian army of more than 100,000 at bay, it had also managed to strengthen its position (Bose, 1994). When the IPKF left Sri Lanka, the LTTE quickly stepped into the void and found itself in almost absolute control of Jaffna. This was also possible because the then President of Sri Lanka, R. Premadasa, had taken the initiative to start peace negotiations with the LTTE. This prevented any large scale military actions, thereby leaving Jaffna peninsula to the LTTE.

This meant that the LTTE actually was in charge of civil administration in Jaffna. In a way had what it wanted to have: a separate Tamil state, even though the Sri Lankan government still paid the salaries of administrators and teachers, and appointed them, but with LTTE approval. During that period there still was war, but only on the periphery of Jaffna, with small—and larger-scale attacks and counter-attacks south of Jaffna peninsula and in the Eastern Province. LTTE administration included legislation, taxing, etc. It excluded any regular, democratic influence from the Jaffna Tamils on LTTE policies. The LTTE is basically autocratic and this might be one of the reasons why it is hardly open to peace negotiations and autonomy, not independence, of Tamil areas in Sri Lanka. In case of autonomy elections would be unavoidable. This would be against the whole internal power climate of the LTTE. It is also likely that an LTTE turned into a political party would be defeated in general elections. Popular support of the LTTE is based on fear rather than on loyalty.

As far as I know, there are no systematic accounts of life in Jaffna in the years 1990–1995. There is a huge, invaluable amount of information regarding events taking place in the north of Sri Lanka supplied by *The University Teachers for Human Rights* (UTHR), Jaffna, but their reports deal primarily with documenting human rights issues (see their latest report, UTHR, 1997).

Like in the case of the JVP there are organizations associated with the LTTE, working abroad but engaged in projects in LTTE controlled areas in Sri Lanka. The first is the Tamil Rehabilitation Organization (TRO). TRO is pro-LTTE but it is not part of the LTTE. The second is the Tamil Eelam Economic Development Organization (TEEDOR). TEEDOR is an LTTE auxiliary. The TRO sponsors rehabilitation centres in Tamil areas, the TEEDOR carries out development projects. Both TRO and TEEDOR collect money and try to engage sponsors in many countries. Both are transnational in their activities although geared to projects in Tamil Eelam.

TRO and TEEDOR are expressions of an important difference between the JVP and the LTTE. The JVP was an almost purely Sri Lankan affair. The JVP did have some contacts with organizations abroad (some helped in military training, for instance), but the consequences of these contacts were in the end of marginal importance. In the case of the LTTE this is very different.

The issue the LTTE was involved in—an independent state—implicated India in the first place. India's role in the LTTE-Sri Lankan government conflict is extremely complicated and cannot be discussed here in any detail (I refer to Bose, 1994; Kodikara, 1989; Muni, 1993). Major issues in the Indo-Lanka relationship pertaining to the LTTE are India's subcontinental ambitions, India's fear that an independent Tamil state in Sri Lanka might strengthen similar ambitions within its own boundaries, and differences in interest between the government in New Delhi and the government of Tamil Nadu that tends to support the Tamil liberation movements in Sri Lanka. All these issues simply did not exist in the case of the JVP insurgencies: the JVP was not an issue for interests outside Sri Lanka. The JVP insurgencies also did not give rise to an exodus of Sinhala. The so-called ethnic conflict between Sinhala and Tamil, however, did lead to a massive displacement of Tamils, many of them fleeing the country, going to South India, Europe (United Kingdom, France), Canada and Australia.

Jaffna Tamils (and especially the people from Velvettiturai—Prabhakaran's place of birth) had always had a transnational network of trade and/or smuggling (Narayan Swamy, 1994: 50) but the exodus after the 1983 pogrom in Colombo and elsewhere made possible a truly worldwide web of relations. This network was quickly used by the LTTE to enlist support—financial support in the first place. The LTTE created a transnational enterprise including propaganda. It extracted money from Tamils abroad. It collected money in other way. And it became involved in weapon and drug trade (see Kloos, 1998). This made the LTTE a resourceful movement.

An important role abroad is played by the pro-LTTE Tamil Coordinating Committees (TCCs) that have been established in at least twelve countries (see Kloos, 1998). These TCCs are a thorn in the flesh of the Sri Lankan government, which regards them as supporters of a terrorist movement. Foreign governments have been asked to have TCCs offices closed, but as long as TCCs do not violate the law they cannot be legally prohibited.

A final element of comparison I will briefly deal with is the acceptance of both movements by the Sinhala and Tamil population respectively. Here I have to rely on impressions. The key word is *ambivalence* with regard to both movements. Ambivalence is probably strongest among Tamils, who have suffered under LTTE violence far more and far longer than the Sinhala under JVP violence (however horrible and traumatic the years 1987–1990 have been for the Sinhala).

For an understanding of the feelings of the Tamils, one should remember that at the moment only the LTTE is still adamant about a separate state. All other insurgent groups, and also the Tamil United Liberation Front (the main Tamil political party) have accepted ideas about devolution of power and a certain form of federalism. The government of Chandrika

Bandaranaike has already been since 1995 working on such a project. The problems of having devolution accepted are manifold. Among the Sinhala, especially the more chauvinist as well as the Buddhist sangha are totally against a plan that threatens the political unity of Sri Lanka. Also party-political interests play a role: the acceptance of devolution of power will mean a fundamental breakthrough in the civil war. The United National Party seems to be unwilling to grant the reigning People's Alliance this success.

If for major sections among the Sinhala the devolution plan goes too far, for radical Tamils it does not go far enough. Although most Tamil parties accept devolution, the LTTE is still adamant with regard to independence.

Especially since in 1995 a good deal of the population of Jaffna was evacuated by the LTTE to the area south of Jaffna lagoon, "the Tamils are tired of this war, they cannot take any more. 'Why do you not go for peace talks'—said a Tamil traveller to a LTTE official" (UTHR, 1997: 6). On the other hand, there is a deep distrust among Tamils regarding the Sinhala majority, and given their experiences with plans for devolution of power in the past they have good reasons to be distrustful. As long as the devolution plan is not agreed upon, Tamils are likely to remain distrustful and are likely to support a movement that defends Tamil autonomy—the LTTE included. There is among Tamils a feeling that although they suffer severely under LTTE tyranny (and more than the Sinhala do), the Liberation Tigers in any case fight for the interests of all Tamils. Hence, the ambivalent feelings and judgements: fear and hatred as well as pride.

As far as the JVP is concerned, one should distinguish between the early period of resistance against the government, and the 1980s and especially the period after April 1989, when the JVP declared that in its fight against the establishment it would also target the families of the armed forces. This declaration has been a strategic mistake of the JVP because it unleashed an unprecedented violence against anyone suspected of JVP sympathy. Before that date there were even in the army and the police many people who in fact felt sympathy for the JVP, if not for its methods, than for its goals. It should be understood that the armed forces recruited from precisely the same category of people as the JVP did, namely, unemployed Sinhala youth, and that the Jayewardene and later Premadasa governments had in the 1980s lost a good deal of their legitimacy. So here too one can observe feelings of ambivalence among the wider population with regard to the JVP: agreement with their protest against established politics, but disagreement with the violence characterizing the *beeshanaya kala*, the 'time of horror' (the late 1980s and early 1990s).

In a way, the comparison suggests many more questions than can be answered in the context of a paper. Many questions will never be answered. It is in the nature of guerrilla movements to be silent about key issues: their members' survival depends upon silence and secrecy. LTTE leader Prabhakaran has given a number of interviews but given the life-and-death struggle that is going on one cannot expect him to be open on relevant issues (apart from being clear about the ultimate goal of the LTTE). Moreover, many key figures are dead (or are likely to die in the struggle in the near future). This applied not only to top figures of the LTTE and the JVP, but also to members of the government, like the late President Premadasa (assassinated on 1 May 1993), and top politicians like Lalith Atulathmudali (assassinated on 23 April 1993) and Gamini Dissanayaka (assassinated on 24 October 1994), not to mention many top military men.

The JVP and the LTTE do show a number of similarities flowing from the fact that both are expressions of youth dissatisfaction and a struggle with the establishment. They also had a common enemy, namely, the Sri Lankan establishment, the government in particular. These commonalities were dwarfed, however, by a fundamental difference: especially in the 1980s the JVP was, its leftist ideals notwithstanding, a fiercely Sinhala chauvinist party that stressed the basic tenets of Sinhala identity. This included the idea that Sri Lanka was the primeval home of the Sinhala that could not be cut up into two states. This idea was, of course, totally at odds with what was basic for the LTTE: a state of their own.

The main explanation for the difference between the two youth movements is that with the LTTE there is the additional factor of ethnic discrimination. This turned their conflict with the Sri Lanka, Sinhala majority into a war in which ideological elements did not play a dominant role: the Liberation Tigers were and are not in the first place revolutionaries, they simply want a state of their own. The leaders of the JVP, however, *were* revolutionaries.

References

Abeyratine, Sirimal, 1998, *Economic Change and Political Conflicts in Developing Countries. With an investigation into Sri Lanka*. Amsterdam: VU University Press. Sri Lanka Studies in the Humanities and Social Sciences, No. 7.

Alles, A.C., 1976, *Insurgency—1971: An Account of the April Insurrection in Sri Lanka*. Colombo: The Colombo Apothecaries, 3rd ed.

Ann, Adele, 1993, *Women Fighters of the Liberation Tigers*. Jaffna: Thasan Printers.

Bandarage, Asoka, 1983, *Colonialism in Sri Lanka: The Political Economy of the Kandyan Highlands 1833–1886*. Berlin: Mouton Publishers.

Banks, Michael, 1971, 'Caste in Jaffna'. In E.R. Leach (ed.), *Aspects of Caste in South India, Ceylon and North-West Pakistan*. Cambridge: Cambridge University Press, pp. 61–77.

BBC, 1991, *Tamil Tigers: Suicide Killers* (broadcasted by the BBC on 23 October 91).

Bose, Sumantra, 1994, *States, Nations, Sovereignty: Sri Lanka, India and the Tamil Eelam Movement*. New Delhi: Sage Publications.

Chandraprema, C.A., 1991, *Sri Lanka: The Years of Terror. The J.V.P. Insurrection 1987–89*. Colombo: Lakehouse Bookshop.

De Silva, C.R., 1978, 'The Politics of University Admission: A Review of Some Aspects of the Admissions Policy in Sri Lanka 1971–1978', Sri Lanka Journal of Social Sciences, 1(2): 85–123.

Dissanayaka, T.D.S.A., 1983, *The Agony of Sri Lanka: An In-depth Account of the Racial Riots of 1983*. Colombo: Swastika Ltd.

Farmer, B.H., 1957, *Pioneer Peasant Colonisation in Ceylon: A Study in Asian Agrarian Problems*. Oxford: Oxford University Press.

Gunaratna, Rohan, 1990, *Sri Lanka. A Lost Revolution? The Inside Story of the JVP*. Sri Lanka: Institute of Fundamental Studies.

——, 1997, *International and Regional Security. Implications of the Sri Lankan Tamil Insurgency*. St Albans, Herts.: International Foundation of Sri Lankans.

Hettige, S.T. (ed.), 1992, *Unrest or Revolt: Some Aspects of Youth Unrest in Sri Lanka*. Colombo: Goethe-Institut/American Studies Association.

Hoole, Rajan, Somasundaram Daya, Sritharan K. and Thiranagama Rajani, 1990, *The Broken Palmyra: The Tamil Crisis in Sri Lanka: An Inside Account*. Claremont: The Sri Lanka Studies Institute.

Hyndman, Patricia, 1985, *Democracy in Peril. Sri Lanka: A Country in Crisis*. Report to the Lawasia Human Rights Standing Committee.

Ivan, Victor, 1989, *Sri Lanka in Crisis: Road to Conflict*. Ratmalana: Sarvodaya Book Publishing Services.

Karunatilake, H.N.S., 1988, *The Accelerated Mahaweli Programme and its Impact*. Colombo: Centre for Demographic and Socio-Economic Studies.

Kloos, Peter, 1994, "Past Political Identities, Present Political Interests: An Indigenous Political Model in Sri Lanka. In M. van Bakel, R. Hagesteijn, P. van de Velde (eds.), *Pivot Politics: Changing Cultural Identities in Early State Formation Processes*. Amsterdam: Het Spinhuis, pp. 223–34.

——, 1997, "The Struggle between the Lion and the Tiger: The Relevance of Inter and Intra-ethnic Conflict for the Construction of Ethnic Identities in Sri Lanka". In Cora Govers and Hans Vermeulen (eds.), *The Politics of Ethnic Consciousness*. London: MacMillan.

——, 1998, "A Secessionist Movement in an Age of Globalisation: The Liberation Tigers of Tamil Eelam of Sri Lanka". In Nancy Jetly (ed.), *Ethno-Sectarian Conflicts and Internal Dynamics of Regional Security in South Asia*. New Delhi.

Kodikara, Shelton U. (ed.), 1989, *Indo-Sri Lanka Agreement of July 1987*. Colombo: The University of Colombo.

Meyer, Eric, 1986, "Seeking the Roots of the Tragedy". In J. Manor (ed.), *Sir Lanka in Change and Crisis*. New York: St. Martin's Press (French original published in 1983).

Moore, Mick, 1993, "Thoroughly Modern Revolutionaries: The JVP in Sri Lanka". *Modern Asian Studies*, 27(3): 593–642.

Muni, S.D., 1993, *Pangs of Proximity: India and Sri Lanka's Ethnic Crisis*. Olso/London: Prio/Sage Publications.

Narayan Swamy, M.R., 1994, *Tigers of Lanka: From Boys to Guerrillas*. New Delhi: Konark Publishers.

Navaratnam, V., 1995, *The Fall and Rise of the Tamil Nation*. Montreal: The Tamilian Library.

O'balance, Edgar, 1989, *The Cyanide War*. London: Brassey's.

Obeyesekere, Gananath, 1974, "Some Comments on the Social Backgrounds of the April 1991 Insurgency in Sri Lanka (Ceylon)". *Journal of Asian Studies, 33(3): 367–81.*

Sahadevan, P., 1995, "On Not Becoming a Democrat: The LTTE's Commitment to Armed Struggle". *International Studies*, 32(3): 249–81.

Schalk, Peter, 1997, "Resistance and Martyrdom in the Process of State Formation in Tamiliam". In Joyce Pettigrew (ed.), *Martyrdom and National Resistance Movements: Essays on Asia and Europe*. Amsterdam: VU University Press, pp. 65–89.

——, 1994, "Women Fighter of the Liberation Tigers in Tamil Ilam: The Martial Feminism of Atel Palacinkam". *South Asia Research* 14(2): 163–83.

Sivarajah, Ambalavanar, 1996, *Politics of Tamil Nationalism in Sri Lanka*. New Delhi: South Asian Publishers.

UTHR, 1995, *The Exodus From Jaffna*. University Teachers for Human Rights (Jaffna) Briefing No. 3.

——, 1997, *Jaffna: A Vision Skewed*. The University Teachers for Human Rights, Special Report No. 9.

Vittachi, Tarzie, 1958, *Emergency '58: The Study of the Ceylon Race Riots*. London: Andre Deutsch.

Warnapala, W.A. Wiswa, 1974, *Civil Service Administration in Ceylon: A Study in Bureaucratic Adaptation*. Colombo: Department of Cultural Affairs.

Wickramasinghe, Nira, 1991, 'Divide and Rule' in Ceylon (Sri Lanka) During the Period of Transfer of Power. *University of Colombo Review* 10: 750–92.

——, 1995, *Ethnic Politics in Colonial Sri Lanka 1927–1947*. New Delhi: Vikas Publishing House.

Wilson, A. Jeyaratnam, 1988, *The Break-Up of Sri Lanka: The Sinhalese-Tamil Conflict*. London: C. Hurst & Company.

——, 1994, *S.J.V. Chelvanayakam and the Crisis of Sri Lankan Tamil Nationalism, 1947–1977*. London: Hurst.

6

Pakistan or Punjabistan

Crisis of National Identity

YUNAS SAMAD

Political instability and ethnic conflicts have been the leitmotif of Pakistan's brief history. The minority nationalities in Pakistan lay the responsibilities for these failures and disasters on the state. This paper argues that the Punjabi hegemony of the state has perpetuated a reductionist view that Punjab's and Pakistan's interests are synonymous. This Punjabi perspective of Pakistan—Punjabistan—treats political opposition by minorities as anti-state opposition, which leaves little room for accommodation and negotiation. The paper examines how, historically, nationalism and ethnicity actually came to co-exist in the first place and then considers the process that reactivated ethnic identification at the expense of nationalism. The role of state power and domination, specifically how Punjabi hegemony over the state was established and sustained, is considered central to understanding the frictions, tensions and conflicts between the state and the regional identifications. The paper, finally, reflects on whether all Punjabis participated in this process of domination.

Official nationalism attempted to locate, fix and objectify an essentialized notion of Muslim identity and traced its evolution from the late 19th century, or even earlier, and its transformation into full-blown Pakistani nationalism in the 20th century. This triumphalist approach saw Muslim nationalism as the desirable and natural political development of a reified homogeneous notion of Islam. These essentialized notions of Islam have led to the articulation of a monological perspective of Pakistan nationalism—a perspective that cannot tolerate hybridity and diversity, and celebrates Islamic authenticity as the only basis for participating in this project of national endeavour. The political processes, however, have been bedevilled by the attempts to elaborate a homogeneous official nationalism premised on essentialized notions of Islam: What kind of Islam? What was the relationship between the state and confessional faith? And, where does ethnicity fit in, if at all?

These were issued that were never clarified and this confusion and uncertainty was at the bottom of the crisis in national identity that was reflected in the different interpretations advocated or imposed by the Pakistani establishment. Under Zulfikar Ali Bhutto official nationalism was taken to mean Islamic socialism while during General Zia-ul-Haq's reign it was re-interpreted, under Jamat-i-Islami's influence, in a far more austere manner, as Nizam-i-Mustafa—an Islamic state. The severest test for official nationalism, however, came from ethnic assertion, or more precisely, from linguistic politics. It was argued that nationalism displaced ethnicity in the run up to partition, but then the question arises why does it episodically reappear to become the central feature of the various conflicts that have overtaken Pakistan. The state was partly responsible for the 200,000 to 300,000 lives lost in the Bangladesh war of liberation[1] and the significant numbers lost in the Baluchistan revolt, the uprising in rural Sind and in the bitter and bloody conflicts raging in Karachi. These figures can be contested, depending on one's view as being too low or too high, but it is incontestable that large numbers died resisting the Pakistani state. This bloodshed was emblematic of the crisis in official nationalism, which has consistently and stubbornly failed to accommodate ethnic identifications.

This paper attempts to come to grips with the underlying cause for this instability by understanding identifications as fluid, contested and dynamic phenomena that were changing over time. This is done by re-examining the notion of Pakistan, showing the diversity of perceptions and how it ambiguously and ambivalently co-existed with regional and local identifications. The fact that these different interests were brought together, at all, was a testimony to Jinnah's genius. However, his successors in Pakistan began to assert an official identification that reflected the interest of Punjab. Punjabi hegemony of the military-bureaucratic institutions resulted in a reductionist perspective that treated Pakistan's and Punjab's interests to be the same. The development of Punjabistan ruptured the tenuous, nebulous and fraught relationship between national and ethnic identification and prepared the way for conflict. However, rather than accepting the minority nationality perspective of Punjabi domination uncritically, the paper demonstrates that only certain groups in Punjab actually benefit from this process of domination. And that some elements within the province were actively involved in challenging this hegemony.

Co-existence of Ethnicity and Nationalism

National and ethnic identities in Pakistan—like elsewhere—were not mutually discrete and homogeneous categories that were fixed over time and context. The ebb and flow of official nationalism reveals that it was mistaken to see Muslim identity as a reified category. Rather, it contained ambiguities, variations, subtleties and overlapped. I want to present an alternative perspective on the relationship between Muslim nationalism and ethnicity, arguing that they were deeply intertwined in a dynamic relationship and perhaps, in some cases, not separable at all. Identities, whether national, ethnic, class, or other loyalties, were considered to be heterogeneous and contested categories with shifting boundaries: frontiers that at times were ambiguous, indistinct and semi-permeable, harden into clearly defined, impenetrable barriers that turn small differences into a vast chasm.

The Janus-faced quality of nationalism which allowed it to present an Islamic or regional face depending on the situational context was an important characteristic of Pakistan nationalism. In the 1940s, the Muslim League brought together many strands of Muslim nationalism. These different hues reflected the different conceptions of nationalism being popularized. They mirrored the contradictory interests of Muslims from different parts of India that were superficially aggregated together because of a common perceived fear and distrust of the Congress. The Congress' ascendancy during the inter-war years confirmed the fears of middle and upper class Muslims that the constitutional safeguards were inadequate. These concerns engaged the minds of intellectuals and politicians and a number of schemes and proposals were promoted. Out of this debate the acronym 'Pakistan' emerged but it only gained popularity when appropriated by the Muslim League.[2]

Three strands ran through Muslim nationalist discourse at the time. Thematically, they represented separatist, federal and confederal perspectives. Chaudhary Rahmat Ali, an imaginative and ardent separatist, invented the acronym 'Pakistan'. During the late 1930s, his ideas, propagated by the Pakistan National Movement, became common currency among Muslim intellectuals, particularly in Punjab and within the League leadership of Sindh and the North West Frontier Province (NWFP).[3] The credit for popularizing the acronym 'Pakistan' in Punjab went to Rahmat and his supporters. The term Pakistan was strongly resisted by Jinnah, mainly due to personal differences with Rahmat Ali. Outside Punjab, Dr. Qadri and Professor Sayed Zafrul Hasan elaborated the Aligarh scheme that was concerned with the interest of the Muslim-minority provinces. In Bengal, Fazlul Huq was not simply thinking in terms of one separate homeland for Muslims but two when he proposed the Lahore Resolution. He wanted Bengal to be independent from both India and what is today Pakistan.[4]

The activities of the Pakistan National Movement provoked a debate, which involved Sikander Hayat, Sayed Abdul Latif, Nawab of Mamdot and Mian Kifayat Ali. The first two proposed a federal solution, while the latter two suggested confederal alternatives. All of these schemes were designed to avoid partition and the transfer of population that was implied in Rahmat's separatist vision.[5] Mamdot and Kifyat Ali believed that federalism left too strong a centre and its powers needed to be further reduced. Sayed Abdul Latif's plan had a cultural premise and this was used to justify the interest of the state of Hyderabad.[6] The fact that the majority of the schemes were proposed by Punjab is not a coincidence. It was the most active on this issue as the province had been the major benefactor of provincial autonomy and most concerned that these powers would be curtailed by a centre dominated by the Congress. It was also feared that ultimately such a centre would break Punjab's monopoly over the army.[7]

By the time of partition the Muslim League was able to establish its hegemony over all the regional parties except in Kashmir and Baluchistan. Sheikh Abdullah remained loyal to the Congress and in the case of Baluchistan most of the Baluch tribes were outside British Baluchistan and hence had no say in the final outcome. States such as Kalat were in touch with Jinnah only because they were interested in independence. Pakistan nationalism was expanding not by displacing old regional, tribal, linguistic, sectarian and familial loyalties but by subsuming them largely intact and by trying to establish new correlations between the local and subcontinental levels. There was also an ambivalence and a number of ambiguities emerging from the overlapping between ethnicity and nationalism in the Muslim-majority provinces. It seems that only the Cabinet Mission satisfied these subtleties in difference and that was why the provincial bosses had approved.

Sikander Hayat's federal proposition could not really be considered to be an example of Muslim nationalist thought. He was extremely hostile to the idea of Pakistan and his scheme explicitly retained non-Muslim minorities so that it was not a Muslim state. In fact, it was a perspective that was rooted in Punjabi regionalism and not Muslim nationalism. In Bengal, regionalism was also moulding nationalism in its own image. The East Pakistan Renaissance Society rejected Muslim nationalism in favour of Bengali identification and inspired Raghib Ahasan's Greater Bengal scheme. Suhrawardy and Abul Hashim popularized these ideas and turned the Bengal Muslim League into a mass party. With partition looming, Suhrawardy disowned openly the two-nation theory, preferring the idea of an independent Bengal outside of Pakistan. This ideological cleavage was the basis for the friction between Punjab and Bengal that plagued the united Pakistan.[8]

Sindhi politicians G.M. Sayed, Ghulam Husain, Hidayatullah and Abdulllah Haroon represented the general sentiment in the

Sindh Muslim League that was unanimously opposed to any centre—League's or Congress'—from interfering in Sindhi affairs. Also, it was clear that Sindh was against being amalgamated with Punjab in a north-western block. The ambivalence between nationalism and ethnicity was epitomized by the political career of G.M. Sayed. He built up the Muslim League in the province and was expelled from the party as partition loomed. Outside the party he reverted to an explicitly Sindhi perspective, focusing on anti-Punjabi and anti-Bihari issues.[9]

In the NWFP, the League and its supporters did not articulate any clear expression of Muslim nationalism. The party remained a marginal force until the referendum of 1947 when it wrested control of the province from the pro-Congress Khan brothers. The Khudai Khidmatgars was an explicit vehicle of Pakhtun ethnicity, which had strong anti-centre characteristics.[10] Dr. Khan wanted autonomy for Sarhad as well (Frontier) as restricted powers for the centre, and refused to concede differences between Hindus and Muslims. When the issue of a referendum was advanced, the Khan brothers raised the Pakhtunistan slogan, mainly as a bargaining counter, but were unable to stop the tide against them. These strong regional identifications in Bengal, Sindh and NWFP were major obstacles for the expansion and consolidation of Muslim nationalism and combined with other issues in Pakistan into anti-centre hostility.

Historically, it was shown that nationalism and ethnicity were not distinct and separate, essentialized categories simply juxtaposed to each other. Nationalism formed an amalgam with ethnicity and a complex relationship was created where influences of both the Islamic and Indic elements were active. There was a need for these issues to be handled sensitively in Pakistan.[11] Instead, this relationship quickly unravelled with ethnicity asserting itself as a competitor to nationalism. Ethnicity was an enduring resource that in the highly factionalized social and political structure facilitated the politics of 'ins' and outs'. These shifts in identifications were not only due to agency but a response to alterations in state power and domination. It was not only a question whether one could or wanted to assert Sindhi or Muhajir identity but also whether structures prevented or greatly limited the participation of Pakistani identity. The primary reason for these shifts in identities was due to the role of the state. The proposition suggested is that groups who were excluded from state power politicized ethnicity in order to legitimize resistance. In doing so they become the 'other', thus justifying their suppression by the state. Conversely, as groups were co-opted by the centre they depressed their ethnicity and emphasized Pakistani nationalism. This simple linear hypothesis is complicated by the class characteristics of the dominant groups. The fact that landlords dominate the establishment made it easier to co-opt ethnic representatives from similar backgrounds.[12]

Since 1947, the military-bureaucratic oligarchy has been the major player in Pakistan politics. It has ruled Pakistan directly and indirectly for over 30 years. The legitimation for this interventionist role has been that it was the true and only guardian of nationalism in Pakistan and that all those that opposed it were allies of the great 'other' India. The state was not ethnically neutral and the dominant linguistic groups were the Punjabis. Approximately, 80 per cent[13] of the army and 55 per cent[14] of the federal bureaucracy were from Punjab. This preponderance was most clearly apparent at the highest level of the establishment. With defence being the largest item of the budget, roughly about a third,[15] the implications were clear. Political intervention ensured that the Punjabi-dominated military-bureaucratic combine was guaranteed that it received the main slice of the cake.

This core group in the establishment co-opted allies but its options were limited by the size of the cake. Thus, a group's co-option by the centre was at the expense of another group. It was their proximity to the centre that ultimately determined political identity. Exclusion resulted in the politicization of ethnic identity and the recurrent issues underpinning these mobilizations were demands for increased autonomy, greater representation at the centre, encouragement of cultural diversity and socio-economic concerns.

It was in the early 1950s that the ethnicization of the state took place, the Punjabis aligned with the Muhajirs, Urdu-speaking migrants from India, against Bengalis. The Muhajirs, 3.5 per cent of the population, had 21 per cent of the jobs in the Pakistan Civil Service and this reflected the historic advantages that this group had.[16] Thus, in the debates at the time, Punjabis and Muhajirs were the most vocal advocates for the construction of a strong centralized state and were prepared to go to any means to achieve this goal. However, the Bengali representatives resisted this move and wanted a more decentralized central government, even if it meant decreasing tension with India and thus negating the call for a larger army. Simultaneously, they attempted to use the political processes to translate their political majority into institutional predominance as well. The crucial turning point in this struggle was the humiliating dismissal of the Bengali Prime Minister Nazimuddin by the military-bureaucratic oligarchy. The exclusion of Bengalis from the centre, the tightening grip of Karachi over East Pakistan, the insensitive handling of the language issue and the economic exploitation of the region pushed East Pakistan along the road of separatism.[17] The resistance went underground during Ayyub Khan's military rule and resurfaced with venom in the general upsurge for democracy a decade later. The essential demands of the Awami League, decentralization, greater representation in the army and respect for a majority decision in the assembly, if accepted, would have undercut the foundation of the Punjabi-dominated military-bureaucratic oligarchy.[18] The class difference between landed elites of West Pakistan and the middle-class opposition made the gulf between the two, a chasm that the military believed could only be dealt with by the mailed fist. The fact that East Pakistan was separated by 1,200 miles of Indian territory made this exercise of brute force a futile affair.

Defeated on the battlefield by India, the establishment was forced to accept a civilian government led by Zulfikar Ali Bhutto. This was a major interregnum in the military-bureaucratic combine's domination of Pakistan. Despite the fact Bhutto was a Sindhi, he was very much the centre's man. A hawk on India and a strong centrist, he initially was quite acceptable to the army. His rise to power defused the tensions building up in rural Sindh as the PPP (Pakistan People's Party) government at the centre provided political access for Sindhis. The recognition of the Sindhi language by the provincial government in 1972 and the quota imposed on Muhajirs entering the Pakistan Civil Service[19] led to a deflation of Sindhi nationalism and the enhancement of their Pakistani identity.

Bhutto's regime came down harshly on the opposition that was primarily located in the NWFP and Baluchistan. The toppling of the National Awami Party—Jamat-i-Ulama-i-Islam coalition in Frontier and the incarceration of Wali Khan on trumped up charges alienated Pakhtuns. Their exclusion intensified the calls for greater autonomy. However, the dismissal of Ataullah Megnal's government in Baluchistan precipitated a rebellion by the Baluchi tribes. Over 9,000 lives were lost in the conflict between 1973 and 1977 that involved the deployment of four army divisions (approximately 80,000 men) including combined operations by the Pakistan and Iranian air forces. The struggle for an independent Baluchistan was led by tribal leaders such as Ataullah Megal and Khair Bux Marri, some of whom were of Marxist persuasion. It was an unequal struggle that forced the Baluchi combatants to retreat into Afghanistan. The heavy-handed approach politicized Baluchis and intensified separatist feelings.[20]

Bhutto's autocratic behaviour also antagonized the military-bureaucratic oligarchy. The creation of the Federal Security Force displacing the army's role in internal security and lateral entry of political nominees into the bureaucracy antagonized the oligarchy. Thus, when the Pakistan National Movement mobilized urban groups against electoral malpractices by the PPP in the 1977 general elections, it provided the opportunity for General Zia-ul-Huq to take over. The exclusion of the PPP from the political process, the execution of Bhutto and the deployment of the army in 1983, and again in 1986 in rural Sindh to suppress opposition, alienated many Sindhis. The perception grew that the province was colonized by the Punjab, accelerating the momentum in ethnic assertion. The expulsion of the PPP, the main political force in Sindh, from the central arenas resulted in the flourishing of a different form of Sindhi nationalism. Two currents emerged: one calling for a Sindhu Desh (independent Sindh), and the other calling for a Sindhi-Baluch federation in a confederal Pakistan.[21]

As this development was accompanied by a realignment of political forces both in the centre and with the centre's relations with other minorities, the Soviet intervention in Afghanistan increased the significance of the western provinces. Sensitive to the possibility that the opposition forces in Baluchistan might become surrogates for Soviet-Afghan plans for the destabilization of Pakistan, Zia made a serious attempt to woo them. Baluchi suspicions were not so easily allayed, but it did have the effect of making them neutral to the regime. In the Frontier, the establishment found its task easier as Pakhtun refugees from Afghanistan swung public opinion in favour of the centre's strategy against the Kabul regime. As the west's conduit of weapons and resources for the Afghan guerrillas was mainly channelled through the province, the Punjabi-dominated army incorporated Pakhtuns into the ruling clique. The fact that Pakhtuns were prominent in the army made this task easier, and Pakhtun generals and bureaucrats played a significant role in the regime.[22]

This inclusion, however, was at the expense of the Muhajirs. The shift against them had been initiated during Bhutto's government by the imposition of an upper ceiling on their recruitment into the civil service. The displacement expanded into other areas during Zia's time. Mainly Punjabi, but also Pakhtun, influence increased in Karachi at the expense of the Mujahirs. They were still influential in the federal government and in the administration in urban Sindh, but their position was being eroded. This process of exclusion ultimately resulted in a shift in identifications. Muhajirs had been the solid supporters of the Islamic parties as Islam was the justification for their presence in Pakistan.[23]

Pakistan Punjab was not a homogeneous entity and three different cultural-linguistic strands were discernible. Some would argue that these differences were dialectical variations and do not amount to separate languages or cultures. In the east around Lahore lies the densely populated heartland that was the traditional home of the 'yeoman farmer' and was also so dear to the colonial administrators. This region was a natural extension of the small farmers' landholding pattern that was found in the Indian Punjab. Only a small part of the heartland of old, undivided Punjab lies within Pakistan. But it asserted its dominance as it contains the provincial capital Lahore—the political hub of the region and the most industrialized area in the province.[24] A significant proportion of this population migrated from eastern Punjab at the time of partition and they have a close affinity with the original Muslim population in that they all speak standard or Majhi Punjabi.[25]

To the north and north-west—Jhelum and Rawalpindi districts—is what can be broadly characterized as the Potohari-speaking region, which extends into Hazara in NWFP and Azad Kashmir. This was *barani* land, hence poorer and sparsely populated and was the principal recruiting ground of the Pakistan army. The martial castes of the Greater Punjab were always closely associated with the state. The military lobby was always able to maintain close relations with successive empires (Mughals, Sikhs and British) and, now, the Pakistani state. The interlude between the Second Afghan War and the First World War saw the dramatic increase in recruitment from Punjab with the majority coming from a narrow range of martial castes, representing less than 1 per cent of the subcontinent's population. The local economy was revolutionized by the multiplier effect of military expenditure. Besides the direct impact of pay and pensions, the demand for commercial agriculture and domestic handicrafts expanded. These inaccessible areas were incorporated into the world economy by the construction of strategic roads, railways, cantonments and even some industrialization. Legislation was also brought in defending the interest of the martial castes. The Punjab Land Alienation Act, along with other pieces of Unionist legislation, restricted the expropriation of agricultural land by predatory moneylenders.[26]

In Pakistan, these patterns persist. The present recruiting policy remains narrow and 75 per cent of the Pakistan army comes from three districts of Punjab, viz., Rawalpindi, Jhelum and Campbellpur and from two districts of Sarhad, viz., Mardan and Kohat. The army remains the biggest employer with about 500,000 men, which represents 9 per cent of the male labour force in the country.[27] It absorbs surplus sons from the poor and hilly agricultural lands that are dependent on rainfall for irrigation. While farmers from irrigated lands were in need of labour, the *barani* areas had a surplus that could be easily absorbed by the army. The army was also an honourable profession for the martial castes with Rajput pretensions. The influx of pay and pensions improved the lifestyles and was a source of economic satisfaction and the army continues to act as a development agency. It has encouraged strategic industries, and defence contractors once mastering the techniques, apply their skill in the civilian sector. The agricultural economy received continuous stimulation from the demands of the cantonments and produces of the Military Farms Department. The army also generated a relatively sophisticated pool of labour: it trained a large number of drivers, mechanics, engineers who then applied their skills in the civilian economy when discharged. The road transport sector has a significant presence of those who learned their skills in the armed forces.[28]

The army was also socially linked to the Punjabi society through the officer corps. The social composition of the Pakistan Army Officer Corps has been changing since the 1960s when it consisted primarily of scions of the landed gentry and urban professionals. With changes in career opportunities attracting elites to the private sector and the professions, their place was replaced by officers drawn from the urban and rural lower-middle class. Since the 1970s many of the junior officers were drawn not from the prosperous central region of the Punjabi but from the northern impoverished districts. These later entrants were less westernized and prone to the religious rhetoric that was the hallmark of Zia-ul-Huq's regime—a development reinforced by the infiltration of the officer corps by student cadres of the Jamat-i-Islami. Its penetration was assisted by the practice introduced by General Zia of sending combat offices to the universities—the stamping ground of the Jamat—introduction of Islamic teaching and training at the Pakistan Military Academy, and at the Command and Staff College, as well as other initiatives by Zia to inculcate Islamic perspectives and values into the officer corps.[29]

Officer loyalty was also carefully nursed by Zia-ul-Huq to a much greater degree than any of his predecessors. Under Ayyub Khan's rule, the military handed power over to the civil service within a short period of 21 months. Ayyub was careful not to offend the bureaucracy as the latter were responsible for the day-to-day running of the country. General Zia, instead, asserted the authority of the military over the civil administration by nominating military personnel to the top positions in the federal and provincial bureaucracy. This was done in a low-key but persistent manner that effectively reduced the civil service to a subordinate position in the running of the country. Besides placing officers into top civilian jobs, Zia kept the 'boys' happy and loyal by organizing the rotation of highly lucrative training assignments in Saudi Arabia and the Gulf states. It was estimated that 30,000 soldiers were seconded to the Middle East and that one out of every six or seven men in uniform benefited from this arrangement.[30]

Landlords were politically the most powerful and well-organized class in Pakistan and Punjab and have a significant presence in the army and bureaucracy, though this seems to be declining. They gained from the economic activity generated by the military but benefited most by their willingness to serve in any government. This group's success in politics was founded on the premise that they were entirely flexible in their political allegiance and willing to change loyalty when it was profitable. They have overshadowed Punjab's political landscape through various political organizations. A handful of families dominate Punjab politics. The Hayats of Wah, the Noons and Tiwanas of Sargodha, and the Daultanas of Mailsi in Multan district, were probably the most prominent. Others that were also politically significant include the Legaris, Pirachas, Kalabagh, Gilani, Multan Qureshis and Dastis. From the three leading families came the leadership of the Unionist Party, and then the Muslim League.[31] Even though Ayyub Khan tried, he could not keep them out of politics and Bhutto's PPP and General Zia continued the pattern. The latter's efforts to inject the Majlis-i-Shura with new blood only resulted in the landlord lobby emerging in a commanding position in the new assembly. These tendencies persisted in the government of Benazir Bhutto, with Ghulam Mustafa Khar and Farooq Leghari being the most prominent from Punjab.

Despite the support of the landed class, the army wanted a countervailing political force. The economic benefits had already converged the interests of the middle class and the army. Winning over and sustaining the support of the Punjabi middle classes was crucial for the army if it was to successfully blunt any opposition to Martial Law. The fact that they did so, perhaps, explains why the Movement for the Restoration for Democracy (MRD) was not so significant in Punjab or that workers and peasants have remained quiet since the 1970s. The military cultivated the emerging industrial bourgeoisie of Punjab to its side. This became more compelling with the announcement of elections after Zia's death. The Islami Jamhoori Ittehad (IJI) was formed by General Hamid Gul, Director General of the Inter-Services Intelligence (ISI), on the explicit order of General Beg. The IJI, a nine-party alliance, consisting of both factions of the Muslim League and the Jamat-i-Islami, did not have a clear political programme other than broad support for the Islamization programme. Out of the various contenders for the leadership, the Chief Minister of Punjab, Nawaz Sharif, was supported by the army at the expense of the former Prime Minister, Junejo, and the former Premier of the Interim Government, Ghulam Mustafa Jatoi. This was not surprising as Nawaz Sharif, who had an enduring animosity for the PPP for nationalizing family industries, was, along with other young aspiring politicians, groomed by General Ghulam Jilani when the latter had been the Governor of Punjab. He was noticed by General Zia when he made significant financial contributions to Zia's December 1984 referendum campaign. In 1981 Nawaz Sharif was invited to become Finance and Sports Minister of the province, and after the 1985 provincial elections, Zia appointed him Chief Minister of Punjab. Once the military-bureaucratic oligarchy installed their men at the head of the Islamic coalition, they used the intelligence agencies to assist his election campaign. Brigadier Imitaz, Additional Director General of Internal Security of the ISI, played a crucial role in Sharif's campaign, especially in Punjab.[32] The fact that Benazir Bhutto won the 1988 elections only demonstrated that the ISI miscalculated the strength of the opposition and the degree of public hostility to all those associated with the older order.

On the debit side, the military lost support of some groups during Zia's rule. Women were considered a soft target and Zia introduced the Hudood Ordinance in 1979. The ordinance provided for severe punishment, including amputation and public floggings, for certain crimes. The aspects concerning women were the provisions concerning *zina* (adultery) and *zina-bil-jabr* (rape). The maximum provision for these crimes that the ordinance provided, irrespective of gender, was stoning to death or a hundred lashes. Guilt of suspects could be established by self-confession or by the testimony of four Muslim males of known moral repute. A woman's witness on its own could not convict a man. The ordinance did not deal with the question of raped unmarried women becoming pregnant. The consequence was that victims of rape were being sentenced for adultery. The ordinance, in effect, gave legal sanction to the sexual harassment of women. The case of Safia Bibi illustrated the point. A blind domestic was raped by her employer and his son. She was charged with adultery and awarded three years' imprisonment and fifteen lashes while the father and son got away unpunished.

This, along with other cases, mobilized women into opposing the Islamization process. In 1981, the middle class and upper class women formed Women's Action Forum (WAF) in Karachi and it spread to the key urban areas (Lahore, Islamabad, Peshawar, Bahawalpur, Faisalabad and Quetta), and crucially it struck roots in Punjab. The All-Pakistan Women's Association (APWA) and other women's organizations supported this development. In attempting to formulate a strategy, the WAF decided to fight the legislation by arguing within an Islamic context. It enlisted sympathetic *ulama* and adopted Islamic idioms and metaphors in mobilizing support. This was vigorously opposed by the Islamic parties, and the Jamat-i-Isalmi formed Majlis-i-Khawatin Pakistan to block WAF's campaign.[33] WAF in 1994 changed track and proclaimed that it was now a secular organization and was also contemplating declaring itself a feminist organization.[34] WAF activities, however, were part of a much wider phenomenon. Women workers from the PPP and the Awami National Party (ANP) and the largest women's organization, Sindhianai Tehrik, played a significant role in opposing these discriminatory laws.[35] The opposition was not able to do more than check the Islamization process, but their activities politicized important sections of women and created new oppositions to the regime. The irony was that Islamization was intended to weld the nation around Islam, but instead it alienated Punjabi women.

The other repercussion of the Islamization process was the rise in religious sectarianism. One of the major issues confronting Punjab was the rise of sectarian splinter groups that were heavily armed and dangerous. Each group was local, but their collective influence spanned a crescent stretching from Sialkot to Faisalabad, covering Gujranawala, Sargodha and Jhang. Some of the organizations, such as the Sipah-i-Sahba Pakistan (SSP), were a breakaway from Jamiat-ul-Ulam-i-Islam (J-U-I), a Deobandi organization. The SSP founded as a sub-organization of J-U-I in 1984, broke away allegedly over ideological grounds from the parent body. While the parent body advocated a generic concept of the Islamic state, the SSP adhered to a much narrower view that demanded all other sects be declared non-Muslim. On gaining its independence it became involved in a protracted and bloody struggle against Shias. Violence was not restricted to opponents; there were fierce leadership conflicts within the organization. Its founder, Maulana Haq Nawaz Jhangvi, was killed and so was his successor. A number of splinter organizations emerged from the SSP—the Harkat-ul-Ansar and the Tanzeem-i-Dawa being the largest of the nine groups that broke away. Most of these organizations were no more than a cover for criminal networks patronized by influential landlords, led by local *maulvis*. A vast amount of sectarian literature, valued in millions of rupees, was circulated by these organizations. This literature targets Shias, Ahmadiyas and Christians. Both the Harkat-ul-Ansar and the Tanzeem-i-Dawa have Arab nationals trained by Afghan Mujahideen and Harkat was believed to be led by an Egyptian cleric living in Karachi. The Shias were organized around the Tehrik-i-Jafri-i-Pakistan, the local chapter of the Khomeini revolution. It came to prominence when it led the Shia protest against the introduction of *Zakat*. Originally, it was confined to the NWFP but it has made major inroads into Punjab and aggressively challenged the SSP's anti-Shia campaign. The third major sectarian organization was the Sunni Tehrik, a product of the Barelvi movement, Ziaul Quran, which has grown dramatically in Faisalabad and Jhang. This organization has been in the vanguard of the anti-Christian movement. While most of these organizations' energies are focused on those who were or perceived to be non-Muslims, the violence has flowed into intra-Sunni rivalry. The murder of a local Deobandi *hakim* by a mob egged on by a rival *Barelvi* mullah was indicative of the dangers of Zia's Islamic pigeons coming home to roost.[36]

The Siraiki-speaking areas, principally in the south-west Punjab around Multan and Bahawalpur, have made a conscious and explicit attempt to distance themselves from the dominant groups in Punjab. In the 1930s the first conscious effort was made to revive the language that Khwaja Ghulam Farid rendered in his mystical hymns. The search for authenticity was impacted by the migratory waves unleashed by partition. Approximately, half of the population in Multan was originally refugees from east Punjab and these refugees dominated the city's industrial and commercial sectors. Their presence downplayed the efforts of the Siraiki-speakers to establish the city as a cultural centre for Siraiki—for the refugees, Lahore was their cultural centre. This sense of deprivation fuelled the initial development of the Siraiki movement in the 1960s. This was institutionalized in a variety of cultural and literary organizations and journals. They were unable, however, to assert their demands for a Siraiki Suba, despite the more relaxed political environment following the downfall of Yayha Khan. This failure meant that their effort remained concentrated on cultural matters, which varied from persuading Radio Multan to increase transmission time in Siraiki, to the activities organized by the Siraiki Academy.[37] It was unclear how, but there has been, recently, shifts back to politics with two organizations becoming active in the Pakistan Siraiki Party and the Siraiki Qaumi Movement. With MQM attempting to make inroads, the indications were that this would polarize the region.[38]

The other area of dissent comes from Azad Kashmir. Administratively, the area of Azad Kashmir was notionally autonomous. In practice, all decisions were cleared or were taken by Islamabad. Even though, culturally and linguistically, Azad Kashmir was part of the Punjabi heartland, it has been treated as peripheral despite the significant contribution it has made to the country as a whole. Unlike other areas of the Potohar, Mirpuri villagers were not, generally, recruited by the British Indian Army. Instead, Mirpuris established a niche in the engine rooms of the British merchant navy. Opportunities did not arise until the acute labour shortage during the Second World War, and Mirpuri ex-seamen enthusiastically filled in these gaps. These pioneers provided the bridgehead for chain-migration that took place in the post-war era. Substantial numbers of Mirpuris left their ships and called their families and clansmen to join in a great wave of migration. A third of a million settled in Britain, which was half the population of Mirpur's villages. The region was not evenly represented and the majority of the emigrants were from Mirpur district or from the southern part of Kotli district. In many villages over half of the population included residents abroad, resulting in significant flows of remittances back to the villages of origin. The paradoxical consequence of this has been that while capital-rich, thus producing short-term increase in the standard of living, there has not been sustained economic growth.

The Pakistanis have not merely overlooked the Mirpuris, but exploited their hard-earned financial and environmental resources. The Mirpuris deeply resented that their considerable financial contribution was not being deployed to stimulate the economic and infrastructural development of Mirpur or Azad Kashmir. Nor had Mangla generated any benefits for the local population. While electricity was being supplied downstream as far as Karachi, the neighbouring villages were connected much later. This frustration boiled over in the short-lived Dadiali rebellion that served as a reminder to the discontent among Azad Kashmiris.

Even though, the boundaries between Mirpuris and Potoharis were largely artificial in cultural terms, there were few, if any, linguistic or cultural differences between those living on either side of the Jhelum. However, Mirpuris assert that they were Kashmiri and hence not Pakistani or Punjabi. This sense of Kashmiri nationalism has emerged not only against Islamabad but it also mixed up with parochial sentiment that makes Muzaffarbad equally undesirable. The result has been enthusiasm by Mirpuris for Kashmiri nationalism, a desire for real freedom epitomized in the slogan 'Kashmir Zindabad! Pakistan Murdabad![39]

Conclusion

Muslim nationalism was not a homogeneous phenomenon. It consisted of several strands that ranged from separatist, federal and confederal perspectives. Besides these variations in the nationalist discourse, there was an array of regional tendencies—Bengali, Sindhi, Pakhtun and Punjabi—that were partially subsumed by the Pakistan movement. The Muslim League was imperfectly able to bring together these diverse perspectives under the ambiguous Lahore Resolution of 1940. Regional, linguistic, sectarian and tribal affiliations remained largely intact and this created a number of ambiguities and ambivalence and points of tension between nationalism and ethnicity which were later to become the historical basis for the opposition to the centre. These antagonisms were to become the enduring resource that was amplified by the highly fluid political environment in the struggles of 'ins' and 'outs'.

The ambiguities and ambivalences between nationalism and ethnicity were episodically hardened into ethnic fault lines due to the insensitive handling and short-sighted priorities of the state. The *casus belli* was the insistence of the Punjabi-dominated military-bureaucratic oligarchy, which has, directly or indirectly, ruled Pakistan for roughly 30 years, of pursing policies that had little support outside the state institutions. Both of these key institutions were quantitatively and qualitatively the preserve of the Punjabis and their allies. Punjabis and Muhajirs initially advocated and then defended vigorously the necessity for a highly centralized state. This was strongly resisted by the Bengali political leadership, and the Punjabi-dominated military-bureaucratic oligarchy retaliated by imposing military rule. Ayyub Khan's regime compounded the exclusion of Bengalis with economic exploitation of East Pakistan. The result was that it diverted the political opposition on to the road of separation. The break-up of Pakistan and the rise to power of Zulfikar Ali Bhutto led to a reformulation of the power relations at the centre. Sindhis were co-opted at the centre at the expense of Muhajirs and his regime's harsh response to legitimate opposition in Baluchistan and the NWFP exacerbated pre-existing grievances. Baluchis resisted the establishment and the rebellion was crushed with a significant loss of life. Bhutto's downfall led to a further reformation of the ethnic composition of the centre. Zia-ul-Haq's exclusion of Sindhis confronted him with a serious revolt in that province and a dramatic increase in separatist sentiments. However, Pakhtuns and Baluch, primarily due to the sensitivity of the western border regions after the Soviet intervention in Afghanistan, were accommodated by the new regime. The Zia regime neutralized the

Baluchis hostility to the centre by its attempts to compensate them for past injuries. Pakhtuns did much better, with members of the establishment being elevated to senior and sensitive positions. However, this was at the expense of Muhajirs who faced increased exclusion. They formed the MQM and mobilized around ethnicity. The army, fearing that they would work collectively with Sindhis, lured them away into forming a coalition with their preferred nominee, Nawaz Sharif. The army's role was a major contribution to the collapse in law and order in Sindh. Realizing that they were losing control of the situation, the army clamped down on its former allies and attempted to discredit and incarcerate the leadership, but had little success.

Punjab, however, was not a homogeneous entity and not all Punjabis benefited equally from the fruits of power. In terms of the rural population, the army's recruiting policy benefited directly and indirectly the population of Rawalpindi, Jhelum and Campbellpur as well as the two neighbouring districts in the NWFP. The officer corps increasingly belonged to the urban middle classes, which always benefited materially from military rule. This policy was developed to a fine art under Zia's rule with officers nominated to senior positions in the civil administration and sent on lucrative contracts to the Middle East. The landed gentry was a declining element in the officer corps, but was a very influential group associated with their counterparts in the bureaucracy and political parties, in which the landlords were dominant. If this was not enough, the army cultivated the support of the industrial bourgeoisie in order to deepen its link with Punjab. Nawaz Sharif was groomed for leadership and for the IJI, which he was to lead, by the military in a desperate attempt to keep Benazir Bhutto out of power.

However, Zia's regime alienated significant sections of the Punjabi society. The introduction of Islamic law, which particularly affected women, politicized them. It resulted in the emergence of a women's movement, which struck deep roots in the Punjabi towns. Though the opposition had little impact on the regime, it politicized a dormant section of society. The other repercussion of the Islamization process was the increase in sectarian violence. A number of violent splinter groups emerged in the small towns of Punjab. Their principal victims were Shias,

Ahmadiyas and Christians. They have been involved in bloody internal power struggles and were increasingly involved in intra-Sunni conflicts.

The Siraiki-speaking areas were increasingly opposed to the dominant groups in the Punjab. This opposition emerged from a variety of Siraiki cultural organizations and recently was expressed by the emergence of the Siraiki Qaumi Movement and the Pakistan Siraiki Party. The other significant opposition in the rural areas came from the Mirpur population of Azad Kashmir. Despite their significant contribution to the Pakistan economy, primarily through remittances, the area has remained underdeveloped economically and infrastructural progress remains marginal.

Finally, ironically, the Punjabi domination of Pakistan has not benefited all Punjabis: it has been underpinned largely by Punjabi elites (bureaucrats and landlords) and co-opted sections of the peasantry. This domination has been the primary cause for the ethnic conflicts that convulsed the nation's brief history and has forced minorities to challenge Punjab's hegemony by propagating alternatives to Pakistan—alternatives that have been rooted in the historic ambiguities and ambivalences of Pakistani nationalism.

Notes

1. R. Sisson and L.E. Rose, *War and Secession: Pakistan, India and the Creation of Bangladesh* (Karachi: Oxford University Press, 1992), p. 306, fn. 24.
2. Y. Samad, *Nation in Turmoil: Nationalism and Ethnicity in Pakistan 1937–58* (New Delhi: Sage, 1995), Chapter 2.
3. K.K. Aziz, *Rahmat Ali: A Biography* (Lahore: Vanguard, 1987), pp. 199–201.
4. Samad, *Nation in Turmoil*, Chapter 2.
5. Sikander Hayat, *Outlines of a Scheme of Indian Federation* (Lahore, np. Nd.). K.K. Aziz, *A History of the Idea of Pakistan* (Lahore: Vanguard, 1987), ii, pp. 545–550. A. Punjabi, *A Confederacy of India* (Lahore, n.p., 1939), pp. 6–17, 195–200. 'A Punjabi was the pseudonym that Kifayat Ali, a government servant, wrote under.

6. S.A. Latif, *The Cultural Future of India* (Bombay, 1938, publisher not known), p. 46. National Archives Pakistan, Quaid-i-Azam Papers, F/49 Mohammad Afzal Qadri to Jinnah 25 June 1939.
7. India Office Records, Mss Eur F 125/88 (Linlithgow Collection) Craik to Linlithgow, 19 May 1939.
8. Y. Samad, *Nation in Turmoil*, Chapter 2.
9. Ibid., Chapter 3.
10. S.A. Rittenberg, 'The Independence Movement in India's North-West Frontier Province 1901–1947', unpublished doctoral dissertation, Columbia University, 1977, pp. 175–76.
11. Y. Samad, *Nation in Turmoil*, Chapter 3.
12. U. Phadnis, *Ethnicity and Nation-Building in South Asia* (New Delhi: Sage, 1990), p. 104. H. Alavi, 'Class and State' in H. Gardezi and J. Rashid (eds.) *Pakistan: The Roots of Dictatorship* (London: Zed Press, 1983), p. 46.
13. S.P. Cohn, 'State Building in Pakistan', in A. Banuazizi and M. Weiner (eds.), *The State, Religion, and Ethnic Politics: Pakistan Iran and Afghanistan* (Lahore: Vanguard, 1989), p. 318.
14. C.H. Kennedy, *Bureaucracy in Pakistan* (Karachi: Oxford University Press, 1987), p. 194.
15. Government of Pakistan, Finance Division, Economic Advisory Wing, *Economic Survey 1992–93* (Islamabad, 1993), p. 61, Table 6.6.
16 R. Braibanti, *Asian Bureaucratic Traditions Emergent From the British Imperial Tradition* (Durham: Duke University Press, 1966), p. 269.
17. Y. Samad, *Nation in Turmoil*, Chapters 4 and 5.
18. R. Sisson and L.E. Rose, *War and Secession*, pp. 66, 76.
19. C.H. Kennedy, *Bureaucracy in Pakistan*, p. 194.
20. S.S. Harrison, 'Ethnicity and Political Stalemate in Pakistan' in A. Banuazizi and M. Weiner (eds.), *The State, Religion, and Ethnic Politics: Pakistan Iran and Afghanistan* (Lahore: Vanguard, 1987), p. 274.
21. Ibid., p. 283.
22. O. Noman, *Pakistan* (London: Kegan Paul International, 1990), p. 198.
23. Y. Samad, 'Military and Democracy in Pakistans' in *Contemporary South Asia* (forthcoming).
24. Rawal Bakhsh, 'The MQM's New Clothes', *The Herald (Karachi)*, Vol. 25, No. 1, January 1994.
25. C. Shackle, 'Siraiki: A Language Movement in Pakistan', *Modern Asian Studies*, 11, 3 (1977), pp. 385, 389.

26. C. Dewey, 'The Rural Roots of Pakistani Militarism', in D.A. Low (ed.), *The Political Inheritance of Pakistan* (Basingstoke: Macmillan, 1991), pp. 261–65.
27. S.P. Cohen, *The Pakistan Army* (Berkeley: University of California Press, 1984), pp. 44, 57.
28. Dewey, 'The Rural Roots of Pakistani Militarism', pp. 271–74.
29. Akmal Hussain, *Strategic Issues in Pakistan's Economic Policy* (Lahore: Progressive Publishers, 1988), pp. 361–64.
30. Dilip Mukerjee, 'Zia's Military Legacy', *The Round Table*, 310, 1989, pp. 182–83.
31. Craig Baxter, "The People's Party vs the Punjab 'Feudalist'", in J. Korson (ed.), *Contemporary Problems of Pakistan* (Leiden: Brill, 1974), pp. 8–25.
32. *The Daily Jan* (London 31 October–1 November, 1992).
33. Ayesha Jalal, 'The Convenience of Subservience: Pakistan' in Deniz Kandiyoti (ed.), *Women, Islam and the State* (Basingstoke: Macmillan), 1991, pp. 102, 104–7.
34. Saira Akhter, 'Celebration of Women', *The Herald*, 25, 3 (March), 1994.
35. Babar Ali, 'Elitists View of Women's Struggle in Pakistan', *Economic and Political Weekly*, May 14, 1988.
36. Aamer Ahmed Khan, 'The Rise of Sectarian Mafias', *The Herald*, 25, 6 (June), 1994. Aamer Ahmed Khan, 'Blind Faith', *The Herald*, 25, 6 (June), 1994.
37. C. Shackle, 'Siraiki: A Language Movement in Pakistan', *Modern Asian Studies*, 11, 3, 1977, pp. 393–400.
38. Rawal Bakhs, 'The MQM's New Clothes', *The Herald*, 25, 1 (January), 1994.
39. Roger Ballard, 'Kashmir Crisis: View from Mirpur', *Economic and Political Weekly*, March 2–9, 1991.

7

Diversities, Ethnicity and Autonomy

K.S. SINGH

Few parts of the world have such a wide range of diversities as the Indian subcontinent. India has been described as a fishing trap into which have drifted peoples and cultures from elsewhere, a meeting ground of many influences.

In this paper we discuss India's diversities, the increasing articulation of ethnicity by groups, and the movement for and institutionalization of demands for autonomy.

Diversities

India has an extraordinary range of diversities in terms of linguistic, biological and cultural traits. Even though, the 'racial' categories have now been discarded, it is appropriate to recall for the purpose of this discussion the country's population is derived from four 'racial' stocks or morphological types. India has five language families. There are as many as 325 languages and dialects and 25 scripts are in use. The country has an incredible diversity of cultural traditions and patterns. There are as many as 2,795 communities in India. There is a wide range of diversities within each community.

The linguistic situation is heterogeneous at one level because Indians have a remarkable felicity for language. Most people in the country speak a number of languages or at least two languages. In situations of language contact the incidence of bilingualism is as high as 65 per cent. It seems that the census data on bilingualism is much too conservative (13% according to the 1981 census). One of the reasons for this could be mother tongue loyalty. Tribals are generally trilingual. No state in India is unilingual in spite of the preponderance of the speakers of the state language.

Since the Indian population is highly mixed in respect of racial composition, it is not advisable to speak in terms of the racial classification the population. Instead, we rather speak of morphological and genetic variations among populations which tend to be more so within a given population or community than between communities. There is a great deal of biological diversity among the people of India. However, the commonalities appear to be more than the variations. The number of genes in which they differ are only a few in comparison with the vast number of genes which are shared in common. There is a much greater homogenization in terms of morphological and genetic traits at the regional level. Most of the communities within a region or state share many of these traits.

The various communities which constitute the fabric of the country have first to be seen in the context of the eco-system and the eco-cultural zones. There are about 91 eco-cultural zones in the country. The communities are rooted in their resources. They derive their identity from their environment, the mountains and rivers, the terrain and its resources and the occupations based on their resources. Even, the migrant groups seek to identify themselves with their local environment except in respect of language they speak at home or marriages. This rootedness in the local eco-system is an outstanding characteristic of communities, which cuts across religious distinctions

By and large, people, regardless of the distinctions of caste and community, share a great deal in common within an eco-cultural-linguistic region or its sub-region. The People of India project identified 776 traits relating to ecology, settlement, identity, food habits, social organization, economy and occupation, linkages and the impact of change and development, the pattern of distribution of such traits was explored. If one takes the communities grouped into religious categories, it is noticed that Hindus share a very high percentage of traits with Muslims (96.77%), Buddhists (91.19%), Sikhs (88.99%) and Jains (77.46%). The shared traits between Muslims and Sikhs (89.95%), Muslims and Buddhists (91.18%) and Jains and Buddhists (81.34%) are also very high.

Therefore, the traits different communities share are far more than the traits that they do not share. Unfortunately, the traits that communities do not share are often played up as markers of their respective identities. In fact, in recent years, differences rather than commonalties are sought to be emphasized. One of the reasons for the sharing of traits on such a large scale could be the fact that most of the communities are embedded in the same ecological and socio-cultural background, even though later they have embraced different religions or ways of life (Singh, 1992).

Ethnicity

This discourse on diversities and linkages among the people of India will put in perspective the ethnic question, ethnic movements and inter-ethnic relations. It is appropriate to recall that the word 'caste' has been in use for the past four hundred years, 'nationality' for the last seventy years, and the term 'ethnicity' for the last thirty-five years. Ethnicity was used initially in a bio-cultural sense and is used now in the socio-psychological context, as an amalgam of feelings and emotions. In the beginning the term 'ethnicity' was applied to define tribal identity. Gradually, it replaced nationality in many discussions. Now, it is being increasingly used to describe all kinds of identities, their relationships, etc. With the Mandalization of Indian polity and society, groups of castes, labelled as socially and educationally backward classes, occupy the centre-stage. Scholars have already started discussing caste as an ethnic category and caste problems and relationships as ethnic in character. In fact, all identities, tribal and caste, have become ethnic now. Similarly, all movements, centring on the aspirations of various groups, are ethnic movements.

In a paper on autonomy movements in Chotanagpur written some years ago, an attempt was made to trace their evolution from a tribal base, as tribal ethnic movements, to a regional movement with a sizeable section of non-tribals draw into it (Singh, 1977). The social base of the movement expanded, generating myths, offering explanations of tribal/non-tribal harmony and setting new goals whereby the two communities hitherto regarded as dichotomous categories would live happily ever after. The transition from ethnicity to new forms of regionalism committed to the goal of autonomy has been underway in some other parts of the country, even as ethnicity has emerged as a strong, vibrant force elsewhere, recognized as such both at levels of national and international research and action.

We may, therefore, now deal with ethnic movements and the transition of some of them, to a regional platform, various models of autonomy evolved to accommodate ethnic and regional aspirations, and prospects and possibilities of doing so in the future. The ethnic demands, strident and clamant, often looking ominous, threatening to tear the fabric of existing political system apart, have been, by and large, accommodated in our federal and democratic polity which has emerged the stronger for it.

Probably, the best known example of transition from ethnicity to regionalism is offered by the Jharkhand movement in Chotanagpur and Santal Pargana area of Bihar which started as a tribal ethnic movement. In its earlier phase from the 1920s to the 1930s covered by Unnati Samaj and Adivasi Mahasabha, it articulated the demands of the tribals as a separate category or as a minority, and demanded separation from the rest of Bihar. The establishment of the Jharkhand Party in the late 1940s represented in principle a transition from ethnicity to regionalism, as the door of the party was thrown open to everybody including non-tribals in the region. In spite of this, the Jharkhand Party remained primarily a tribal party dominated by tribal Christian leadership and led by three major tribes in their respective regions: the Munda, Santal and Oraon. The minor tribes generally kept out of the movement and joined the Congress. The Jharkhand Party swept the polls in two general elections, polled about 8,00,000 votes in both, and captured about 30 assembly and 3 to 5 parliamentary seats. It was thus at its peak in the 1950s. The impact of development programme to a large extent ended the feelings of alienation of the tribal people. All-India political parties appeared on the scene. The opening up of Chotanagpur and Santal Pargana was yet another factor. Jharkhand started losing ground from the third general elections. The merger of the Jharkhand Party and the Congress Party was a corollary to the processes mentioned above. The party broke up; it became like a splintered glass. It is not necessary to go into the processes of split that occurred in the 1960s and the 1970s even though their various factions succeeded in getting representation in the state government and in positions of power. In a way that testifies to their skill as strategists.

A remarkable development that occurred in the 1970s and which crystallized further in the 1980s was the growing consciousness of a common cultural heritage that unites the tribals and non-tribals in Chotanagpur and Santal Pargana and in their periphery. The tribals do not form more than 30 per cent of the population of this region comprising 21 districts of Bihar, West Bengal, Orissa and Madhya Pradesh. For over 200 years the tribals were told that they were different from non-tribals. The colonial ethnography structured a notion of duality that conditioned tribal perceptions until recently. It is only during the last 15 years that the consciousness of Jharkhand as a cultural area where various communities have shared cultural spaces and traits and have lived together in harmony but are now facing a common threat to their identity has sharpened. It is being reinforced by researches in the languages of Chotanagpur which today speak of convergence of linguistic traits. A similar convergence is being discovered in respect of all cultural traits, such as kinship norms, folk religion, life style, values and world view, festivals and festivities, etc. Many a common space is being explored in ethnography and other social studies.

All this comes through in the works of artists and tribal and non-tribal scholars, poets, and in the performing arts which have received a fresh impetus. Therefore, this area today has for the first time become sharply conscious of its 'authentic' cultural vibrations. Such a resurgence of literary and artistic activities had not occurred earlier. This is a development which deserves to be studied.

An example of the coming together of the communities of Chotanagpur is offered by the changing perceptions of

Kurmi-Mahato community over the last six decades. About 60 years ago they were a tribe. Just before the census of 1931 they claimed the Kshatriya status and sought a pan-Indian identity. They were consequently descheduled as a tribe. Now, they are clamouring for the restoration of their status as a tribal community, have dissociated themselves from their pan-Indian moorings, and have discovered many commonalties they claim to share with neighbouring tribal groups and non-tribal communities. The Kurmi-Mahato community of Chotanagpur is spread over a sizeable part of Jharkhand territory now divided between Orissa, West Bengal and Chotanagpur and therefore the importance of this community and its perceptions in the developing movement have a great significance.

Yet another development has been the articulation of the regional factor by almost all political parties except the Congress in recent years. The Jharkhand movement as a tribal movement started by highlighting the regional factor. They spoke for the region as a whole and the grievances and exploitation of its people, particularly the tribals. In the last three decades the feeling of alienation of almost all communities in Chotanagpur from the local establishment and the government has increased manifold. Complaints about deprivation in all matters of job, reservation, representation, self-employment, etc., have mounted. It is therefore little wonder that almost all political parties today stand for either autonomy or for the formation of a separate state of Chotanagpur-Santal Pargana. The Bharatiya Janata Party (BJP) has spoken up in favour of Vananchal, which is coterminous with Chotanagpur-Santal Pargana and which it insists is different from Jharkhand with its claims to the peripheral areas of West Bengal, Orissa and Madhya Pradesh. The ethnic dimension has thus been replaced by the regional perspective on backwardness and the need for accelerated development. The Janata Dal, always in favour of smaller states, has recently pledged support to the formation of Jharkhand and other smaller states in the interest of rapid development. The CPM is against the break up of West Bengal and not in favour of Jharkhand state. The CPI is in favour. The Naxalites and ultra-Left perhaps support the cause of a separate state. Even within the Congress there is an appreciation of the uniqueness of the situation in Chotanagpur and Santal

Pargana. Sometime ago, about 86 Congress MPs and MLAs demanded a Union Territory (UT) status for Chotanagpur, but later backtracked.

The Government of India set up a Committee on Jharkhand Matters (COJM) in August 1989, which submitted its report to the Union Home Ministry in May 1990. The COJM considered a whole range of possibilities for granting positive, substantial and meaningful autonomy while maintaining and strengthening the safeguards for tribal populations. In this connection, three points are noteworthy. First, the whole of Jharkhand comprising 21 (now 22) districts spread over four states should be recognized as a distinct culture area which should be developed as such irrespective of the political and administrative boundaries into which it has been broken up. The people here share a tradition, a history and a rich and vibrant folklore. The efforts made so far for the preservation of its culture and the promotion of its language, literature and performing arts have been regrettably uneven. Hence, a dynamic cultural policy should be framed, appropriate cultural institutions should be established and all efforts should be made to preserve and promote the cultural identity of the people of this region. Tribal and regional languages should be introduced at all stages in schools, colleges and universities. There should be interaction across the borders and cultural authorities may be set up under the aegis of the Zonal Cultural Centres located at Shantiniketan.

The second is the recognition of the political and administrative identity of the Jharkhand region within Bihar. At the third level, even within the framework of an autonomous Jharkhand, efforts should be made to strengthen the safeguards for the tribal people who will form 30 per cent of the population. In fact, such safeguards should be under constant review and be strengthened and new strategies should be evolved continually to safeguard the interests of tribal people. Development authorities like Jhargram Development Authority or even Chotanagpur Development Authority should be introduced in all tribal areas of adjoining states. There should be constant interaction among such authorities across the borders to promote composite development.

The COJM was of the view that a new politico-administrative structure could be conceived of in terms of autonomy, comprised of the 13 districts of Bihar. An autonomous model in Bihar should become a prototype for replication in the three states of West Bengal, Orissa and Madhya Pradesh, if the three state governments wish to consider the matter.

Five years after the submission of the report by COJM, the Bihar government established the Jharkhand Area Autonomous Council (JAAC) on 9 August 1995. No elections were held, sufficient powers were not delegated and adequate funds were not allotted to this body. Therefore, the demand for a full-fledged state, supported by the major parties like the Congress and the BJP, grew.

It is in this context that we should analyze the momentous results of the 9th Lok Sabha elections which revealed the four major trends. First, Jharkhand parties emerged in a big way after their disastrous performance in 1984. The reason for their rout was the sympathy factor in the wake of the assassination of the late Prime Minister Indira Gandhi in 1984 who was regarded as a friend by tribals. All Jharkhand parties except the JCC were able to register significant gains by playing up the Centre's initiative in setting up the Tripartite Committee on Jharkhand Matters in August 1989 and mobilizing their cadres on an impressive scale during the tour of the committee to different areas in Chotanagpur and Santal Pargana. They told their voters that the Centre was sympathetic to their demand for autonomy. This message seemed to have gone home.

Another factor was the Jharkhand Mukti Morcha's (JMM) alliance with the Janata Party, the unprecedented mobilization of the OBCs, Muslims and the tribals in Jharkhand. The Jharkhand parties in Chotanagpur and Santal Pargana captured four seats. All of them put together polled about 13.64 lakh votes, a record performance. Among Jharkhand parties, JMM continued to be the major political force with three of its candidates being elected to the Lok Sabha as against none from other parties. However, the second trend continued to be the dominance of the BJP as the largest political force—a process that started in the mid-1960s with the fragmentation of ethnic tribal community into its Christian and non-Christian segments, the former perceived as the more advanced cornering all benefits by the latter which supported the cause of a separate Vananchal state. They polled 17 lakh votes in Chotanagpur and Santal Pargana and captured six seats. Together with the Jharkhand and Janata Dal, which also supported the Jharkhand movement during the election and afterwards, these parties captured 11 seats out of 13 and polled 39.14 lakh votes, i.e., more than 50 per cent votes, which demonstrates the preference of the majority of the people of the region for autonomy or a separate state. The CPI was supported by JMM. Janata Dal with two seats and 4.6 lakh votes emerged third, and the CPI with one seat and 3 lakh votes came fourth. Thirdly, the Congress was able to get only two seats, of which one was from Shingbhum; even here, the attitude of the Congress candidate was reported to be ambivalent on the question of links with the rest of Bihar. He was an old Jharkhand leader himself. The other seat was from Lohardagga where the candidate supported the Centre in this initiative. The Congress polled less than the BJP but more than the Jharkhand parties, about 14.6 lakh votes. Fourthly, the Jharkhand parties were wiped out in the 'peripheral' areas of Madhya Pradesh, West Bengal and Orissa, which they claim will constitute the Jharkhand state. Their performance was the poorest in the two constituencies of Madhya Pradesh, where one of their candidates who contested as an independent lost. In Orissa JMM polled 2 per cent votes; there were Jharkhand independents in Mayurbhanj and Santal Pargana who did not do well either. In West Bengal they polled about 5,000 votes. Part of this may be explained by the boycott by JCC which was reportedly strong in Mayurbhanj and Midnapur. The emergence of the Janata Dal in Orissa, of the BJP in Madhya Pradesh and the Leftist parties in West Bengal areas of the proposed Jharkhand state was strongly favoured by the electorate. Tribal separatism, therefore, had no significant electoral support in these three states.

The results of the subsequent elections to the 10th Lok Sabha held in the context of the disruption of the alliance of the Janata Dal and the JMM, confirmed the domination of the BJP which swept the polls. The JMM could win only one seat in parliament. The BJP emerged as the champion of the Vananchal state. Thus, it appears that there was a strong groundswell of support for autonomy and even for a separate state consisting of Chotanagpur and Santal Pargana district of Bihar.

Other Movements

We shall now briefly discuss some other movements. There are no movements of any significance in the rest of middle India or in the south because, except for occasional demands for a separate state raised by the Bhils and the Gonds and by some tribal groups in Gujarat, there has not been any significant mobilization of tribal people in favour of such a demand in the rest of the country. In the last general elections tribal self-rule emerged as a major demand in parts of Gujarat. In fact, the tribal people who seemed to have been accommodated 'rather well' within the linguistic, cultural and political framework of the states in middle India are now articulating demands for self-rule. The prospects for the formation of autonomous territories in the tribal belt cutting across middle India, which includes northern Andhra and some other areas in the south—there are two tribal majority districts (Bastar and Jhabua) and about 200 tribal majority taluks—have brightened up. We will discuss the matter a little later.

We now turn to the ethnic situation in the north-east. It has been a dynamic situation with tribes discarding old names and assuming new names, coalescing to form new and larger identities even if these cut across existing boundaries of states, the seven sisters and now probably the eighth sister with the inclusion of Sikkim in the region. The Constitution of India provides for the formation of autonomous district councils under the Sixth Schedule. For many years it worked well. The formation of Nagaland in the mid-1960s and the constitutional amendment to provide for the non-application of laws without the consent of Nagaland Assembly was a landmark. It went a long way in accommodating Naga aspirations within the framework of India's federal polity. Later, Assam broke up as the Assamese language was sought to be imposed on other communities inhabiting the once Great Assam. The creation of the states of Meghalaya and Manipur is again another landmark in the application of the principle of ethnicity in the formation of states. Recently, Mizoram has been recognized as a full state and the provisions applicable to Nagaland have also been extended to this new state. Elsewhere, the demand was for the extension of the provisions of the Sixth Schedule to Tripura which have been extended to that state. The cultural and political autonomy of Arunachal Pradesh is cited as an example of the success of Nehru-Elwin policy of tribals choosing the timing and laying down their own conditions for coming to terms with the larger national identity.

Assam continues to face the threat of further division. The Bodos are demanding a separate state. It is an extraordinary case of a community with a population of not more than 29 per cent in one particular area demanding the creation of a state covering most of northern Assam. It is a case of heightened ethnic self-awareness extending beyond the limits set by demography and ecology. The self-perception of the Bodos also goes beyond all sense of history. But myth making has been a part of ethnic movements and what is happening in case of smaller communities such as the Bodos reflects the scramble for a share in political power in the Brahmaputra valley, aided and abetted by forces which are not difficult to identify. As a distinguished administrator from the north-east pointed out, the high—probably the highest—rate of investment by the Government of India has produced distortions in the relatively egalitarian societies that existed once upon a time, and has spurred the demand for increasing autonomy by more and more ethnic communities in order to attract more and more of central assistance. Probably a measure of autonomy for the Bodo territory where they are present in sizeable numbers and a sharing of power at Dispur may help meet the aspirations of the Bodo people within the framework of a unified Assam.

The model of autonomy under the Sixth Schedule within the framework of a united, multi-ethnic Assam is being deepened and widened to meet tribals' demand for further share in power and resources. In April 1995, the tribals of Karbi Anglong and North Cachar Hills, which have an autonomy of their own under the District Council, were further granted, under a tripartite agreement, transfer of legislative powers in respect of 14 other subjects, direct access to the governor to discuss their problems and to participate in discussions about financial location to the councils with the Planning Commission.

In spite of occasional bloody attacks launched by Bodo militants against non-tribals, the negotiations undertaken by the moderate Bodo leadership, which reflect the majority Bodo view, with the Government of India, are going ahead. The Bodos are likely to settle for a Bodoland Territorial Council under the Sixth Schedule with some modification that would empower the governor to override the state government in respect of 'reserved' subjects.

In 1995, as autonomy was granted to some Assam tribal areas such as Lalungs (Tiwa), Mising and the Rabha-Hasongs, the first two with satellite areas of village council with separate compact areas or boundaries, and the third with more than 50 per cent tribal population. The village council will be governed by the executive council and funds will be provided for development from the tribal sub-plan and other sources. The interests of non-tribals and their rights will be protected by the council and the government. This is a unique experiment in granting autonomy to individual tribes, and has been justified on the ground that this will curb the trend towards tribal alienation and is in conformity with the creation of Zila Parishad under the Panchayati Raj system for the general population.

The movement leading to the formation of Gorkha Hill Council offers the most vivid example of the extension of the principle of autonomy to an area lying outside the north-east. It is not necessary in this paper to go into the history of the development of the movement which goes back to 1917, culminating in the acceptance of the demand for autonomy. Our objective is restricted to the elucidation of the principles of autonomy. The accord for setting up the Darjeeling Gorkha Hill Council was signed on 22 August 1988. There is a provision for the constitution of the Hill Council of 42 members, of which 28 would be elected and the remaining 14 will be nominated by the state government. The Hill Council covers the whole sub-division of Darjeeling, Kalimpong and Kurseong. The executive powers of the council cover land use, management of forests, use of canal, water resources, schools buildings, hospitals, tourism, vocational training, public works, development and planning, roads, transport, education and small-scale and cottage industries. A notable feature of the accord is that it preserves the integrity of West Bengal as a state while conceding the principle of autonomy to resolve the identity problems of the Gorkhas. The demand for a separate state of Gorkhaland has been dropped and the nomenclature Darjeeling Gorkha Hill Council suggests the acceptance of the identity of the Gorkhas in the area. The agreement speaks of the Gorkha rather than Nepalese as the new category of ethnic identity. The reason for dealing at length with the provision of the accord is that this model has wider implications for the whole of middle India where ethnic problems are acute. It seeks to marry the two concepts, which were considered irreconcilable until recently, that of maintaining the existing structure and boundaries of a state and resolving the ethnic issues by granting autonomy that establishes the concerned community's control over their environment and resources, and over the pattern of growth and development that vitally concerns them.

Territoriality as a basis of identity has been recognized in the notification recently issued by the Government of India conferring on almost all communities of Ladakh the status of Scheduled Tribes (STs). There are both Buddhists and Muslim segments of the same community or there are either Buddhists or Muslims. An autonomous council has been set up for the Buddhist dominated area. The benefit of the recognition of an area as a whole as a scheduled area irrespective of the socio-economic status of various communities had been extended earlier to the Jaunsaris and Kinnauris and for the Gaddi. In Arunachal Pradesh all tribes are scheduled on a territorial basis. In all these cases, almost all communities within a territory are recognized as STs creating an anomalous situation, for elsewhere it is the principle of backwardness and ethnicity, and not territoriality that determined the status of a tribe.

Pluralism

We may, at this stage, refer to an important landmark in the ethnic scenario as it developed from the mid-1980s, the Indo-Sri Lanka Agreement of 29 July 1987, which was designed to end ethnic discord. Its historic significance is two-fold. First, it recognizes, probably for the first time in international law, or at least in the context of South Asia, "the multi-ethnic and multi-lingual plural society" of Sri Lanka, consisting *inter alia* of the Sinhalese, Tamils, Muslims (Moors) and Burghes. It further states that each ethnic group has a distinct cultural and linguistic identity which has to be carefully nurtured. It provides for a separate administrative dispensation and political autonomy for the Northern and Eastern Provinces, areas of historical habitation of Sri Lankan Tamil-speaking peoples "who have at all times hitherto lived together in this territory with other ethnic groups". All this has to be achieved within the larger context of the unity, sovereignty and territorial integrity of Sri Lanka. The treaty strengthens its "character as a multi-ethnic, multi-lingual and multi-religious society in which all citizens can live in equality, safety and harmony, and fulfil their aspirations". It is not the purpose of this paper to discuss the aftermath of the accord and the recent moves to devolve more powers. The purpose of this brief foray into international relations is to point to the nature of ethnic formations for a South Asian country; substitute Sri Lanka by any other country in developing world, the issues are the same or similar.

Review of Models of Autonomy

In this part of this paper we briefly review various models evolved in recent years to accommodate ethnic and regional aspirations in the country. We have referred to the provisions of the Sixth Schedule earlier. Article 370 deals with the special dispensation for the state of Jammu & Kashmir.

We may refer to the models of regional autonomy for the purpose of removing the sense of grievances of people of a region. In 1956 the Constitution was amended to provide for the constitution and functions of Regional Committees of Legislative Assembly of many states to satisfy regional aspirations. Separate development boards were established for Vidarbha, Marathwada and the rest of Maharashtra and for Saurashtra, Kutch and the rest of Gujarat. Other measures included equitable allocation of funds for development of such areas and equitable arrangements to provide technical and vocational training, opportunities of employment, services, etc. However, as is well known, these development boards have not performed their functions entirely to the satisfaction of the people concerned. The Development Board for Telangana remained a non-starter. In September 1973, a six-point formula was worked out by leaders of Andhra Pradesh for accelerating the development of backward areas, the institution of informal arrangements in the matter of admission to educational institutions, and the constitution of a high-power administrative tribunal to deal with grievances of services and so on.

Of historical interest was the formation of the regional committees in Punjab in 1957. There were two regional committees, one for the Punjabi region and other for the Hindi region consisting of the members of the Legislative Assembly to deliberate over scheduled matters which covered a wide range of subjects such as public health, agriculture, primary and secondary education, cooperative societies, development of economic planning, etc. This also did not function. Punjab and Haryana were created as separate states. A similar experiment was undertaken in 1969 by creating a sub-state or an autonomous state comprising of Meghalaya within the state of Assam. This experiment lasted for two years. The reorganization of the north-east areas was undertaken in 1971 resulting in the granting of statehood to Manipur, Meghalaya and Tripura and in the creation of the Union Territories of Mizoram and Arunachal Pradesh. In 1958, the Sixth Schedule was extended to the states of Tripura and Mizoram. The model of autonomy applied to Nagaland was extended to Mizoram when it became a full state, as mentioned earlier.

The State Reorganization Commission in 1956 recommended the formation of a separate development board for Chotanagpur-Santal Pargana region. It took nearly 16 years for Chotanagpur-Santal Pargana Development Authority to be established. In later years this authority was delegated with powers and allocated larger funds to ensure the effective implementation of programmes for the development of this region. The authority, however, was not able to make an impact. Its trifurcation, i.e., splitting into three branches, undermined its effectiveness. In fact, people's representatives from the region demanded that this experiment be scrapped and replaced by an agreement that involves people's participation in control of development apparatus. The Jharkhand Area Autonomous Council was established in 1993, armed with more powers, but it is now no substitute for a separate state. However, it should be noted that this autonomous model of the seventies inspired the creation of Tribal Development Authority in Assam, which also has not been able to make any significant impact. A similar development authority, Jhargram Development Authority, was constituted in West Bengal in 1975.

It is in this context that we may further discuss the formation of autonomous councils within a state. This experiment has two aspects. First, it recognizes ethnicity as a factor in polity. Secondly, it recognizes the need for the devolution of power, decentralization of authority, and the transfer of resources to meet the people's needs. The story starts with Gorkha Council in Darjeeling. Assam has announced the formation of autonomous councils for Bodos, Rabha, Lalung, Karbis and so on. The Jharkhand Autonomous Area Council, criticized as a parody of the model earlier suggested, a glorified development authority, is, nevertheless, a step forward in granting a measure of, if not a substantial measure of, authority to local people. The Leh Autonomous Council is the latest in the series combining the sub-regional and ethnic dimensions to meet a long-standing demand.

All over the country, today, people want a share in power, a sustainable role in the actual working of institutions, old and new, that constitute the apparatus of power. This is a universal trend, highlighted by the movements of the indigenous people and environmental movements. This is all to the good. It is to the abiding credit of our people and the democratic system that it has generally been able to respond to the challenge and craft appropriate strategies and build up institutions. But, the test lies in the implementation.

Therefore, we may now discuss the autonomy processes at work among the other communities. Once we are aware of the identities and their dynamic interaction among people, we will appreciate the strength and relevance of the traditional institutions. The caste sabhas or tribal councils are ubiquitous and functional. However, the traditional village panchayats or panchayats organized around collective management of resources such as forests, like Van Panchayat in the Himalayas, have almost become dysfunctional. Jayaprakash Narayan once wrote approvingly of the ancient panchayats in Tamil Nadu, which enjoyed autonomy and a measure of respect from the rulers. In the tribal areas, however, the tribal councils variously known as Munda-Manki or Manjhi-Parganait, function at two levels, the hamlet/village level and the inter-village, in areas populated by the tribal people.

However, it is the formal statutory panchayats which have come to occupy the centre stage. The inclusion of the panchayat in the Directive Principles is often described as an act of absent-mindedness, because it was a stray afterthought. It took almost a decade to introduce the two-tier Panchayati Raj system at the block and district levels. The experiment generally failed. The Sarvodaya workers suggested the corrective in the form of a three or four tier Panchayati Raj system starting from the hamlet/village level. However, nothing happened. The Panchayati Raj system stagnated in the 1970s and early 1980s, the states refusing to part with their power or resources to what they feared would emerge as a rival centre of power.

Therefore, the 73 amendment came as a breath of fresh air. It is truly path-breaking in the sense that it makes the Panchayati Raj Institutions (PRTs) strong, viable, functional bodies, elected with a substantial representation of women and weaker sections, with sufficient devolution of power and transfer of resources.

But it must be remembered that everything in the country functions within the cultural context and the local structure of power. Therefore, the need for vigilance, to ensure that funds are not diverted, and that panchayats do not degenerate into an oligarchy.

The Bhuria Committee Report has made recommendations of far-reaching significance about setting up a four-tier Panchayati Raj system from the hamlet/village upward in the tribal areas covered by the Fifth Schedule. It is rather silent on the Sixth Schedule and the need for enmeshing the traditional and modern institutions in tribal areas. The upcoming middle class in tribal society also wants a share in traditional power structure dominated by tribal chiefs. The middle class youth are adept at playing the political game in modern democracy, and seek to control resources. Therefore, there is now the demand for strengthening the Six Schedule in the north-east by linking it up with the traditional institutions, from the village upward, and for extension of the Sixth Schedule to tribal middle India where the Fifth Schedule is widely perceived as having failed.

We have, therefore, three models before us. One is that of the development authorities which have failed to make any impact and which, it is suggested, should now be replaced by institutions that involve control of the apparatus of power and development by the people's representatives, elected directly or indirectly. What people now want is not only development, but a share in power. The second model is that of autonomous councils created right from the inception of the constitution to the establishment of the Gorkha Hill Council. The third is the creation of states. The State Reorganization Commission recommended the constitution of the states on the basis of language as far as major languages were concerned. Jawaharlal Nehru later regretted having supported the reorganization of states and called it as one of the two blunders he had committed in his life, the other being complacency on the frontier matters. India, he said, should have remained a federation of states which reflected its multi-lingual, multi-ethnic character. Part of Nehru's apprehension that major languages would submerge smaller language groups has been borne out by the treatment meted out to them and to the linguistic minorities. Regional identities based on major languages have been accentuated. Even so there could be another point of view. Language riots have not occurred, and the country as a whole has gained from the linguistic reorganization. The second phase of reorganization of states in the north-east proceeded on the basis of the application of the principle of ethnicity, but it was the ethnicity of major tribal groups. Minor tribal groups such as the Zailiangrong and Konyaks were left out. Now, they are clamouring for recognition of their homeland divided between more than two states as a culture area, and for setting up institutions for preserving their identity, customary laws, and so on.

The third model which is now being increasingly talked about is that of smaller states to be formed out of bigger states for the purpose of accelerating the pace of development. It adds a new dimension to the formation of states in India. Until recently, the dominant view seemed to be that no matter what happens, the existing states should not be broken up and that the demand for autonomy should be accommodated within their existing framework. Now, we have among the supporters of the United Front and among parties such as the BJP dominant elements calling for the formation of smaller states to speed up the process of development, in the larger national interest of eliminating poverty and removing backwardness. The Janata Dal has also demanded the formation of smaller states. At first the prospects of breaking up Bihar to create a Jharkhand state looked daunting because of the likely repercussions on states like Jammu & Kashmir where there is a demand for granting a UT status for Ladakh. However, the Bihar Assembly passed a resolution on the creation of a Jharkhand state, and Jharkhand has come into existence. Uttar Pradesh has accepted the demand for the creation of Uttarakhand (which has also been established as a state). But Maharashtra with its problems in Marathwada and Vidharbha has steadfastly refused to accept the creation of smaller states. However, the idea of smaller states has been gaining ground.

It should be however noted that the creation of a separate state or UT is not likely to solve entirely the problems of backward communities like tribes. They will continue to be protected. Therefore, a combination of the model of autonomy and the provision of the Sixth Schedule may become necessary to satisfy both regional and ethnic aspirations of the communities concerned.

Ethnicity and regionalism articulate the aspirations of communities for the preservation of their identity and the protection of their rights and those of the region as a whole. While ethnicity postulates the recognition of the uniqueness of a community, it also requires of its constituents the recognition of the others, of the imperatives and compulsions of nation-building, which is a continuous process, carrying all with it. There are limits to ethnicity and regionalism in a complex multi-ethnic situation. In the task of nation-building, all regions and communities should be treated fairly and equally, as far as possible, given the constraints of resources. The constituents of the nation-state should show an understanding of the infinitely complex process of nation-building. Our track-record in this respect, particularly in the resolution of ethnic conflicts in the north-east and language problems—if not caste and communal problems—has generally been worthy of a stable civilization and resilient cultural system like India's. The current spate of difficulties therefore calls for still greater efforts to understand ethnic aspirations and to make various groups realize that they are a part of the larger nation-state. The task of political management of a large plural society such as India's has never been an easy one, but it should continue to be performed in a spirit of accommodation, wisdom and goodwill.

References

Institute of Social Sciences, 1993 (March) Report of the Committee of Members of Parliament and Experts constituted to make recommendations on law concerning extension of the Provisions of the Constitution (Seventy-Third Amendment) Act, 1992 to Scheduled Areas, *Panchayati Raj Update*.

Singh, K.S., 1966, *The Dust-Storm and the Hanging Mist: A Study of Birsa Munda and His Movement in Chhotanagpur* 1874–1901, Calcutta: Firma K.K. Mukhopadhyaya (Second Edition); 1983 *Birsa Munda and His Movement 1874–1901: A Study of Millenarian Movement in Chhotanagpur*, Calcutta: Oxford University Press.

——, 1977, "From Ethnicity to Regionalism: A Study in Tribal Politics and Movements in Chhotanagpur from 1900–1975", in *Dissent Protest and Reforms in Indian Civilisation*, Simla: Indian Institute of Advance Study, pp. 317–342.

——, 1979, "Tribal Ethnicity in a Multi-Ethnic Society: A Study in the Processes of Conflict and Integration in Post-Colonial Chhotanagpur", in *Trends in Ethnic Group Relation in Asia and Oceania: Race and Society*, UNESCO, pp. 56–69.

——, 1982, "Transformation of Tribal Society: Integration vs Assimilation", *Economic and Political Weekly*, August 14–21; (A summary) *Voluntary Action*, 1982, 24(8–10) March-May, 27: 1–17.

——, 1982, "Tribal Identity Movements Based on Script and Language", *Man in India*, 62(3): 243–45.

——, 1982, *Tribal Movements in India*, Vol. I (edited), New Delhi: Manohar.

——, 1983, *Tribal Movements in India*, Vol. II (edited), New Delhi: Manohar.

——, 1985, "Script Reform and Development: A Study of Two Movements Among the Ho Tribe in Singhbhum", *South Asian Anthropologist*, 6(2): 111–23.

——, 1989, "Ethnicity and Polity Formation in Tribal India", *Human Science*, 38(1): 77–82.

——, 1990, Ethnicity, Identity and Development, IV Verrier Elwin Memorial Lecture, New Delhi: Manohar.

——, Ethnicity, Regionalism and Autonomy: A Preliminary Presentation, Workshop on Ethnic Identities and Social Transformation, Institute of Peace Research and Action, Chandigarh, January 12–14, 1990 (mimeographed).

——, 1990, "Tribal Violence", *Journal of Anthropological Survey of India*, 39(2 and 3): 127–32.

——, 1990, Report of the Committee on Jharkhand Matters, Ministry of Home Affairs, Government of India.

——, 1990 (May) with Dr. Bhupinder Singh and K.N. Prasad, Report of the Committee of Jharkhand Matter, Ministry of Home Affairs, New Delhi (mimeographed).

——, 1992 "Cultural Policy, Cultural Pluralism and Visual Anthropology: An Indian Perspective", in *Visual Anthropology and India*, edited by K.S. Singh, Anthropological Survey of India.

——, 1992 (March) with Dr. Bhupinder Singha and A.M. Gokhale. Report of the Expert Committee on the Plains' Tribes of Assam set up by the Government of India (mimeographed).

——, 1992, *People of India: An Introduction*, Calcutta: Anthropological Survey of India.

——, 1994, Ethnicity and Nation-building: Issues and Response (mimeo). Seminar organized by Centre for South and Southeast Asian Studies, University of Madras and U.S. Educational Foundation in India.

——, 1995 (September), Unity in Diversity: Making Grassroots Democracy a Reality (mimeographed). Centre for Democratic Studies, Madras.

——, 2001 (24 August), The Jharkhand Dream, *The Times of India*.

8

Reification and Ways of Living

Secularism, Tolerance, Religion and Identity in Contemporary Indian Scholarship and a Village Community

LEE I. SCHLESINGER

Knowledge, especially for social scientists, is always situated knowledge. Knowledge arises and takes shape in accord with habits and traditions and, interests and powers. It springs sometimes from positions of influence, control participation or action and sometimes from positions of remove, renunciation, observation or contemplation. Although this general point needs no elaboration here, the argument below depends on remembering that even the knowledge that appears or presents itself as the least situated, as emanating from nowhere in particular, as applying to or comprehending almost everything in general, as being the most rational, objective, unbiased, and natural, is itself knowledge that is nonetheless situated.[1] In the following three sections I consider knowledge in different situations, and I try to display the significance of the situatedness for some current discussions about ethnicity and cultural pluralism and for some current studies and understandings of South Asian societies.

The immediate framing situation for what I am claiming to know and profess here is the occasion of a conference organized by the Department of Sociology of the University of Bombay in December 1995. Distinguished scholars from around the world gather to share ideas, opinions, and a little research relating to cultural pluralism and ethnicity in contemporary South Asia. My own discomfort with the confines of the conference framework, however, leads me to turn directly to some less noticed, less admitted situations that mater to me and that I wish would matter much more to others. One of these is a single village where I have done social anthropological fieldwork. One of these is the modern bourgeois world. One of these is where I would like some scholars and intellectuals to meet and build a better science of society and attain a more sensitive view of the understandings, values, habits, and actions of particular people living together in particular ways. I conceive of these three situations as *Somewhere in Particular, Somewhere Else, and Somewhere in Between*. (And I confess that my own position/interest in situating knowledge is motivated by the contrast I find between a view from somewhere and a view from everywhere, which is to say a view from nowhere in particular).

Somewhere in Particular

In the same day's mail that brought the invitation to participate in the Bombay conference, I received a letter from a close friend in the village in Satara district where I did ethnographic field research first in 1975–76 and where I have returned for briefer visits in the mid-1980s and mid-1990s. I had recently written this friend, whom I rename Ganpati, to inquire whether a date had yet been set for the inauguration of a new Ram temple, whose construction was nearly complete. In his reply (the letter that arrived along with the conference invitation), immediately after the traditional epistolary courtesies, Ganpati wrote in Marathi and without much punctuation or discipline to control his stream of thought as follows:

> The auspicious time for the installation of the image of Sri Ram is not yet fixed, but it could be similarly seen that whatever good or bad happens on the surface of this earth is by the grace of Parmeshwar, and then if some say this Parmeshwar is Ram or

> some say Yesu (Jesus), then some say Rahim, then a few people say Gautam Buddh, then a few people say Guru Nanak, but the meaning of all this is one and the same, and this means that although the names of the creator of the world are all different and that although each sect and religion (*panth dharm*) may be different, all religions say one and the same, and this means humanism (*manavta*), which means every person should behave with each other in a human way (*manushyapramane*). Humanism means to behave with love to everyone, to help someone in times of danger, to participate in his happiness and suffering, to tell him to behave well, and not to give trouble to another. These truths (*tatva*) are in the Hindu religion (*dharma*), and accordingly (or similarly) they are in other religions. It is said that the Hindu religion is the most superior (*shrest*) (in the world).
>
> Even if I worshipped Allah or Jesus, the god of the Hindu religion would not make trouble for me, and so there is no problem (no obstacle arises) if I just worship the creator of the world.

This unsolicited and extremely uncharacteristic outpouring in my friend's letter was then followed by a hesitant inquiry, equally unprecedented, asking whether I might want to join all the other villagers, who hold me in such high regard, and offer a donation now to help finish the construction of the Ram temple. (I must add that in the twenty years of our friendship, this is the first time that this friend, unlike some other villagers, had ever suggested that I give anything to the village).[2]

Villages, village life, and village culture are both familiar and strange to most urban Indians and to Indian scholars. The familiarity, whether derived from personal experience and relationships or from other common images, tends often to obscure the strangeness, especially in some areas which are a bit resistant to immediate conceptualization and which could challenge sharply or be most critical of the ideas and ways of inferences of outsiders.[3] The ideas excerpted from my friend's letter are not likely to be strange to most educated Indians or even to most who have been somewhat educated about India.

They compose almost a common litany, even if this is not one that we expect to come in the mail everyday, much less on the same day as an invitation to an international sociology conference. Similar remarks appear in the sermons of Swami Vivekananda and Mahatma Gandhi, and this kind of generous preachy formulation arises on many less lofty occasions too. I heard such universalist and syncretic theistic humanism quite a few times during my village field research; it comes easily to the tongue and probably also to the inner thinking of many villagers, especially when provoked, for example, by the presence of a foreigner, to consider that other people may have other gods, other holy scriptures, and other ritual practices. Nonetheless, the familiarity of an expression is not always an index of how easy it is to understand all of what is being expressed. I shall offer some additional context for what my friend Ganpati wrote in order to help appreciate what it means it relation to issues of religion and identity and whether it may have any broader political relevance or theoretical implications for thinking about modernity, the nation-state, and its social (ethnic, pluralist) composition or decomposition.[4]

At the very top of the piece of paper, as begins almost every personal correspondence I have seen in Maharashtra, Ganpati wrote, and this was certainly the first thing that he wrote, 'Sri Ram Prasann' (invoking the favour or blessing of Lord Ram). This, or the similar invocation, 'Sri Ram, Jai Ram', has appeared also on the other three letters I had received from Ganpati since I resumed an interrupted correspondence with him a few months earlier. Ten years earlier, however, this was not how his letters began. Then they either had a simple 'Sri' at the top, which invokes Ganesh, or they included one of the variants of the name of the village goddess, the *gram devata*, Injabai (whose own temple stands immediately next to the site of the old and new Ram temples). My friend seems clearly not quite as indifferent to the particular name of the deity as his prose text might indicate. Sri Ram now has a greater significance, even if only in the common, perhaps automatic (or unreflected) act of beginning letters, than he used to.

In other ways too, my correspondent, like so very many Maharashtrians I know, is sometimes quite sensitive to particular names.[5] On the envelope that contained his recent letter, Ganpati wrote the word 'Sambhajinagar' in parentheses after 'Aurangabad' in my address. His previous letter to me did not do this, although in an even earlier letter this year as well as in a conversation when I was visiting him in his village for Divali (in October 1995), he mentioned Sambhajinagar, the new appellation which the Shiv Sena has proposed to replace Aurangabad. This particular pairing of city names establishes a blatant religious context and conflict. It opposes the name of a devout, even famously fanatic, conquering Muslim emperor as joined to a Persian form of a city-suffix and the name of the Maratha Hindu *raja* whom that same Muslim emperor captured and killed as joined to the Sanskrit form of a city-suffix. My friend, like a number of other villagers who also spontaneously raised the topic of the proposed new name for Aurangabad as soon as they learned that this was where I was living, has clearly chosen to identify himself with something that Sambhajinagar represents. Whatever this is, however, it is almost certainly not the Shiv Sena as a political party or movement. Ganpati has no interest in, much less affection for, Bal Thackeray; and he is aware of the hate, the anti-humanism, in this supremo's politics.

At this point, two observations pertinent to the larger picture are worth noting explicitly, before considering Ganpati's character and beliefs in slightly more detail. Namely, the village is not isolated; and this one villager's religious attitude is not simple. The penetration of outside ideas and news is as obvious in my friend's notion of the oneness of the creator and of all religions being basically a common human moral code as it is in his sensitivity about the name of the largest city in Marathwada, over 300 km away from his village. Similarly, each of these same two specific subjects suggests, in their ambivalence (if not inconsistency), a complex disposition regarding sectarian or religious differences (or identities). That is, the attitude which he readily reveals to me comprises different elements that do not all fit together to reveal a single, or apparently simple, whole. Despite widespread outside opinion concerning rural simplicity and rural simpletons, the evidence I have at hand shows that the complexity and indefiniteness of an attitude of a not very educated villager regarding how names identify things when the things are not always visible or tangible (e.g., things like a deity, a city, or a social group, things whose naming can raise basic and profound philosophical as well as moral-religious problems) is no more implausible than the observation that the village or village life itself has no very definite borders when it comes to matters cultural or political.

Ganpati, almost 50 years old, has lived his entire life in his native village. He was educated up to 10th standard, which he failed. Both his parents were totally uneducated. His father, who died long before I met Ganpati, worked most of his life in the Bombay mills to make a better living than he could in the village, where his three sons grew up. The family was both poor and low status, on the far margins of the village's economy, politics, and ritual life. Indeed, in relative terms it remains so today. Because this family has been the only representative of its caste in this village, I shall maintain some confidentiality and note only that Ganpati belongs to one of the less prestigious traditional village service castes, one of the balutedar jatis that is associated with a relatively impure occupation. In current official parlance, he is an OBC, along with about 10 per cent of the village population.[6]

In the last two generations Ganpati's family has improved its economic condition significantly, although certainly not to an unusual degree relative to changes in many other families in the village. Initially almost landless, his father was able to acquire several acres of land and build a solid two-room house. The three sons, of whom only Ganpati has been in the village since the early 1970s, have all fared much better than their father. One son rose to a high rank in the army, one is a high school teacher and lives permanently in the taluka town, and Ganpati, the youngest, farms in addition to holding a menial salaried job in the irrigation department. These brothers have almost nothing to do with each other now, following several quarrels, and the family has been split ever since the father died. All three have had good marriages, and all have sons, indeed they have only sons.

Ganpati is a religious person and has been so far at least the twenty years of my acquaintance with him. Moreover, his own life has improved greatly in the past two decades, and he readily admits this. Yet he is not a generally happy person and frequently expresses frustration and anger, whose roots I do not comprehend. At the same time, he does consider himself fortunate in many respects and understands his good fortune to be a blessing from Parmeshwar, the one god. Ganpati both practices and thinks much about his religion, taking time each day for the rituals of domestic worship as well as reading sacred Marathi texts and a modern magazine devoted to interpreting the Bhagavad Gita. He is not, however, unusually devout or religious in the village setting, where many others are as fastidious in daily practices, in holiday observances, and in regional pilgrimages as he is and where quite a number devote much more time, study, or effort to religious matters.

Ganpati, along with his wife, takes care of an assembly of household deities, not only the dozen or so sculptural images (*murtis*) in the wall-niche (*devil*) and the framed pictures (*fotos*) on the wall but also an unusual small Shiva lingam of indeterminate material which rests on the floor beneath the devil in the main room of the house, next to which are kept several copies of the *Jnyaneshwari*, wrapped in cloth and placed on a low wood platform (*pat*). Food is offered to the household deities represented by divine objects every day, though unlike many village families, Ganpati's makes offerings to the gods in the village temples only on special occasions. The first brightly coloured sacred picture on the wall is of Jnyaneshwar, and it is garlanded and worshipped every morning, as are the adjacent images of Datta, Shikhar Shingnapur (a major Maharashtrian Shiva temple complex not too far away from the village), Shiva, and Jotiba (the *kul devata*). Starting sometime in 1994, Ganpati takes time every evening to read to himself a passage from the *Jnyaneshwari* before his meal; he does this without fail, no matter how much it delays the meal for his family or guests. (He tells me that he understands only a little of the original text, but he sometimes reads the marginal commentary, written in modern Marathi. Yet he believes he is learning, improving himself spiritually, and also gaining peace and satisfaction through his time with the *Jnyaneshwari*).

Ganpati's worship includes the recitation of prayers, and these intervals in his daily routine appear heartfelt, sincere and meaningful as a break from mundane pressures, and not just as formal ritual gestures. Often it seems that he becomes a different person after he addresses his gods, since his anger, sarcasm, and chronic headache disappear for a while. My understanding and interpretation of the depth and effect of his religious feeling also derives from having joined him in years gone by on pilgrimages to other deities, which he takes very seriously. Indeed, unlike many, he believes it is less important to show up at Shikhar Shingnapur on one of the Shravan Mondays, the days most holiest to Lord Shiva, than to have a peaceful moment of prayer and darshan of this deity at a quieter ti.ne during that month. Similarly, he does not go to Pandharpur or Alandi on an *ekadashi*, the appointed pilgrimage day for Vitthal and Jnyaneshwar, but at times when it is much less crowded; and he visits the nearby Kartikswamy site when he can be alone and solemn. While his religious practice is less social and more personal and private than that of some in the village, his own attitudes and practices are shared by many others. Ganpati feels especially close to Shiva, Datta, Jotiba (his family deity), Jnyaneshwar, also to the *gram devata* (Injabai), and now, it appears, to Ram as well. In his mind sometimes he also accepts Allah, Yesu, and all other names and images of the one god, Parmeshwar.

Since 1975, when I first met him and he was struggling as a farmer and could barely feed his mother, his wife, and himself, his family has grown and his economic condition greatly improved. Then and now he reads daily newspaper and continues to be a well-informed villager concerning regional and national events, but he takes no role in village politics or social affairs. Except for expressing immense admiration for Lal Bahadur Shastri and praise of Atal Behari Vajpayee (at least prior to his 13-day prime ministership), Ganpati is cynical about politicians and all political parties, and he feels at odds with the state and its organs (such as the banks where he could not get loans and the State Transport Corporation which failed to fulfil his youthful dream of becoming a bus conductor, and almost any other office where he is treated poorly because he does not have the right kin and caste connections). Although in recent years public works have benefited him greatly (including in some ways he is unlikely to recognize, such as improved transport service to the village), he credits the gods more than the state as responsible for his relative good fortune. This is despite the fact that a World Bank project has been the direct source of most of the material improvement, not only bringing irrigation to his land and making him a sugarcane farmer, but also providing him additional employment and a regular government salary as a watchman/clerk in the local irrigation department. These changes that have raised his standard of living greatly in the past ten years, just as the birth of two sons in the 1980s and his good health, are blessings of the gods, of God.

There are, of course, countless other things to say about this rather ordinary, this hardly unusual, villager who wrote me that "all religions say one and the same thing, and this means humanism" and "that the Hindu religion is the most superior". For example, he contributed one month's salary to the construction of the village's new Ram temple. He also recently spent more than a month's salary to feast neighbours, friends, and relatives on the occasion of completing his first reading of the entire *Jnyaneshwari*. In the past few years he has bought some new steel vessels for storing grain and for cooking and a new traditional wood-burning copper *bumba* for heating bath water but no fancy clothes or electric appliances. He never sees films, watches no television at his neighbours, and does not follow any sort of modern popular culture; he condemns the music which his elder teen-aged son plays on a borrowed cassette player. Ganpati still lives quietly and mostly with himself, his family, his gods, his religious thoughts and feelings which he will only rarely articulate, and his short temper and some other conflicting opinions. He considers, for instance, untouchables as generically filthy people, although he describes the personal and household behaviour of some of his wealthy Maratha neighbours in exactly the same terms. When a newspaper story or some other matter draws his attention to Muslims, he will have nothing good to say about them, although this is an attitude that appears to differ only slightly from a general contempt for the ways of recent history and the modern world; and he does not hesitate to contradict himself with his occasional confessions of humanism, equality, and the universal love which he believes some of his gods and saints embody. Ganpati is a vegetarian, but everyone else in his family does eat meat, and he does not object or even criticize.

In some small part, this is the village friend who wrote me the letter excerpted above. While we imagine and try to understand who else (and how else) he might be, we must take into account the limits of terms used by people who do not live in a village, or with other villagers, or with gods, because the terms, in substance and form, of such other people might not readily capture or reflect the somewhat limited and yet by no means simple realm of experience that envelops this Ganpati and many who live near him. Before considering such terms more directly, however, and thus leaving this village as one particular situation of knowledge, two other quick observations about this place in the mid-1990s should be noted, since they too are useful to suggest how, depending on one's situation, what one knows seems either simple or complicated, insignificant or pervasive.

First, the construction of a new Ram temple, part of the reason for Ganpati's recent letter and one of the major current collective endeavours in the village, is part of the village history that predates most interests in Ram temple throughout India today. Although I have not done all the research necessary to summarize what this village's new Ram temple does mean, this *mandir* is certainly not simply a local consequence of the *Ramayana* television serial or the Ayodhya events of recent years. Actually, it is slightly misleading to call the Ram temple just built in this village a new one, because it replaces an old Ram temple, a mud-brick but substantial structure which collapsed in the 1960s or early 1970s. In 1975, rubble and fragments of the walls remained on the site, and villagers told me then that they would build a new temple and instal a new image of Lord Ram. (The old *murti* had been immersed and abandoned in the Krishna river, not too far away, after the temple collapsed). The concrete slab for the floor of the new temple was built in the early 1980s, although it is, in fact, the roof of the village's new gram panchayat office, built at that time exactly on the site of the old temple and built in such a way to support a future temple above it. For the next ten or more years, nothing was added to this slab while the villagers went about collecting funds (or promises) to insure that they could raise enough to complete the project. Less than three months after I received Ganpati's letter and, I can add, with no material help from me, the construction was finished, and the temple was inaugurated with the installation of images (Ram, Sita, Laxman, and Hanuman) in February 1996. (The *murtis* were donated by a major Bombay industrialist). Having emphasized already that the village is not a closed or isolated place and that outside ideas and forces penetrate easily, I certainly would not conclude that the *Ramayana* TV serial or the Ayodhya events have not influenced what the old/new temple means to the villagers (or have not affected the fund-raising and timing of this temple's construction). Yet these certainly do not tell the whole story, which in a fuller account would include the role of one particular village leader as well as the local impact of the irrigation scheme and new sugarcane wealth.

Second, the other major new building in this village, the largest single structure in the community, should also not go unnoticed here. Finished in 1994, this prominent pukka stone and concrete edifice, painted bright white and occupying a nicely-fenced compound, fills a large plot amidst newly irrigated land along the main entry road into the Gavthan (settlement). This is the first real *karkhana* (factory) building in the village, housing an innovative entrepreneurial venture devised by one villager for extracting starch from tapioca by adapting a process developed in Thailand. The big bright bold red letters boast twice, once in Devanagari and once in English, that this is Shri Sai Enterprises. Other signs several kilometres distant on all the roads connected to the village also point the way, for bank loan officers and truck drivers hauling raw product, to Shri Sai Enterprises. I believe that given all the attention social scientists have directed to the position of some sacred powers or images in contemporary India, these signs should be seen as pointing for us too, although perhaps in a somewhat different direction, namely, to make sure that we do not forget Shirdi Sai Baba. If as social scientists we are to keep our commitment to understanding the functioning of systems as wholes (or perhaps merely the processes of complex arrangements in institutional relationships), we must observe the Ram temple and the Sai factory in relation to each other and in relation to the village as well and not only as they can be seen across the nation or in the market. They both suggest paying more attention to a broader context comprising all the other smaller new projects with gods in them or holy names on them, and then too, even in relation to all the pictures of devotional subjects in cars, trucks, buses, rickshaws, pan stands, tea stalls, and computer monitors also. At this point, though, we are obviously on the road, perhaps even approaching some information highway, and we shall leave behind, for a short while, the village and my village friend.

Somewhere Else

The somewhere else that must be recognized is a much larger and much different domain than the village that I know in Satara district. I shall not, however, consider it in any detail, because it is reasonable to presume that my readers are more familiar with this somewhere else, even though there may be no general agreement on how best to label or represent it. Here I want simply to situate some terms and quickly characterize the substance and form of knowledge which their use produces or represents; I want to indicate some things and possibilities which, despite claims (or assumptions) about universality and comprehending the nature of the world, are nonetheless excluded.

I am of two minds about what to call this somewhere else, and yet in being bi-valent or two-minded, I feel, I am actually fitting in, reflecting a basic, if often disguised feature of the place. This worldly situation itself makes for things and notions to have a double character, and it almost always presents one face with an immediacy, efficacy, and authority that overshadow or even work to mask the other. Admitting this characteristic operation at the very outset, I mean to evoke Marx's analysis of the double character of commodities in capitalism and Lukacs' application of this analysis to the categories of modern thought. That is, the somewhere else of this paper is either the domain of sociology or the modern bourgeois world, and there is little need to distinguish sharply between these. What matters most is that sociology itself does not succeed in hiding the modern bourgeois world from which it has grown and to which it belongs.

This somewhere else contains, as did my mail on the same day that I received Ganpati's letter, the words and ideas of cultural pluralism, ethnicity, and nation-building. This is the world of the papers in this and may other recent publications and of discussions in university seminars, policy institutions, and government offices. Cultural pluralism and ethnicity, however, are not terms or notions (even if we could render them in the appropriate vernacular) that appear in Ganpati's village. Given their own sociological and bourgeois situation, it seems proper to question how well they may apply to matters of identity, inter-group relations, or value commitments in the village today. If we are interested in the phenomena that terms like cultural pluralism or ethnicity denote or in phenomena linked closely to them, then we must take better note of how South Asian villages and villagers relate at present to the modern bourgeois world.

To do this anew, from a perspective of the world and our concerns in the 1990s (i.e., and not in relation to the modernization models of the 1950s), we must pay greater heed to the terms we use so that we can examine the differences and the ties between the village and the world with somewhat less partial categories and with somewhat less universalizing interests. (Indeed, a reflective critical sociology of knowledge itself can suggest that universalizing interests, or other generalizing schema, especially social evolutionary or developmental ones, make it almost impossible to grasp and appreciate the facts, meanings, and structures which organize, regulate, and animate societies that operate in many respects within smaller horizons and more modest limits. Seemingly general terms may be no less partial, i.e., particularly situated or oriented, than seemingly much more specific ones). We should attend both to the terms' effects and meanings that inhere in the specific contents (their semantic or substantive features) which define them and to those other characteristics which determine these terms' reach, definiteness, integrity, explicitness or immediacy, and other relational capabilities (in short, what appear as the syntactic or perhaps more formal, even metasyntactic, features of these terms).

The situation in which culture and cultural pluralism and ethnicity are salient, at least as social science understands these, is a situation where the nation or some other large region or large population is involved. These notions and things are rarely, if at all, thematized or sensible in South Asian villages like the one I know. To consider diverse cultural practices in that situation (such as differences in dress, diet, house style, ritual, or language) as indications of cultural pluralism or ethnicity would be highly misleading, because to those living there and to those who would care to observe, such differences do not sufficiently congeal into separate patterns or units of differences, or into deeper bases of identity, which form something distinct or integral enough to rate as a culture or ethnicity. Such differences do not overcome or outweigh all the common practices, shared knowledge, mutual ties, or structured variations which hold together the people and the ways of living in a village or even in a region of nearby villages. That is, the significance with regard to the semantic content of these notions can be suggested by hypothetically considering each caste in a village as composing a culture or ethnicity of its own and then trying to observe what some notion of cultural pluralism or multi-ethnicity might achieve by way of efficiently describing both the regularities that appear in relations among castes (e.g., matters of status, purity, occupational specialization, endogamy, commensality, etc., which is to say the fields of inter- and intra-caste social relations) and the features of village life where caste or caste differences are either unimportant or totally absent (e.g., agriculture and political or social factions). I believe that merely evoking this possibility should make clear that such terms do not help much even in explaining contemporary casteism (which involves categories like forward and backward, castes, OBC, creamy layer, etc., none of which come out of village social relations), much less the caste system or caste order in the rural situation. Furthermore, the significance of cultural pluralism or ethnicity for occupational, class, political, and devotional differences, considered apart from caste identities and as social factors in themselves, is difficult to discern in small communities where practically everyone shares a language and where non-caste-based differences in dress, diet, house-style, or other indicators or consumption and display are most likely to reflect the influence of wealth and urban (or merely foreign) models. The effect of applying these terms without further qualifying them is to obscure if not efface most of the differences and similarities which empirical work on social relations in South Asian villages reveals and strives to explain.

All these negative remarks about the meaning of cultural pluralism and ethnicity, noting what they fail to include and also the gap between rural and other settings in South Asia that they suggest, do not imply, however, that they have no positive sociological relevance for studying villages or villagers. Instead, it just becomes necessary to move a bit beyond or behind these terms and consider whether some of the elements or processes these terms comprise might themselves pertain more immediately to another particular situation. If cultural pluralism or ethnicity is significant for the social and political life of nations and cities today, then its positive relevance in relation to rural areas in South Asia has to derive from some of the components that constitute what comes to appear as culture or ethnicity in these other locations. In this particular instance, a broader, less partial, and more relevant conceptualization of the sociological interests that cultural pluralism and ethnicity introduce includes concerns with identity, community, and the repositories (incarnations, images, objects, institutions) of ultimate value (or values).[7]

That is, the meaning of the initial interests here elicits a kind of basic affiliation or association of individuals with groupings, categories, roles, or ideals; and the process or product that incorporates or manifests these can be that of a person or of a collective social subject, involving the definition of and relations among individuals as well as groups, and expressing itself as an identity or community. These concerns with identity, community, and matters of ultimate value can help us to observe and possibly to connect, or perhaps to decide to keep separate, my friend Ganpati or the social groupings in his village situation and those in Bombay, Delhi, or the nation or the larger region as a whole. The South Asian discussions of cultural pluralism and ethnicity, like those in the United States, presume a sense of something very deeply rooted and therefore basic to an identity or community and to those values that are the hardest to modify or renounce in everyday beliefs and practices. Thus, to get beyond the negative implications of these terms and not conclude solely by noting all that they hide or miss, it is appropriate, if not even necessary, to include gods and religions into the present remarks and to recognize that the meaning of cultural pluralism and ethnicity in South Asia, as long as this South Asia is one that includes villages and villagers, must be considered explicitly in relation to gods and religions, to these expressions of identity, community, and value in some ways which rural people live.

Moreover, it is not only appropriate but necessary to look beyond the semantic or substantive features of the terms that focus our attention upon a subject. The situation of knowledge suggests not merely that some terms other than those of cultural pluralism and ethnicity should direct a study relevant to rural South Asia but that some other kinds of terms—terms differing in their more formal or syntactic properties—must be conceived and put to use. To substitute for the terms 'culture' or 'ethnicity' some alternate terms like 'identity', 'community', or 'religion' can make little difference as ıong as the latter represent the same kind of referent, something with formal properties like those that the first terms cover. The use of 'culture' or 'ethnicity' in recent sociological discussion, and especially in contexts where pluralism or nationality pertains, represents thing-like entities or processes. That is, they designate identifiable wholes, observable, distinct (at least conceptually distinguishable, i.e., even if in reality it may be possible for some subjects to be multi-cultural or multi-ethnic), and possibly even measurable (since the scope of a culture or size of an ethnic group quickly enters into consideration) and able to relate directly to each other in some orderly manner. They thus form acceptable objects for a positivistic social science and, following Lukacs, belong to a particular ideological realm, one characteristic of the modern bourgeois world and consequently one with specific limits in its critical potential.

Lukacs' analysis of the antinomies of bourgeois thought and the constitution of modern western philosophical categories from the double character of the commodity-form reveals from within this particular realm some of its own limits, including those which prevent or contradict recognition of the limits. The categories render social and historical subjects into objects that unavoidably become second nature to us, to us modern bourgeoisie or to us inadequately critical (or insufficiently dialectical) sociologists. Based upon Marx's disclosure of the secret of the commodity, which can do nothing otherwise than to present social relations between persons as objective relations between things, Lukacs' epistemological extension of this critique shows that concepts and categories which appear given, natural, and objective or object-like are themselves but necessary manifestations of social relations and social structures. In particular, such concepts and categories compose another basic factor of the same commodifying, capitalizing apparatus, one that produces knowledge for exchange value, for dividing and dominating classes of people, for exploitative applications and instrumental technologies, for a world market.[8]

Consistent with (and developing from) the totalizing dynamic of capitalism, this analysis of its forms of consciousness and thought includes and exposes even the category of nature itself; "nature is a social category", a product of the ideology which sustains the modern bourgeois world. This realm of somewhere else that presents itself as a nowhere in particular, viz., as a given, natural, and objective viewpoint with a universalizing claim to comprehend and hold true everywhere, is also the ground of current notions like culture, as this pertains to 'cultural pluralism', and ethnicity (and even many understandings of 'the nation' too). But with respect to the village ways of living, to a situation that still insists that this larger somewhere is a somewhere else, these kinds of terms and ideas are especially problematic and hard to accept because they introduce both aspects of the reification that Lukacs describes, that is, the naturalization of the world and the rationalization of the world.

Ethnicity as well as an entified notion of culture are themselves too easily understanding as natural units and almost inevitably evoke a natural order. They come with natality and thus appear as given at birth. Although for some, modern social science can correct modern bourgeois common sense and effectively show that social or historical rather than biological factors constitute one's ethnicity or culture (i.e., explaining how these are actually social or historical constructs), this social science does not and cannot diminish the sense of primordiality which they convey. Indeed, these terms' significance in and for social science itself consists mainly in their distinguishing those identities taken as primordial, basic, and fixed in a particular way of life from roles or duties which are established in either wilful action or accidental circumstances. (During the last two or three decades, the greatly increased attention to ethnicity and cultural identity in many views of modern society and history does not reflect a sense that these are phenomena which have been recently produced or invented, but rather that they have always been there, in these societies and their history, and that their importance has only been recently discovered).

Moreover, a focus concentrated on ethnicity and culture tends to impose a rational perhaps even governing order in the social world. Such notions represent discrete specifiable objects (immediately identifiable objects of identity) or discrete products of a particular kind of social process (such as boundary definition or maintenance in situations of migration or urbanization), and in either case, these are taken to interrelate in certain consistent and non-contradictory ways. They can be counted, classified, and arranged, such that a coherent system appears. Thus, the ethnicities or the cultures can serve not only intellectual or contemplative interests in problems of establishing and maintaining social order (the predictability necessary for rationality) but also practical political or administrative interests in such problems (the law or efficiency which makes governing possible). Consequently, such notions can direct the exercise of power in a manner indifferent to, and perhaps even in violation of, those parts of a population living with other notions, habits, and values concerning who they are and how they want to use, assert, deny, twist, or transform their identity or identities.[9]

Thus, as these terms reflect and bring to mind discrete entities (whether things or thing-like processes, all given in the nature of things, in the way things must be), they obscure other kinds of processes drawing upon the dynamics, uncertainties, inconsistencies, and possibly even the ideals and more implicit or practical forms of understandings which also shape, organize, and animate the identities and relationships of people in many communities. Ethnicity and culture are also generally used as homogenizing and levelling notions, which quickly draw attention away from internal differentiation and internal relationships within a social setting and from any other powerful structuring factors with both meaning for actors and impact on the life of the larger society. In all these respects, such notions and terms belong to a situation and to the situated knowledge which do not relate well to much that goes on in South Asian villages. Furthermore, even if these terms may be meaningful in certain urban, national, and international contexts, they are not adequate for understanding the links of any of these domains to the people who compose not only the majority of the present population of South Asia but also those who bear and sustain the ties to most of the pasts and traditions (and possibly the most original accomplishments too) of this region as a whole.

The situation, therefore, of ethnicity and of the sense of culture that appears in cultural pluralism is something similar to the place in which T.N. Madan put secularism, as he attempted in his 1987 lecture to put 'Secularism in its Place'. Namely, this situation is someplace that is not faithful to the traditions, institutions, history, and values of South Asia. So, where should, or where can, we go from here?

Somewhere in Between (and Somewhere where Between Matters)

With no immediate prospect of arriving anyplace very conclusive, I want to indicate some directions that follow from what I have learned from Ganpati, his fellow villagers and the ways they live together. To help clarify my concerns about how and where to proceed, I shall first draw a contrast with some important essays by T.N. Madan and Ashis Nandy on religion and secularism (viz., the Madan essay that I just mentioned and Nandy's 1992 paper on "The Politics of Secularism and the Recovery of Religious Tolerance"). I share their deep discomfort with applying both categories from the western world and an uncritical scientific method to comprehend South Asian societies (and to intervene in their political, economic, social, and cultural lives).

Cultural pluralism and ethnicity appear to me to belong where Madan puts secularism and where Nandy locates development, progress, technology, and science. This is someplace with only limited relevance to much South Asian experience and yet someplace with tremendous possible consequences, because it is someplace that connects this region (by means of a part of its own population and some of its own institutions) to a wider world that is unstable and deteriorating ecologically, unbalanced and exploitive economically, violent, and not moral. I find much in the critique and condemnation that Madan and Nandy aim at western and modern ways persuasive, even though many of the implications remain unclear, uncertain, and profoundly problematic (with regard especially to matters of liberty and equality). Yet in trying to represent more positively something Indian or South Asian as an alternative, the ideas in the Madan and Nandy essays strike me as struck too close to the national capital and its scholarly/political discourse and researches not moving quite enough (and also not quite moving enough) to approach and appreciate much of what appears important in Ganpati's village. Thus, as I seek a somewhere in between, I want to direct attention toward a few of the not so modern or not so bourgeois things that seem to matter but that remain ignored in some important contemporary Indian scholarship.

Madan asks about the place of secularism (and other such products of western ideologies and science) in order to understand much better how South Asia's religious traditions view "the relationship between the categories of the 'religious' and the 'secular' " (399). He considers the difference between what he labels as exclusivizing and totalizing situations, where the former is expressed in notions of tolerance and intolerance as both of these reject the hierarchical relationship between the religious and the secular (or between the sacred and the worldly political order) which Madan discerns in South Asia's religious traditions. Similarly, cultural pluralism and ethnicity also clearly express a situation of exclusivism and hence, for Madan, would have little if any relevance for South Asia, whose tradition totalizes instead. The surprising weakness in Madan's essay, however, is how he reifies tradition itself, excluding too much of social life from it, making it an exclusively cultural subject.

Madan here accepts Dumont's not only inadequate but also dangerous account of most of Indian society (dangerous because it reifies—and, in a structuralist manner, crystallizes, essentializes, India—as it idealizes and de-politicizes and denies attention to economic and welfare issues). Hierarchy also needs to be put in its place, which in India is not every place, as Madan's other writings on non-renunciation and domestic issues argue so convincingly. Hierarchy may require a totalizing situation, but the opposite, that a totalising situation is exclusively or even predominantly hierarchical, does not hold, and Madan's point that India's religious traditions are totalizing can be accepted without falling under the whole cloth mantle of Homo Hierarchicus. Furthermore, in this essay on secularism, with an uncharacteristic turn for him as an anthropologist, Madan looks only at the classic South Asian religious traditions, the great traditions, whether as represented in the *Vedas* and the *Arthashastra* or in the Indian Constitution and Pandit Nehru's writings. He does not come very close at all to my friend Ganpati's letter, to Ganpati's worship of Datta, Kartikswamy, Mahadev, and Jnyaneshwar or to his village's Ram temple and Shri Sai Enterprises, in any of their polysemic vitality and/or confusion or in their totalizing implications. The South Asia that Madan depicts as not the place of secularism is also not the place where many South Asians, their societies, and even their religious practices live today.

Moreover, Madan's essay appears to remain under the sway of secular thinking, even holding to a version of exclusivism, because despite his opening caution that "by modernity I do not mean a complete break with tradition" (p. 394), he depends nonetheless upon just a minor revision of the modernity/tradition dichotomy. "Secularism as an ideology has emerged from the dialectic of modern science and Protestantism" (p. 403). For Madan the place of secularism is the part of the modern world which cannot deal with and which seems to oppose tradition and religious traditions, even if these can persist and occupy another part of a modern world. Madan's reliance on Dumont in this essay further reinforces the impression that a major binary opposition is at work (separating India, mainly traditional and Brahmanic India, from the modern West, even as science and religion exclude each other within the modern West), and it hardly matters this is primarily an intellectual rather than an empirical (or existential) dichotomy.

Ashis Nandy breaks further away than Madan from the constraints of secular thinking as he tries in his paper on "The Politics of Secularism and the Recovery of Religious Tolerance", (conference paper, 1987, published, 1992) to rescue religious tolerance "from the hegemonic language of secularism popularized by the westernized intellectuals and middle classes under the influence of nation-state interests" (p. 67). In seeking the conditions which support a tolerance outside "the scope and limits of the ideology of secularism in India" (p. 73), he introduces a number of points in accord with some hard to capture aspects of life in the village I have studied and thus appears to approach more closely much that matters there.

For example, there is not much distance between Ganpati's ramblings about his religious beliefs or identity and Nandy's portrayal of "somewhat fluid definitions of the self". Nandy writes that "such a self, which can be conceptually viewed as a configuration of selves, invokes and reflects the configurative principles of religion-as-faith" (p. 73). (This self is a negation of western and other regressive South Asian elements that accept a "definition of the self as a well-bounded, individuated entity clearly separable from the non-self", a notion compatible with 'religion-as-ideology', which in turn involves well-bounded and mutually exclusive religious identities). Nandy's 'more fluid definition of the self' does not involve a well-bounded, individuated entity clearly separable from the non-self. Moreover, "it is the self in conjunction with its anti-selves and its distinctive concept of the non-self which together define the domain of the self", and this domain rejects well-wounded and mutually exclusive religious identities. It is this self who is compatible with what Nandy calls religion-as-faith (p. 73).

As a second point, the image of faith, which opposes a notion of religion as ideology, also pertains to Ganpati's village. Faith for Nandy means "religion as a way of life, a tradition which is definitionally non-monolithic and operationally plural". Indeed, he asserts that in larger societies, like India's, religion as a way of life has to turn into a "confederation of a number of ways of life which are linked by a common faith that has some theological space for the heterogeneity which everyday life introduces" (p. 70). Ganpati's everyday life confederates a number of heterogeneous theologies, the differences or even chaos among which cannot diminish the significance or the strength of his devotion and worship. Perhaps the non-exclusive and non-monolithic qualities even make them more adaptable to changing times and more vital.

Third, Nandy explicitly attends to "the non-modern majority of a society" (p. 84) in examining "the traditions of tolerance in Indian society" (p. 85). He claims that its response (or 'sort of response') to secularism and the modern policies or politics of state that appear to deny religion "does not keep religion separate from politics". [This response "does say that the traditional ways of life have, over the centuries, developed internal principles of tolerance and these principles must have a play in contemporary politics" (p. 84)]. Certainly, no consideration of the separation of religion and politics had much impact on the villagers' decision to build a new gram panchayat office on the site of the collapsed Ram temple and then to build the new Ram temple atop the slab roof of the office itself.[10] Nandy's essay observes the indifference of secularism to culture and discovers a certain kind of "religious tolerance outside the bounds of secularism". What Ganpati's letter and his overall way of life present is described precisely by Nandy's key idea—that is, not only a "tolerance of religions but a tolerance that is religious". My evidence supports Nandy that here, in this part of South Asia, people are living located in "traditions, outside the ideological grid of modernity" (p. 91). (This point is consistent also with his observation that the violence between religions in India is largely an urban and industrial phenomenon). Nandy's description of an "accommodative and pluralist meaning" for secularism as understood by a majority of Indians applies; the secularism accommodates religion and the diversities and co-existence in the matter of faith (p. 74).

Thus, Nandy's account comes closer to the somewhere in particular with which this paper began and confirms the more general relevance of some of my narrowly-based observations. He is developing a set of analytic (if not even scientific, despite how dirty a word this might be for him) notions that help conceive and depict a relationship between the part of the South Asian subcontinent which seems not absorbed in or hegemonized by the modern bourgeois world and that world. And yet, as close as it comes, in two crucial ways Nandy's work does not go far enough.

First, despite his knowledge and appreciation of Frankfurt School sociology, he seems to have lost sight of the importance of more dialectical notions, of the working of contradictions in the experience and structuring of social life or culture. Even his major analytic notions are too pat and too clear-cut for a complex world where Hindu deities, global capitalism, or rationalizing science and bureaucracy may run rampant. His own self, positively identified in a negative manner, as he proudly proclaims "I am not a secularist" (p. 73), lacks the very fluidity that Nandy portrays and values as distinctive of South Asian cultures. (He continues just as determinedly, "In fact, I can be called an anti-secularist").

His version of the split between faith and ideology resembles the heavy-handed slicing of a traditional social scientist (i.e., a modern one) and of a structuralist, who sees things only in terms of us and them, traditional and modern, secularism and anti-secularist, cold and hot. Possibly, the crudeness of the analysis (despite the brilliance of the argument) is an artefact of Nandy's rhetoric and his sense of what current politics demands, and yet to the degree that the rhetoric itself thus stands apart from the dialectic, my point is established. The author's position itself is not grounded in his own words or thought, and so as a political preface, it lacks persuasive critical punch.

Second, Nandy is largely indifferent to matters of social structure, power (politics), and resources (economics) as he confines his attention to areas of culture and psychology (of symbolism and individuality). As important as these are, they cannot suffice. Culture and psychology do not take us all that far from the modern world which, as ideological or discursive figures, they routinely dominate. (They reflect much more than they transcend the distinctive immediacies of this world, even as, or perhaps precisely as, they do appear to go beyond or to delve within, and thus to relativize either symbolically or personally, the more vulgar everyday social constraints and needs). Neither the fluid selves nor the way of life which comprises faith (as religion) nor religious tolerance, as Nandy describes all these non-modern processes, can survive on spiritual resources alone (on anti- and non-selves, on philosophy and theology, or on the opposition to ideology). What he illuminates and describes is sufficiently open, complex, and dynamic to draw from and interact with the rest of society and social life, the organization of persons, the structures of power and wealth, and the ongoing transformation and reproduction of these. Yet his argument, in this political preface as in other writings, appears as an ideological critique of an ideological phenomenon. Nandy's tolerance, as a matter of faith, does not reveal itself to be a matter of faith as a way of life, because he does not approach the ways of living, the people, their fluid selves, their diverse and multi-dimensional social relations and different kinds of groupings, the real world of real others and non-selves, and the economic and political pressures and institutions without which no way of life can go on for long. In looking for the conditions which support a tolerance outside "the scope and limits of the ideology of secularism in India", he overlooks the more material and social structural dimensions, i.e., what generates and supports such conditions and what can erode or destroy them. He seems unable to look outside the scope and limits of ideology itself, reflecting and reproducing (despite his anti-secularist self) a modern situation, a strong interest in (or predisposition towards) culture and psychology, and hence his observations and values, as perceptive and critical as these are, do not point to where social scientists need to go and to where sociologists or social anthropologists in particular are best equipped to go.

With a few observations, some posed as questions, I want to conclude more positively and yet also return closer to where this paper started by beginning to point one way to a somewhere in between. Regardless of the current situation's persistent antinomial thrust which almost forces us to consider ourselves and our worlds as either modern or post-modern, colonial or post-colonial, rational or religious, liberating or coercive, meaningful or absurd, serious or playful, doomed or improving, evil or good, I urge a departure from the fixations of such dilemmas in order to contemplate or entertain where and how someplace(s) in between may also matter. I seek a situation somewhere in between the village and sociology, that is, a situation of knowledge and for knowledge which belongs between a somewhere in particular and the somewhere else that represents itself as both nowhere and everywhere. This place is where most of our modern bourgeois categories and science, on account of their own situation, have yet failed to reach. Somewhere in between the village and the modern bourgeois world, another sociology (a different reasoning on society, a new social saying/knowing) should emerge to help account for how these two relate, where and when they come together, where and when they do not, what happens when they do or do not, and why. Moreover, this situation in between would not ignore, as such categories as cultural pluralism and ethnicity almost force us to do, the complex of thoughts, beliefs, names, temples, factories, and social relations of rural South Asia. It would take us outside and beyond the village community, which was never an isolated, self-sufficient, independent republic in any case, but it would not leave it behind or alone. It is where ideas like those Ganpati expresses and the ways in which he puts them together might more closely approach the ideas and reasoning that sociologists rooted in the modern bourgeois world believe in and use.

Here are three aspects of life that are important in a contemporary village community, which are absent from much important contemporary Indian scholarship, and which may matter greatly for learning about and acting in South Asian and other societies in the contemporary world.[11] These are just three indications of the kind of phenomena that South Asian social science must consider, especially if matter of identity and community and the ideas and values expressing these are to be taken seriously. Indeed, my experience and study suggest that notions of identity and community may help to compose a less partial, more neutral or comparative, situation in which to locate and respond to interests in secularism, religion, cultural pluralism, or ethnicity. In particular, my experience and study suggest that more relevant and critical concepts, analysis, theorizing, and understanding of identity and community will result from more attention to:

> devotion and the associational effects of faith (the effervescence which collects as well as collectivizes representations, a Durkheimian point); ritual intensification as a conjunction or collaboration of new wealth and more religion, e.g. Shirdi Sai Baba (a somewhat Weberian point, since the economic and spiritual affect each other); and social relations and the structures of association, whether these be caste, clanship, kinship, or village community, economic class or political faction (also a Durkheimian point, but one that draws more immediately from Evans-Pritchard and Srinivas).

First, rulers and ruling perspectives, the kings and the codifiers, often tend to claim all the associating, integrating, and unifying responsibilities for themselves, leaving the rest to see themselves in terms of differences and divisions. Scholars and other intellectuals usually follow the former and make their living on the basis of distinctions. Divide and rule, divide and analyze, divide and, from above, comprehend. Yet there are other sources and forces of association in the social life and religious practices of villages and villagers, of small communities and lesser individuals. In the village and in Ganpati's life there are bhakti and the religious-cum-ritual-cum-routine daily complex of activities that join Shiva and Vishnu (in the sometimes confused understandings of who Vitthal/Vithoba is), that join Shiva/Mahadev and Jotiba, that join Jnyaneshwar and Tukaram, and then that even join these to Ramdas Swami and Vivekananda. On less everyday occasions there are the expressions that join Ram and Rahima and Buddha and Guru Nanak. There are many other links or fusings (I hesitate even in my choice of terms) that I have not yet mentioned but which also remain absent from contemporary discussions of religion, secularism, community, and identity. Defeating my own modern intelligence, categories, and reasoning, widespread village understandings join the pure universal spirit to a rock in the corner of a millet field or insist on the simultaneous truth of one god and 33 crores of them and of a *nirguna* and *saguna* (formless and formed) divinity. More noticed and yet still not sufficiently probed and with implications quite difficult to trace, are the common beliefs expressed in everyday practices involving both *andhashraddha* and *vijnyan*, say astrology and astronomy or ghosts and psychological rationalizing.

I urge that we consider these associational habits and ask what they may have to do with the common display, in houses and not only in public building, of portraits of Mahatma Gandhi next to that of Netaji Bose or of Shivaji beside Dr. Ambedkar. What about Bal Krishna with the butter and Lord Krishna with the chariot; is there more than a name that unites these objects of devotion? What about the names that interchangeably identify lingams as Shiva, Mahadev, Mahesh, Shankar, and many more particular regional and local persons (Siddheswar, Omkeshwar, Grashneshwar)? What about the thousands of timeless and local devis, and then the new position in Maharashtrian religion of Santoshi Ma or of Durga? If the precise names of the one lord or all the divine beings do not really matter, then, what about the names of people (where in the village there is a complex and yet flexible system of personal calling and referring names), of social groups (castes, *jati*, in particular), and of places, and of the different logics or contexts which determine what is in a name, whether the rose or the railway terminus smells the same by any other name? Why must Mumbai efface Bombay for some? Why does, or how can, my friend Ganpati, who professes humanism in the most generous and noble terms, be concerned that Aurangabad become Sambhajinagar?

What kind of tolerance (or intolerance) is it that tolerates both tolerance and intolerance, non-violence and violence, and preserver and destroyer? What kind of reasoning (or non-reasoning) is it which itself draws inferences from rational and irrational procedures? My purpose in raising such questions here is to argue that such phenomena of undeniable importance in villagers' everyday life make the case anew for more dialectical, dynamic, open, and always contextualized, always contextualizing, concepts and descriptions. Most notions of ethnicity or of culture in relation to cultural pluralism and certainly most applications of such notions import and presume senses of thingness (even if the thing is a process) and reason and quantity and givenness which defy the currents of values, the associations of social intensity and identities, as people in particular places, small or large, generally live and animate them.

Second, a more specific sense of ritual intensification deserves attention. (I am adopting this term and ideas from the work of R.F. Salisbury on the effect of the introduction of steel axes in tribal New Guinea; he showed that this technological development meant that tribes had more wealth and hence more time with which to elaborate their ritual practices). To me it is surprising, even shocking, that social scientists continue to be surprised and shocked whenever they find a positive mutual relationship between increasing wealth and increasing faith. The aftermath of an enlightenment episode in the early modern West, emphasizing the advance of reason, science, and the apparent secularization of society, still blinds many to the larger sweep of modern western history and, indeed, to the historical aspects of the Weber thesis itself. In the hurry to get on with modernization, or for some even in the rush to reject it, many forget that the disenchantment of the world was a much later consequence of adopting new vocations. The birth and growth of western industrial capitalism accompanied radical religious reforms, religious innovations, religious wars, and also witchcraft crazes and fanatically intolerant puritanical fundamentalisms. Despite all the dichotomies canonized in modern scientific views and sociology textbooks, namely, those that set apart faith and reason, sacred and profane spheres, spiritual and material values, or religious and economic practices, many basic technological and economic changes can both expand and transform ritual and other unreasoned or irrational activities.

By accepting and applying a notion of ritual intensification, contemporary social science would not so easily marginalize or reject the roles of religion in less traditional or rapidly changing societies. We would have to attend more to both the building of religion, as it becomes something more or even something new or renewed in people's lives, and to the buildings of religion, the obvious tangible objects which display and may also further inspire the new accumulation of wealth and forms of collective activity in the society. We would be able to avoid viewing, as both western and western-looking non-western social scientists are prone to do, the current manifestations of faith, even in its more fundamentalist guises, solely as the impact of cultural forms from abroad, as a result of post-modern or late capitalist communication media and trans-national flows. Without denying the possibility of some role for these, we would also consider the internal or local logic of certain kinds of socio-economic transformation which produce conditions of greater affluence, both in respect to cash and time. We would see religion within and not opposed to modernity and modernization and could accept and further investigate how temple building and pilgrimage go together with factory building and tourism. Consequently, our categories, of thought and of perception too, should be more dialectical, or at least more two-sided, so we never neglect that the coin, or the paper currency, or now even the credit card, always has two sides that appear to face in different directions, with different meanings, uses, and effects.

For all the serious academic attention in recent years to Lord Ram, where is the equally serious scholarship that would begin to consider Sai's significance in the life of modern Indians and contemporary India? Throughout western India at least, from Dharavi to Malabar Hill in Mumbai, from a *kisan's* god house to a jawan's rucksack in the Desh, and in the rickshaws, tea stalls, lottery stands, factories, markets, corporate suites, and government offices, this Sai Baba blesses all and seems addressed by all. His place at Shirdi is the inclusive, perhaps totalizing and confederating, traditional, modern, and post-modern village and city, and it is not Ayodhya. In Shirdi and elsewhere on the way to Shirdi, not only Hindu and Muslim and Sikh, but also Marwari and Maratha, merchant and peasant, movie star and peon, cosmopolitan and provincial, and Vedic sacrifices and *bhakti* exertions assemble together under the consolation (and the consoling visage) of a single *malik*, one lord, for all. This *malik* means material wealth and physical health as much, if not more than spiritual peace.

Yet social scientists in India have been largely neglecting this religiosity, such as pervasive mundane embodiment of miracles and faith, for other more partisan gods and godmen, their politics, and the drama of the small (and sometimes the large) screen which they occupy in serials and newscasts.[12] The modern opposition, largely ideological, of religion and science, or sacred and secular, or traditional and modern, which makes phenomena of ritual intensification appear anomalous, when not actually barring them from appearing at all, is an especially problematic, consequential reification. This obfuscates, if not denies dialectical relations and possibilities that make sufficiently significant space for religion and ritual for faith and habits, in the workings of modern society, and thus, on the one hand, it implies an approach to culture and discourse either as autonomous realms ungrounded in social, political, economic, or perhaps even moral structures and logics or as holistic realms that just depend upon and automatically reflect such other structuring principles or interests. Or, on the other hand, such an opposition seems to compel viewing ritual and other expressive or textual phenomena within a world of spiralling or cascading ambivalences, unstructured and destructuring fragments, and play, where seriousness and serious consequences seem ever transient, passing fancies (and this may be the price and the fruit of freedom, of living in a world ungoverned by traditional constraints of givenness and structured heritage). Opening more sensitively to the complexities of both local and less localized ways of living in contemporary South Asia and leaving aside the modern opposition of spirit and matter or sacred and secular, social scientists concerned with this part of the world might develop better ideas, terms, notions, or concepts to handle the structures, dynamics and manifestations of religion and identity than those in the current repertoire that relies on ethnicity or culture as derived from largely American interpretations of American society.

Finally, the third kind of phenomena important for village life which requires more attention in our social research is the realm of social relations and the structures of association. The more complex and subtle factors and products of identity and community should be brought once again into the centre of our overall framework and not be ignored or replaced on account of broader or more immediate categories that appear to come from nowhere and appear to apply everywhere.[13] Notions like ethnicity and culture, in their composite generality, may deter us from distinguishing many more particular, indeed themselves more distinguishing classifications and relations among persons and groups. For me, one main question concerns what is gained, either analytically or comparatively, by submerging or translating caste, clanship, kinship, or village community, economic class, political faction, or devotional sect in much of South Asian social life into the contemporary academic discourse of ethnicity and culturalism. (My question aims not to deny all applications or relevance of such terms to contemporary phenomena in this region, since some persuasive use appears in considerations of life in and around Delhi, among academics and professionals in national institutions, within some other rapidly growing urban or industrial centres, during the Republic Day parade and national *utsavs*, and regarding high fashion, advertising, and cuisine. My point rather is to prevent the perspective that comprehends appearances in some specific bourgeois areas of interest from dominating and comprehending how societies and social differences throughout the region are seen, since this specific focus obstructs considering how the bourgeois or professional or more completely commodified spheres themselves may fit within, relate to, or count against other ways of living as so many other people in nearly the same place know and practice these).

Leaving the subcontinent for a moment, we can recognize immediately the difference that a less social and more cultural concept makes as Peter Ekeh describes one in a 1990 article, "Social Anthropology and Two Contrasting Uses of Tribalism in

Africa" (*Comparative Studies in Society and History*, 1990). The contrast is between a notion of a tribe as composed and structured by lineages, clans, and territorial units and a notion of a tribe as a cultural or linguistic group, defined by the presence or absence of traits, unstructured within, and significance in opposition to other tribes outside rather than in opposition to other social groupings that exist within it. In recent scholarship, the latter version of tribe and tribalism, the one which conceives it as a cultural or ethnic unit, has replaced the former, with its greater sensitivity to the social relations and social differences that organize everyday life. This African example is hardly remote from moves in Indian sociology or anthropology. For many, today, any village in particular, which is also to say the village in general, represents or is imagined to be a single cultural element, a product of stable and fairly integrated habits and beliefs (those timeless rituals and superstitions), that is set apart from the city, or the forest, the market, the state, or other cultural realms which together compose the larger society or civilization. This view neglects, unfortunately, almost everything that the earlier social anthropology of rural South Asia discovered regarding the significance of kinship, clanship, factions, and caste structures in village life and also the diverse and changing links—social, political, economic, and religious—of villages and villages with others, whether *sadhus*, *shets* or *rajas*. Similarly, the complexity of caste in rural settings is itself erased in those views from afar or above that regard all castes as pretty much each the same sort of social grouping and see any caste primarily in relation to other castes or multi-caste groupings (and not in relation to the clans, marriage circles, or other sub-groupings which it contains). These views are the ones that catalogue and schedule castes or that care most about vote-banks and reservations but that lose all sight of the sources and structures or solidarity and division within such groupings.

In particular, certain views or approaches lose sight of the social situatedness of the groupings that in turn organize social life. Much recent scholarship has very little interest in the range of identities and varying patterns of relations that sustain communities as people regularly live together with and in terms of each other. The example and influence of another African study is especially salient here. Evans-Pritchard introduced the idea of structural relativity in order to depict the dynamic and contradictory—that is to say the dialectical (the contextually varying and therefore not necessarily consistent across contexts)—dimensions of Nuer identity and their social and political relations. His notion of dominance, pertaining to clans for the Nuer and reflecting their structural relativity, proved immediately useful to Srinivas for depicting the local aspects of caste and faction and other group relations in rural India. For considering either the dominant or the dominated (and such categories are, of course, inherently relative and situational) in a small community, the relational and situational factors upon which intra-group as well as inter-group relations mostly depend must be disclosed, because these govern when and how different identities appear and affect people's lives. Recognizing these factors then reveals and helps explain how a person can be both a member and not a member of a group and also how a person can be a member of one group and also a member of a group opposed to it. These inherent possibilities in much social life are crucial where relations are not so completely one-dimensional, instrumentalized, or commodified, although they too are not unknown in the modern bourgeois world either. Yet these are the possibilities that tend to escape the grasp of those who are preoccupied with matters of culture and who have come to depend upon the naturalizing primordial reifications in cultural categories.

Notions and terms like cultural pluralism and ethnicity are oblivious to the ways of living in which this kind of structural relativity operates. In much of South Asian social life, for example, the relations between brothers, the relationship of being brothers (which by extension includes the relationship between the sons of brothers), is a pivot (or a fulcrum or an idea) on which much of the actual organization of social life for almost every person, in almost family, and in every village depends. Fraternity is here a relation with a dialectic of its own, including an opposition of solidarity and conflict such that each of these depends largely upon the other for its significance and practical effects. (This is far from the ideal of fraternity, the simpler utopian notion, that appears in the Indian Constitution). Many brothers share much together, in terms of their background, status, property, and personal characteristics, and they may usually cooperate and occasionally even be friends. Many brothers, on the contrary, compete or feud with each other, distrust and at times hate one another; and in rare circumstances one brother may even kill another. Sometimes brothers can both love and hate each other, or they may oppose or merely ignore each other only until some outsider enters the picture, when they set their enmity aside. The dynamics and contradictions of this sort of relationship—the properties of fission and fusion animating such a social category as male sibling and also the tensions between the status equality of brothers as others regard them and the seniority or other sorts of inevitable differences that arise within the family—deserve more serious attention in studying South Asian social life and history (and culture). The relations between brothers or cousins are central for the morals and social ideals expressed in the *Ramayana* and *Mahabharata*, have determined the fortunes and misfortunes of many *rajas* and *badshahs*, continue to organize political factions and artisanal and domestic service bonds in many villages, and also popularly symbolize the hopes and fears surrounding certain contemporary inter-communal and international relationships (as in the *bhai-bhai* of Hindu and Muslim or India and China). Such social relations, with all their potentials and meanings, are what the current more cultural, more solid, thing-like, and exclusivist, more naturally homogeneous, more rationally consistent, more simply and thoroughly (and ideally) differentiating ideas cannot penetrate as they determine (and limit and obscure) basic understandings of identity and difference.[14]

Regarding many other social relations too, the significance of dynamic and possibly contradictory qualities like those characterizing the relationship of brothers should be considered in discussions of identities and the ways in which groupings relate to one another and compose a larger society. Gender, while perhaps in certain circumstances quite significant as such (i.e., as such an internally undifferentiated notion, where it indicates either all the males or females in a population or all the values involved in what is simply masculine or feminine), can hide the nearly equally meaningful differences in a society that may exist between father and brother and son or those between mother-in-law and daughter-in-law and between wife and mother and sister. Yet such intra-gender positions also have a tremendous effect on how society, family life, and personal experience are structured. Without attending to the patterns and contingencies of social relations within social groupings, and hence to what contextually composes and realizes any social category, a view of a society that presumes (or beings in terms of) such groupings or categories themselves, those determined by ethnicity or culture or even gender or class, cannot begin to reveal how they are situated or how much they matter in the course of a way of living.

For a social science to include and possibly to comprehend Ganpati and his words and beliefs, his village and its temples and factories, and the names and notions that all these express, embody, or sometimes institutionalize, it seems necessary to move beyond the sociology of the modern bourgeois world, the knowledge and pursuit of knowledge as situated in, possessed by, and attentive to this world. Recognizing (even in the sketchy suggestions noted here) devotion, the conjunction of wealth and religion in ritual intensification, and the dynamics of social relations helps to bring out some of the associating phenomena and situations that the external, less sensitive, less sympathetic, less penetrating, and more fixed interests in cultures avoid. Moving back from the reifications dominating so much contemporary social science may thus help take us beyond the situation of some of the most immediate expressions of contemporary bourgeois concerns—including those of secularism, religion, ethnicity, or cultural pluralism—and bring us closer to the identities, communities, and values that together sustain, organize, and orient the ways of living of most of the people in South Asia at present. The direction for a more relevant social science to follow points towards accepting the totalizing (not exclusivizing) and confederating (not mixing or uniting or encompassing) and contextual relativizing of identities, meanings, groupings, values, and practices. It points away from some basic bourgeois antinomies, including that which necessarily separates form and content or culture and nature. (Forms and categories for living people matter in the situations that compose and constrain ways of life; sociologists who can abstract themselves from such messy situations and think primarily about the forms or represent data in terms of them, such as when exhibiting what culture or ethnicity *per se* reveal, do so at the risk of losing both the situated meanings of these reifying forms and the structures of differences within the groups and between the groups that they designate). Consciousness and experience, no less than institutions and texts (prayers, proverbs, legends, philosophical poems), can take different forms in different situations and can give different form to their contents/subjects and can even dissolve (or render insignificant) any difference between form and content by making them mutually dependent.

A sociology whose terms (i.e., the terms in terms of which problems are perceived and questions addressed) are open to these options should not so easily exclude, for example, *bhakti* or Shirdi Sai Baba or bickering brothers as matters relevant both to a particular village and to its relations to a much larger country, society, and sweep of history. For South Asia, we must seek a sociology that can observe, for example, that the logics that identify all gods as one and the same and yet make one of them worth killing or worth dying for (or that accepts all *dharmas* as one but with one of these superior to all others) may operate far away in naming cities or identifying religions;[15] and that the construction of a Ram *mandir* and a Shri Sai starch factory at one time in one place implicates a much larger ritual-political-economy which is a sphere of powers and values not clearly distinguishable as either ritual or political or economic; and that the structural relativity of caste groupings, clans, and factions in a village has ways of both linking with an separating from the district, state, and national politics of caste and parties. From a village one Ganpati writes me a letter about all the names of God referring to a single creator and yet puts Lord Ram on the top of the page and asks for a donation to a new Ram temple below; and Ganpati worships the Truth of Humanism and quietly studies love and oneness in the verses of Jnyaneshwar but is almost always angry at the world and feuds with his brothers. Where is the sociology—and what will be the shape and substance of its sociological terms—that can span his home and our modern bourgeois world and in doing this also illuminate the village and other communities that connect or divide, and that can value or criticize, both the ways people live in all these situations and the things they can know?

Notes

1. Knowledge, howsoever situated, includes concepts and intuitions as well as the relations among these. As concepts or intuitions are juxtaposed, sequenced, or otherwise brought and used together, the relations among them generate significance and permit inferences. The situatedness of concepts, intuitions, and their possible relations (the meaningful and logical ways of relating) implies that both their substantive and formal properties may differ or vary, including even the character of the relation between what may appear as substance or form. Notions of definiteness and vagueness, quality and quantity, giveness and arbitrariness, and consistency, ambivalence, and self-contradiction, among many others, indicate some of the ways in which the constituents of knowledge may be made and shaped (in substance and/or form) depending on the situations.
2. In turn, this is the first time that this good friend of mine, someone for whom I have deep affection, appears in my writing as a representative informant, as I make of him now an example and subject in a case study. Because I believe it absolutely necessary to consider the particular and the local in regard to the larger subjects at issue, I reluctantly focus on this one particular contemporary South Asian villager as the only means I have at present to direct attention to a village and this little piece of the contemporary South Asian world. Thus, I am offering an illustration, not a research report. Thus, too, I am neglecting much of the social, the interpersonal and collective, features in the way of living, although these are crucial for any fair depiction of the situation of village knowledge. My village friend is simply an indicator of some of the things that I feel we outsiders need to think about, and it pains me to use him and his words in this way.
3. Difference and strangeness are not the same. The former may be just a matter of being the opposite of what is already known and hence not actually strange to it. For example, being many (plural) is different from, although not strange in relation to, being one (singular). Being both many and one, however, is rather strange in relation to, for example, any situation where Aristotelian logic holds, since this does not allow for being both A and not-A. Depending on the situation, being Muslim (or being rural) could be either strange or just different in relation to being Hindu (or being urban).
4. Because I wish to avoid taking sides in the modern versus post-modern *jugal-bandhi*, especially where the *rag* is the one that spans the scale from coherence to incoherence (or order to chaos), I am not going to argue either for or against the presence of consistency or reason in Ganpati's words. Nor am I going to construct or deconstruct any authorial intention. I merely posit that these words make sense, and I

hypothesize that they can say something to us as social scientists. They may tell us a little about a part of South Asia that we do not often watch or listen to as carefully as we might, and more particularly, this expression, as generous, humanistic, positive, and even naïve as it may be for its author or in his immediate context, may have, nevertheless, some critical import for us (in our own situation).

5. The contemporary practice of changing names of public places, almost an obsession, deserves greater scholarly attention in relation to other habits of naming and nicknaming individuals and to understandings and uses of names as indices of identities. Precisely how, that is, in different neighborhoods and for different groups, does Mumbai differ from Bombay? Why were so many people willing to die and why were so many others killed.
6. I include this much caste information merely to satisfy the likely curiosity of Indian and sociologist readers. I doubt that Ganpati's caste matters for anything I write about him here, and I believe that within the scope of the present discussion, in which the particulars of village social structure remain in the background, he can represent villagers from almost all of the mid-range castes, including the dominant Marathas.
7. This conceptualization is broader because it can apply to a more inclusive social situation, and yet it is not necessarily a totalizing or universalizing understanding of the initial terms, since the kind of broader application it defines may not be the appropriate way to broaden them in respect of social life in other parts of the world where the modern bourgeois world situation confronts other sorts of limits or frontiers in relating to other local or regional ways of living (e.g., where movements of material goods rather than of people and ideas establish connections in such a way that identities and values can remain quite fixed). The rendering that I propose in terms of identity, community, and value (as in religion) may not be the sort of analysis of culture (as this notion informs cultural pluralism) or ethnicity that applies well for other parts of the world. I am primarily in search of terms other than those washed up in this latest global sociological wave, terms, other than this flotsam of culture, pluralism, and ethnicity, as these slosh around in either the stew pot or the salad bowl containing certain societal concoctions. Other terms will prove most appropriate to understanding the connections and disjunctions between and among the range of different communities, classes, and classifications (and types thereof) in South Asia and will facilitate more critical analysis and more comprehensive and sensitive comparisons all across the region. These can, moreover, contribute to sociological comparisons of phenomena in this region with some in

North America, western Europe, and possibly other parts of the globe, and yet such terms need not be construed as elements of some universal social theory or be judged in regard to whether they are applicable to every comparison (or generalization) involving different societies or cultures.

8. With concern for, or at least interest in, Indian village ways, our inquiry could, to the contrary, carry us beyond this situation of bourgeois knowledge (and terms of knowledge) as long as we remain open and sensitive to other possibilities. Seeking terms that are not so reified or reifying or dividing or dominating, we may accept and attempt to use some that do not determine, that do not terminate or deliminate, too strongly what they label. Not everything in the grasp of human consciousness or the span of human experience is clearly bounded, distinctly set apart from its environs, impervious to conflicting forces, internally consistent, predictable, stable, or quantifiable. Consequently, in certain situations social science requires terms with properties different from those that seem adequate to the situation of the modern bourgeois world in which sociology first appeared. In respect of these different terms, a quasi-scientific, or at least rigorously disciplined, understanding which works by abstracting certain features and constructing simpler forms of objects, processes, and regular conditions, would remain possible. Thus, I do not deny the possibility that certain notions of cultural pluralism and ethnicity which are not so reified might be relevant to the majority of South Asian people and social circumstances. Yet I do wonder, nonetheless, why we sometimes feel them desirable or necessary—why we bother with reformulating notions deriving from (and applying to) very different historical locales—in order to address the cultural complexity, the communal politics, the religious (and some would say fundamentalist) fervour, and the range of divisive trends or other factors that challenge democratic, or secular, or national values throughout contemporary South Asia. Instead, I propose exploring first more of what we might learn from some ordinary folk and some overlooked locales in the subcontinent itself, since this might not only fit the regional reality better but also even contribute more critically to understanding western or other more fully bourgeois societies and demonstrate certain limits of the conceptual tools which those economies and academies can produce.
9. Sociological concepts like cultural pluralism, ethnicity, or even secularism can easily enter and become part of the world of action outside the sociological discipline, part of much more general formulations and applications of knowledge and power and violence. In some instances they may even originate in the larger world, be picked

up by social science and endowed thereby with grater validation, and then returned with even greater efficacy, for either good or harm or both, to that society at large. With missionary, colonial, imperial, or far-reaching commercial interests, the situation of knowledge and its terms becomes yet more complicated, making situatedness itself more difficult to establish, as concepts originally applying to or even originating from the larger non-academic world in one region are picked up by scholars, rulers, and traders and carried into societies far away.

10. Presenting secularism's indifference to culture and calling it 'ethnophobic', Nandy makes a point that would not in a literal sense apply to notions of cultural pluralism or ethnicity, since these would seem hardly indifferent to culture. Yet given the rather simple and static representation of culture upon which these notions are usually based, it is hard to consider them very ethnophilic either. These notions tend to erase or at least to formalize cultural particularities or differences in the very act of using their existence to identify social groupings, and thus they too may be indifferent to the sort of culture which is lived by persons with more fluid selves or who confederate in their faith and habits a number of ways of life.
11. I am concerned more with matters of sociological substance than method, but without digressing to attend to the latter, I doubt we shall ever adequately grasp much of the former. My sense of the current state of South Asian sociology demands this review of a methodology platitude. If we are serious about connecting our social science to the societies we seriously study, then our research must be more closely in touch with these. For South Asia this means that many more social scientists must live for some time where most of the people and social life are. Not only more contextual and sensitive fact-finding but more meaningful conceptualizing and relevant theorizing depend upon living with people more as they live. In this regard surveys, the dominant, nearly exclusive, data-generating method for Indian social science today, cannot suffice because responses are almost always necessarily categorized, if not determined, even before we obtain them by how others live and by the interview situation which others create. Instead, how people in a particular situation live, think, feel, believe, interact, identify, associate, and differentiate themselves should affect the categories that the others, the social scientists, use to analyze, generalise, and compare. Precisely because the discipline did not come from the villages or the bastis of South Asia, i.e., precisely because it did come from the bourgeoisie of the industrial capitalist west, we social scientists must reform the disciplining ways of seeing and reasoning it has imposed if we and our social knowledge are to be

open to the alternatives and challenges from elsewhere to the modern bourgeois world and if we ourselves are to challenge it with critiques of our own. Only then can we become better and more nomothetic social scientists, can we be more generally relevant to truly different societies, situating the categories and findings that make best sense of one society, one part of our world, in relation to those pertaining to another. Only then, too, can we decide if the trendy or even not so trendy notions that emerge from one part of the world, notions like secularism, cultural pluralism or ethnicity, are significant in another. (Reforming our social science to make it less rooted in the history of the modern west and to make it less compliant to the interests that rule that world demands a collective and dedicated effort. The cards are stacked against us, and these include besides the interests of that particular globalising dynamo which is capitalism, the nature of academic fields and the inertia and contentment they induce.)

12. As that faction of social science which has realized that surveys cannot answer, or even ask, all the important questions has turned so rapidly to cultural studies and discourse histories/genealogies, its focus concentrates upon the kind of mythic, if not romantic-exotic productions, the staged performances, and the hot higher-tech media and jump-cut texts which the trendy theory players in Paris, New Haven, and other misty, steamy, elite saunas seem to require in order to make sense of themselves in suffering their own privileges. I fear that the somewhat different situation and dynamics of societies in South Asia, especially the politics, economics, values, and beliefs that generate and follow from ritual intensification, may be too easily colonized, which is to say, of course, post-colonized, in the already globalised, fully liberalized academic market, which in itself marks a surrender to remote (often foreign) situations of knowledge and knowledge production. I see in the attractions of flashy fashions of culture and its studies, especially including those brands which ethnicize, multi-culturalize, or otherwise culturally pluralize themselves, new avenues of homogenizing and hegemonizing analyses and understandings, that is of putting (or representing) the whole world in a mall of imported wares and notions and of forgetting anyone not able to join the shopping spree of consumer capitalism. Not only do Ganpati and his village still live and belong elsewhere, where they deserve to be respected and represented with different ideas, but it is likely that significant parts of the lives of even those who chose or are forced to buy and consume in the foreign marketplace (to take the Thums Up bungee plunge) still depend to some degree on other values and still relate to other people, groups, communities, and institutions and thus deserve still to be grasped in some other, which is to say, some more grounded, rooted, or locally relevant terms.

13. Kinship or clanship may certainly appear to some to be no less categorical, primordial, or natural components of any human society than ethnicity or cultural identity; and yet generations of anthropologists have worked and argued to contextualize and reconstruct understandings of such notions. These are now widely construed and used in local and practical terms, with dynamic meanings and variable effects pertaining to practices and the difficult conceptual realms spanning between rules and strategies, prescriptions and preferences, structures and sentiments, official and domestic, and even male and female. Unfortunately, much of the recent scholarship on ethnicity and culture (especially when it is pluralized or multiplied) ignores the consequences of such categorical critiques and the place of these terms themselves in political, social, and cultural (symbolic and ideological) struggles.
14. How categories themselves are understood and used limits or opens the kind of attention possible. The qualities and potentials that are expressed in the relations between brothers (or other kin or similarly established social positions) are hardly evident in one kind of categorical thinking that is often used when representing comprehensively a society or other universe of relations by generalizing from some kinds of relationships. Thinking in terms of essences and essential properties of relationships—especially as given primordially or in the nature of things themselves and as fixed by conditions or forces above or beyond (transcending) every immediate situation (of acting or thinking)—is not always necessary or adequate. Wittgenstein's formulation of another sort of category, which he so suitably named 'family relationship', allows for bringing things together on the basis of no one thing, no entity or no distinctive feature, that is common to all that are so related and associated. Instead, what is needed is just a range of qualities, some of which are shared among some, though not all, in the grouping. Moreover, depending on the circumstances or on the project at hand, particular qualities will or will not be significant and consequential, and hence whether or not a category (e.g., a culture or ethnicity) either can be seen to exist or really matters, also depends on the circumstances. By recognizing this (conceptually) possible and (empirically) plausible alternative to the rationalizing and naturalizing inclinations of a modern reifying consciousness of the world and society, a critical sociology gains some ground to pose a positive question regarding certain contemporary social crises. Namely, the challenge appears and takes shape as one of how both most social extremists and most social extremists and most social scientists, each tending in their own thinking towards fundamental simplifications and each acting, when the situation toughens, as simplifying fundamentals, can realize,

value, and perhaps identify increasingly with this other form of human knowledge, consciousness, and experience?

15. The Hindutva dilemma—the matter of way of life-cum-culture versus religion or of being inclusive and insistently egalitarian to all versus oppressively insensitive or genocidal to some—cannot be discussed here, although approaching it might also require, or at least benefit from, some other logical than is usually found in the arguments and reasoning of either Hindutva's opponents or proponents (since in many regards both sides appear equally modern and bourgeois). I can, however, refer quickly to one unexpected research finding from a survey taken in several hundred villages in Satara district which included a question about the caste composition of each village. In situations of absolutely minimal observer interference (because the survey was sent by mail and completed by villagers on their own), lists provided in response to the item requesting all the surnames and castes in the village included not only reports of Hindu Marathas, Hindu Ramoshis, Hindu Sonars, Hindu Sutars, and Hindu Chambhars, but also mention of Hindu Bodhs (Buddhists) and Hindu Musulmans. (From the 1976 survey data, in one taluka where 46 villages reported Muslims present, 5 of these wrote 'Hindu Musulman' in its listing. In a much smaller 1996 mail survey, I also have found one such response in reply to the same item). Without beginning to choose among the possible interpretations of how such an expression could occur and what it might mean, I ask here only whether fixed notions of cultural pluralism or ethnicity or religious community can account for the occurrence of a Hindu Buddhist or a Hindu Muslim in India at present and for its significance in the lives, thoughts, or verbal habits of some villagers.

Contributors

Lionel Caplan, School of Oriental and African Studies, University of London, London.

Peter Kloos, Former Professor, Vrije Universiteit, Amsterdam.

A.R. Momin, Emeritus Fellow, Department of Sociology, University of Mumbai, Mumbai.

T.K. Oommen, Former Professor, Centre for the Study of Social Systems, Jawaharlal Nehru University, New Delhi.

Bhikhu Parekh, Emeritus Professor, University of Hull, UK.

Aparna Rao, Universitat zu Koln, Germany.

Yunas Samad, University of Bradford, UK.

K.S. Singh, Former Director-General, Anthropological Survey of India, New Delhi.

Lee I. Schlesinger, University of North Carolina, USA.

Index